LOUIS

Printed and bound in Great Britain by
TJ International Ltd, Padstow, Cornwall

CATHERINE HANLEY

LOUIS

THE FRENCH PRINCE WHO
INVADED ENGLAND

YALE UNIVERSITY PRESS
NEW HAVEN AND LONDON

For Edwin, Charlotte and Adela

For information about this and other Yale University Press publications, please contact:
U.S. office: sales.press@yale.edu   yalebooks.com
Europe Office: sales@yaleup.co.uk   yalebooks.co.uk

Typeset in Adobe Caslon Pro by IDSUK (DataConnection) Ltd
Printed in Great Britain by TJ International Ltd, Padstow, Cornwall

Library of Congress Control Number: 2016932441

ISBN 978-0-300-21745-2

A catalogue record for this book is available from the British Library.

10 9 8 7 6 5 4 3 2 1

CONTENTS

ILLUSTRATIONS

Plates

Maps

Tables

ACKNOWLEDGEMENTS

I am delighted to acknowledge and to express my gratitude to the Authors' Foundation of the Society of Authors for awarding the grant that enabled me to buy a significant period of time in which to collate, finish and edit the manuscript of *Louis*.

Both Heather McCallum at Yale University Press and my agent, Kate Hordern, saw the potential in a story from a period of history that others might consider unfashionable, for which I remain very grateful; this book would never have seen the light of day without them. Rachael Lonsdale at Yale has been a tower of strength throughout the publication process, and copy-editor Ann Bone's meticulous attention to detail was much appreciated.

I owe a great debt of gratitude to my friend and colleague Sean McGlynn, who also writes about this period of English and French history. When I first mentioned to him that I wanted to write a biography of Louis he could have become territorial, but instead he supported the idea wholeheartedly and has subsequently supplied references, sources, encouragement and enthusiasm, as well as discussing various obscure points in tea rooms up and down the country.

Many others have provided assistance in specific areas so I would like to take this opportunity to thank Susan Brock and Caroline Gibson for reading early drafts of the text and providing many useful comments on them; Andrew Buck for information and references on the crusader states; Glyn Burgess for correspondence on Eustace the Monk; Julian Harrison at the British Library for locating Louis's surviving English charter; Malcolm Mann for tracking down an elusive article I needed; Colin Middleton for discussions on (and practical demonstrations of) thirteenth-century armour and weaponry; Sarah Peverley for information and references on medieval childbirth and twins; Louise Wilkinson for correspondence on Nicola de la Haye; Sam Wilson for a discussion on siege camps; the team of the Magna Carta research project, especially Sophie Ambler, for references to some primary sources I was having difficulty in finding (not to mention making available all the fabulous information on their website); and the team at Guédelon Castle, especially Sarah Preston and Florian Renucci, for practical advice on the building and repairing of castles and for assistance with the translation of some particularly obscure Old French terms. Any errors which remain in any of these areas are of course entirely my own, and I'll be happy to defend them in single combat.

The sourcing of images for the plate section in this book was made immeasurably easier thanks to those generous and patient individuals who sent photographs, found manuscript illustrations and smoothed the permissions process: many thanks to Anne-Catherine Biedermann and Barbara Van Kets in Paris, Jackie Brown at the British Library, Elizabeth Dumas at the Parker Library, Julian Humphrys, James Mears, Beth Spacey and Sam Wilson.

My husband James has been extraordinarily patient while I have been researching and writing, and did not even mind when I replaced the photo of him on my desk with a framed picture of Louis; he has probably heard enough about the thirteenth century to last him a lifetime. And finally I would like to thank my children, who have over the past couple of years put up with me with great tolerance, and who have confused and infuriated several schoolteachers by arguing quite vociferously that there was once a king of England called Louis. This book is dedicated to them.

Map 1 England in the thirteenth century

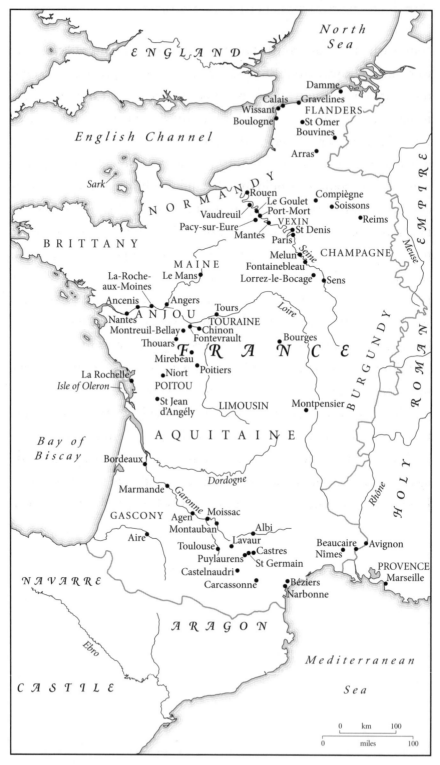

Map 2 France in the thirteenth century

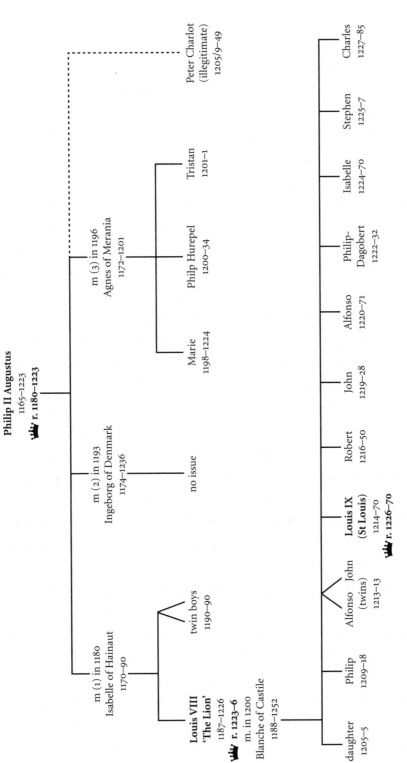

Table 1 The Capetians

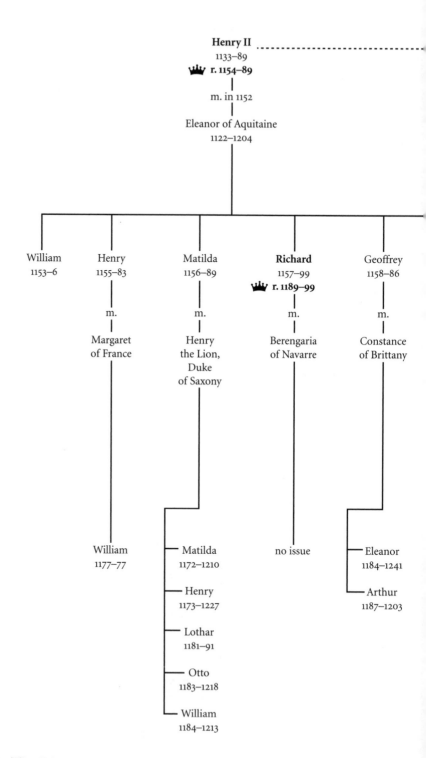

Table 2 The Plantagenets

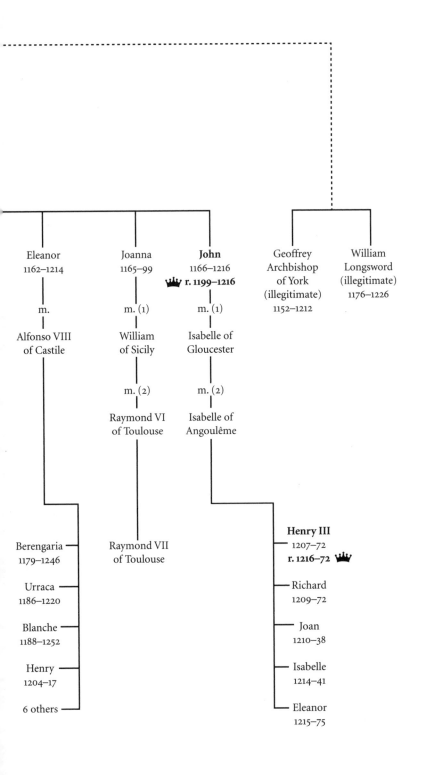

Eleanor
1162–1214

m.

Alfonso VIII
of Castile

Joanna
1165–99

m. (1)

William
of Sicily

m. (2)

Raymond VI
of Toulouse

John
1166–1216

👑 **r. 1199–1216**

m. (1)

Isabelle of
Gloucester

m. (2)

Isabelle of
Angoulême

Geoffrey
Archbishop
of York
(illegitimate)
1152–1212

William
Longsword
(illegitimate)
1176–1226

Berengaria
1179–1246

Urraca
1186–1220

Blanche
1188–1252

Henry
1204–17

6 others

Raymond VII
of Toulouse

Henry III
1207–72
r. 1216–72 👑

Richard
1209–72

Joan
1210–38

Isabelle
1214–41

Eleanor
1215–75

INTRODUCTION

IN AUGUST 1216 Alexander II, King of Scots, rode south to offer his homage to the man he acknowledged as the new king of England; the official recognition of one monarch by another. The journey was a long one, and it took him and his sizeable entourage several weeks to travel all the way through the country; that he managed it in peace was testament to the authority of the man who held much of England in his grasp – a seasoned and respected warrior who was waiting for him at Dover. When Alexander arrived many of the most powerful lords of the realm were there to witness him kneel and give homage for the lands he held in England to the man he acknowledged had the right to bestow them.

The man in question was the son of the king of France, and his name was Louis.

* * *

Today, few people in Britain have heard of Louis. His name, so emblematic of France and of all things 'foreign', sounds odd in the context of English history. But if he had been more successful in his

1

quest for the crown then we might now be as familiar with the name Louis as we are with others such as William and George which were just as foreign-sounding in their time. For, following in the footsteps of William the Conqueror, Louis sailed across the Channel to invade England and claim the throne. However, in contrast to his predecessor's experience, there was for him no immediate and decisive battle, no swift coronation and no complete victory. Instead there was an almighty struggle punctuated by sieges and battles; there were vacillating barons who changed their allegiance from one side to another; there was devastation and suffering across the land as the war went on. Although he never succeeded in occupying the throne officially, Louis was in control of large parts of England from May 1216 until September 1217, and he was recognised as king not only by Alexander of Scotland but also by a large proportion of the great landholding barons. Indeed, it was these very barons who had invited him to invade.

It may seem incredible that England once reached a point where its lords sailed to the Continent and invited the son of the great French king Philip II Augustus to invade and take the throne, but this is exactly what happened: they made the offer, Louis sailed, landed unopposed in the south-east, marched to London and was proclaimed king by cheering throngs of people. He fought his way across much of the country and battled against the remaining adherents of King John and, later, of John's son Henry. The story of how these events unfolded, and of how and why the barons decided that the most attractive candidate for the crown was a Frenchman, is a fascinating and under-explored one which we will investigate in these pages. Who was Louis, where did he come from, why was he invited to take the throne, what happened when he attempted to, what happened afterwards, what was his legacy, and why, crucially, do we not know more about him and about this pivotal era of English history?

Most of the narrative of this period centres on the English King John, with Louis a shadowy antagonistic figure in the background, but we will examine events from Louis's point of view, exploring his life before, during and after the invasion; an invasion which we will investigate in some detail in the central section of the book. Louis himself will be the main focus of our attention, but we will also look at how he fits into the wider narrative of the relationship between kings and kingdoms at this time, and give some background detail to put his actions in context. Once our story of his life is complete we will discuss the question of why he is not called King Louis I of England, even though he held for some time as much or more authority than some of the monarchs who are officially recognised. We will conclude by exploring and analysing Louis's profound and much under-appreciated influence on the course of English history.

In order to tell our story we need to draw on a wide range of evidence, and fortunately for us there are a number of contemporary sources available which can help us to reconstruct Louis's life and his English campaign. Although he left no diaries or personal corre-spondence, numerous official documents from the period survive: charters, financial records, public letters, royal acts, papal bulls and so on. These sources form our factual base and are useful for confirming matters such as who, where and when, and also for identifying areas of agreement and disagreement, alliances and enmities. But they create only the skeleton of our story; in order to put flesh on the bones we must also turn to the more narrative sources of the period, the chronicles and texts written by contemporaries who were observing events as they happened or who had first-hand experience of them. Of course, these writers were not necessarily objective or even striving to be so: they are often biased and their narratives can be highly personal. But if we take this into account then we can safely use them to add colour and depth to our tale.

Let us, then, meet some of the men whose works we will consult. In this particular case they are all men: there were more women writers in the thirteenth century than is generally supposed, but those who wrote the chronicles and the great narratives of war were more likely to be monks in an abbey or clerics attached to an army, and therefore male. Our chroniclers hail from a variety of places – they are French, English, Welsh, Breton and Occitan – and they wrote either during Louis's lifetime or shortly after his death. We will give a general introduction to them and an overview of their work here; further details on the texts, their languages of composition and their availability for consultation may be found in the Note on Sources at the end of this volume.

The best sources for Louis's boyhood and youth are the two great chroniclers of his father Philip's reign, Rigord and William the Breton. Rigord was a monk at the abbey of St Denis in Paris who spent many years compiling his *Deeds of Philip Augustus*; it is generally sober in tone, with Rigord realising he was writing for posterity and rarely offering a personal opinion. However, a gradual change in attitude can be discerned: the earlier part of the work portrays Philip in a very flattering light, but a few hints of criticism appear later on as the king acts in ways which do not meet with the Church's approval. Rigord died in 1209 and so his chronicle of Philip's reign is incomplete and it covers only the early part of Louis's life.

William the Breton was also a cleric, but as he was a chaplain in the household of Philip Augustus he travelled around more than Rigord and is able to offer eyewitness accounts of some events, making him all the more valuable. He wrote two major works: another *Deeds of Philip Augustus*, which enlarged and expanded on Rigord's work, and also an epic poem, the *Philippide*, which focuses mainly on the battle of Bouvines in 1214 and portrays Philip in the style of the heroes of antiquity. William's work is useful to us and very readable, but we have to remember that he was among Philip's greatest supporters, so anything he writes can be guaranteed to put Philip in the best light possible. This is sometimes to Louis's benefit and sometimes to his detriment, as we shall see. Most of our references to William's work will be to his *Deeds of Philip Augustus*; references to the *Philippide* will be noted as such.

Much of Louis's life was dominated by the ongoing conflict between his dynasty in France, the Capetians (most recently represented by his grandfather Louis VII and his father, Philip II), and that of the Plantagenets – Henry II and his family – who at the time of Louis's birth held not only England but also Normandy, Aquitaine and other territories on French soil. We should probably note that members of this family did not at the time refer to themselves by the name 'Plantagenet', although it had been the soubriquet of Henry II's father (Henry generally called himself Henry FitzEmpress after his mother), but the name is now so well known that it seems sensible for us to use it in this book. A number of chronicles depict the hostilities between the rival dynasties, and specifically Louis's invasion of England, and they were written by supporters of both sides.

In the Plantagenet camp are Roger of Wendover, Matthew Paris and the author of the *History of William Marshal*; the third ends his account in 1219 and the other two continue and cover some of the later periods of Louis's life. Roger of Wendover was a monk at the large and influential abbey of St Albans, and his *Flowers of History* covers the period up to 1235; he died in 1236 and his work was continued by Matthew Paris, who was a monk at the same abbey. Roger is firm in his support of the Plantagenets against the Capetians and does not like Louis or his companions much; however, he is also in places critical of King John personally. His work has often been considered unreliable as there are demonstrable factual errors in places, and it is full of anecdotes and accounts of miracles which are meant to prove various points; however, the most reliable part of his chronicle is the section he was composing about contemporary events between 1202 and 1234, and he does provide a reasonably coherent account of the military encounters. He also, more unusually, includes a number of passages expressing sympathy with the common people caught up in a war not of their own making.

Matthew Paris (a slightly misleading surname as he was English) took up Roger's work after his death and continued it, expanding it into his *Chronica Majora*, which is one of the finest works of historiography of the whole thirteenth century. As he was not writing until the late 1240s he had the benefit of hindsight, so he was able to portray Louis in a fairly negative light, safe in the knowledge that he was not around any longer. Matthew spices up Roger's earlier text by adding comments, opinions and direct speech, and has some colourful prejudices. He also wrote a *Life of St Alban*, which has some snippets of interest to us, and numerous other works.

The *History of William Marshal*, as the name implies, is a biography of William Marshal, who was a knight and later an earl in the service of several generations of the Plantagenets. It was composed in the 1220s, based on the reminiscences of his squire John of Earley, and contains vivid descriptions of various events during Louis's invasion of England, in which Marshal played a major role. However, the undisputed aim of the author of this work was to eulogise Marshal and to paint him in the most flattering light possible, so the author often twists his account to this end and can therefore be unreliable in places.

Siding with the Capetians in their depiction of the campaign were William the Breton, whom we met earlier, and Gerald of Wales. Gerald was a clergyman and, despite his Anglo-Gallic origins, was a firm supporter of the Capetians; possibly this had its origins in a snub from the Plantagenets when his bid to become the bishop of

St David's was rejected personally by Henry II. Gerald was later appointed a clerk in the royal household by Henry, but despite – or perhaps because of – knowing Henry and his sons personally, he presents the whole family as brutal representatives of a malicious dynasty, while comparing them unfavourably to the Capetians and to Louis in particular, whose invasion he positively welcomes. Gerald travelled widely and is the author of many works, but the one which will concern us most here is his *On the Instruction of a Prince*, which includes both a history of Henry II's reign and a number of pointed reflections on how a king ought to behave.

With a foot in both camps is a writer known only as the Anonymous of Béthune. He was a cleric in the service of Robert of Béthune, who as a lord in Flanders was on different sides of the Plantagenet–Capetian conflict at different times. The Anonymous wrote both a *Chronicle of the Kings of France* and a *History of the Dukes of Normandy and the Kings of England*, which means that effectively he tells parts of the same story twice but from different points of view and without a particular axe to grind either way, which makes his work especially valuable. He was in England from 1215 to 1217, and his chronicles are hugely detailed, so we owe him a great debt for his exact descriptions of various sieges and other events. For clarity, we will refer to each of his works by title.

There are also some other contemporary writers who, although not having the campaign as the main focus of their work, touch upon events and are therefore of service to us. These were predominantly monks who were writing chronicles of or for their own abbeys, but who could not help including mentions of the war as it touched all of them in some way. We know the name of only one, Ralph of Coggeshall, who was the abbot of Coggeshall Abbey in Essex; the others are known simply as the Barnwell annalist (based in Cambridgeshire), the Waverley annalist (Surrey) and the Dunstable annalist (Bedfordshire). As their primary purpose was not documenting the war and they did not have strong affiliations one way or the other, their work is useful for its neutrality.

Both before and after his English campaign Louis was involved in the Albigensian crusade, the war which pitted the Catholic Church against the Cathar heretics in Languedoc, the southern region of France. Three great contemporary writers documented the crusade. William of Tudela started his *Song of the Cathar Wars* but died before it was complete, leaving it to be carried on by an anonymous continuer; what is particularly interesting about the work is that although their writings comprise a single text, William was a supporter of the French royalists fighting against the southerners, while the continuer is a southerner himself and virulently anti-crusade. Another writer recording the same war was Peter des Vaux-de-Cernay, with his *History of the Albigensian Crusade*; Peter also died before the conflict ended.

Taking up the story of the remainder of the Albigensian crusade and documenting Louis's reign as king of France are Nicholas de Bray, with his *Deeds of King Louis VIII*, and the *Life of Louis VIII* written by an anonymous monk. In order to avoid confusion we will refer to Nicholas de Bray's work by his name, and the other by its title. They could hardly be more of a contrast in style: the *Life of Louis VIII* is terse and factual, while Nicholas's text is difficult to work with as he employs a high poetic style packed with hyperbole and confused references to ancient mythology, often while in the middle of describing a contemporary event. The result is chaotic, but occasionally he returns to earth long enough to include a more prosaic passage from which facts can be gleaned. Nicholas was an eyewitness to a number of the events he describes, which is helpful to us, and his work and the *Life of Louis VIII* can usefully be consulted in combination with each other. Louis's reign is also mentioned by William of Puylaurens, another chronicler of the Albigensian crusade, and by another monastic text known only as the *Chronicle of Tours*; we will make passing reference to both of these works.

And finally, of assistance and of much entertainment value is the lively text known as the *Tales of a Minstrel of Reims*, dating from around 1260. In marked contrast to the mainly clerical and mostly sober chroniclers of the thirteenth century, the Minstrel of Reims was very much the 'tabloid hack' of his day, never afraid to exaggerate wildly or to stir up a scandal, and writing very much for the town and the street corner rather than the court. For this reason his work has generally been overlooked or dismissed as unreliable, but if used with caution it can give us a real idea of what the ordinary person on the street was thinking, even if some of the Minstrel's character sketches might not have met with the approval of the nobility at court. He wrote some years after Louis's death but his work covers almost a century so it is the only one which encompasses the entire span of Louis's life.

* * *

The spelling and usage of names in the early thirteenth century can sometimes be inconsistent, so it is worth noting briefly here how we will approach this. Where a modern English version is available, French and German names have been anglicised: thus we have (among others) Philip, William, John and Peter rather than Philippe, Guillaume, Jean and Pierre; Henry and Frederick rather than Heinrich and Friedrich. More unusual names which do not have a standard modern English equivalent – such as Blanche, Falkes, Berengaria, Guala, Amaury and so on – have been rendered in the form used most commonly in modern English texts, rather than their Latinate forms such as Falcasius. Of the various spellings available to non-Welsh speakers such as myself, I have gone for Llewelyn and Gwladys for the prince and his daughter.

Where relevant, surnames retain their *de*, rather than being anglicised to 'of', for both French and English lords: thus Robert de Dreux, William des Roches, Saer de Quincy and so on. Where 'of' is used it refers either to a geographical place rather than a surname (Blanche of Castile, Raymond of Toulouse), or a title: William the earl of Salisbury, Thomas the count of Perche. Each French comital house tended to use a restricted range of first names, so where relevant I have included numbers as well as names (Hugh IX, Theobald IV, and so on) for clarity.

Although the English 'earl' and the French *comte* might be considered equivalent ranks I have used 'earl' for English titles and 'count' for French ones to avoid confusion. In France, not all counts were equal: the counts of Flanders, Champagne and Toulouse were among the six great lay peers of France (there were also six ecclesiastical peers), and were therefore the equal of the dukes of Burgundy, Normandy and Aquitaine and superior to the holders of the more minor counties. The word 'prince' did not, in the early thirteenth century, have the same meaning of 'son of a king' as it does now; at that time it was used more generally to mean 'ruler', and had been adopted in places as diverse as Wales and Antioch. However, its modern usage is now such common parlance that I have felt free to employ it in this way, and have on occasion referred to Louis and others as princes (or princesses) on account of their birth. Ecclesiastical ranks were the same across western Europe so standard terms such as bishop, archbishop, abbot, cardinal and so on have been used. Place names have been anglicised where a suitable form exists (Normandy, Castile), and left in the original (Mantes, Pacy-sur-Eure, La-Roche-aux-Moines) where not.

Those of us who were raised in the era of decimal currency might also appreciate a note on the money which was in circulation in the early thirteenth century. In both England and France there were twelve pennies (*deniers*) in a shilling (*sou*) and twenty shillings or 240 pennies in one pound (*livre*). However, a French pound (*livre parisis*) was worth slightly less than an English pound sterling so the amounts were not quite equivalent. A denomination also mentioned frequently in contemporary writings is the mark, which was 13s 4d (160 pennies) or two-thirds of a pound. Having said all that, we should note that other than a few gold pieces which had made their way over from the east, the only actual coins in circulation were the silver penny in England (which could be cut into halves or quarters if necessary), and the silver *denier* (1d) and *obol* (½d) in France. Transporting money therefore involved the inconvenience of carrying around large and heavy sacks or barrels of pennies.

I have made no attempt to give modern equivalents of thirteenth-century amounts of money as such conversions are inevitably approximate at best. Instead, I have made comparisons with contemporary daily wages, annual incomes or purchasing power, which should help to give a sense of perspective.

* * *

The structure of this book is chronological, following Louis from his birth to his death and concluding with an analysis of his life and reign. And so to begin, let us travel to Paris in the late summer of the year 1187 . . .

CHAPTER ONE

THE SHAPING OF A PRINCE

THE KING OF France was a man under pressure.

In September 1187 Philip Augustus was twenty-two and he had already been on the throne for seven years. As was the custom of the ruling Capetian family he had been crowned and associated with the throne during his father's lifetime, but the elderly Louis VII had died within months of the coronation, leaving the fifteen-year-old Philip in sole charge of a small French kingdom sandwiched precariously between the Holy Roman Empire to the east and the Plantagenet domains to the west. These were held by a rapacious Henry II of England and they sprawled all the way from the Scottish border to the Pyrenees; Henry controlled more of France than Philip did.

That Philip had so far survived, managed to hold his own and even made a few gains against his vastly more experienced opposite number was a positive sign for the future of France, but in one crucial aspect of medieval kingship Henry held the upper hand: he had sons. Indeed, some might argue that he had too many sons – four of them survived to adulthood and they fought constantly either against him or with each other – but Henry had done more than enough to ensure the succession of his dynasty, while Philip had lived through seven childless years of marriage.

But now all that was about to change. Philip's queen was with child and near her time, and France was holding its breath. The older citizens had lived through this before, of course: Philip himself had been a very long-awaited male heir, born to huge celebrations as Philip *Dieudonné*, the God-given, the product of his father's third and somewhat desperate marriage. Philip had five sisters, the eldest twenty years his senior.

Queen Isabelle's lying-in was to take place in the royal palace on the Île de la Cité, the island in the middle of the River Seine in Paris. The birthing chamber was an exclusively female space in the late twelfth century; an expectant mother would retire to a darkened room ahead of the birth, and would be shut in along with her female attendants and midwives – literally 'confined' – until it was all over. Husbands and fathers, even royal ones, could do nothing but wait outside for news, and Philip was no exception.

Giving birth was a painful and dangerous experience which as many as one woman in eight did not survive, so prayers were said both inside and outside the palace as nobles, citizens and clergy awaited the heir. The queen's labour began, and in the early evening of 5 September 1187 she gave birth to a boy. She is said to have wept for joy on being informed of the baby's sex, as well she might. As the news filtered out of the chamber, raced around the palace and spread throughout Paris, bells began to ring. Even the normally sober chronicler Rigord was moved to emotion: the city was filled with such great happiness, he tells us, that for seven days and nights the whole population did not stop singing, dancing and offering praises to God; messengers were sent out to all the provinces to announce the king's great joy. Once again the crown could pass from father to son in a line unbroken since Hugh Capet's accession in 987. Philip could accept the congratulations of his nobles and start work on his dynastic plans.

* * *

Possibly the only person in France who was even more pleased and relieved than the king was the queen. Isabelle of Hainaut had been presented to Philip as a bride in the spring of 1180, when she had just turned ten and he was fifteen. As queen consort her primary role was to produce male heirs, but given her age the consummation of the marriage was delayed. Although not for long: in 1184, when she was still only fourteen, the continuing lack of a child was causing concern among the nobility and this was one of the factors behind Philip's public announcement in the spring of that year that he intended to divorce her. As a consolation he would give her as husband any of his nobles that she cared to name. But Isabelle was not about to be dismissed without making some effort to keep her crown: she retorted that she wanted no other, and walked through the streets barefoot, dressed only in her shift, praying and distributing alms, publicly begging for forgiveness. The sight of the beautiful teenager in such a pitiable state turned opinion in her favour and she was reunited with the king.

But it was to be nearly three more years until she carried a baby to term, years filled with pressure to conceive and with the accompanying worry over her position. So her feelings as she recovered from the rigours of labour, shut in the dark and quiet chamber while the jubilations went on outside, and looked down at the swaddled form in the cradle surely included relief as well as love and pride. As the mother of the future king her status had increased and her position was strengthened.

The new prince was named Louis in honour of his grandfather and other illustrious ancestors. As Isabelle was descended from

Charlemagne and Philip from Hugh Capet, Louis could claim descent from both of France's legendary kings, so his great destiny seemed assured and prophecies began to circulate about his future. The queen's ancestry manifested itself in another way: Louis was pale and blond like her, small and more slender in appearance than the robust Capetians with their trademark mops of uncontrollable dark hair.

The dangers of infant mortality in the twelfth century were many: a conservative estimate would be that some 15 to 20 per cent of babies died in their first year (many within days of the birth), and that a third of all children did not reach the age of fifteen. Death was no respecter of rank, so from the very beginning the young prince, a fragile thread upon which to hang the future of a dynasty until he had any brothers, was to be guarded from harm as closely as possible. This does not necessarily indicate that Louis was a particularly sickly child; rather that he was valuable, a treasure beyond price.

The first great event in Louis's life was his baptism. A ceremony essential for all newborns, not just the royal ones, it was generally carried out within weeks or even days of the birth. Christening drove out original sin, made a child a member of the Church, and provided it with godparents who would make promises on its behalf and act as spiritual mentors and advisers. The infants probably did not enjoy the ceremony much: as well as being stripped and anointed with oil they were immersed fully in the water of the font three times. Louis would have had a number of godparents, but we know the name of only one: Stephen de Tournai, a theologian who later became bishop of Tournai.

At this time babies and young children spent the first few years of their lives in a predominantly female environment. As Louis was suckled and weaned and as he learned to walk and talk he would have been surrounded by the women of the royal household: a wet-nurse, other nurses, his mother and her ladies-in-waiting. Royal children were not generally nursed by their mothers – thus enabling queens to return to a fertile condition all the sooner, for the production of more heirs – but Louis's carefully guarded state meant he was kept in the royal palace, rather than being sent away to form his own household, so it is likely that he saw his mother on a regular basis, and his father as often as convention and royal duties allowed.

When Louis was two and a half years old there was further good news for the realm: the queen was pregnant again. It was to be hoped that she would bear another son in order to secure the dynasty. In March of 1190 she went into what may have been a premature labour ... and unexpectedly delivered not one son, but two. Twins, although by no means unheard of, were more of a rarity in the twelfth century than they are now; most cases would have been diagnosed only at birth, with the appearance of a second baby coming as a surprise to all concerned. Unfortunately, as twins were generally smaller than singleton babies and were liable to be born earlier, the lack of adequate medical care meant that very few of them survived, even if they were born without complication. We do not know the details of what went on in the royal birthing chamber that day in 1190, or how many hours Isabelle suffered and laboured, praying for deliverance, but we do know that the nineteen-year-old queen died, and that both babies followed her to the grave shortly afterwards. France had no more heirs and Louis was left motherless.

* * *

Louis was surrounded by servants and nurses, and had not been brought up entirely by the queen; but losing a mother, as common an experience as it may have been during the twelfth century, would have a traumatic effect on any two-year-old. This loss was compounded only months later when his father left Paris to go on crusade to the Holy Land, not to return for nearly two years. Louis was left in the care of his grandmother Adela, the queen mother, and her brother William the archbishop of Reims. Philip, no doubt aware of the dangers of battle and disease he would face, drew up his testament: if he were to die, the regents and the citizens of Paris were to guard his treasury and keep it safe for his son until he was of age to govern the realm, with the help and by the grace of God.

After travelling to Sicily in September and spending the winter months there, Philip arrived in the Holy Land in April 1191 and was shortly joined by Richard the Lionheart, now king of England after the death of Henry II in 1189. Together – or in competition with each other, depending on how you look at it – they laid siege to the city of Acre, the major port in the Holy Land and therefore of pivotal importance to the crusade. Richard had been delayed on his way by illness, and now Philip succumbed to the same disease, which was to change both his life and Louis's. Called *arnoldia* by contemporaries, it was an early form of sweating sickness, causing fever, chills and the loss of hair and nails; it also seems to have caused nervous disorders. Philip's body swelled, his lips became sore, the unruly hair for which he was famed fell out in clumps and his skin began to peel off in strips; he was afflicted by a paranoia which was to be lifelong. But as he lay sweating on his camp bed in the heat of the Holy Land, perhaps fearing for his life, he can have had little idea that his young son was also hovering near death in Paris. For Louis, approaching his fourth birthday, had developed a life-threatening bout of dysentery, a common cause of infant mortality.

As the little boy lay suffering, with no parent to comfort him, the monks of St Denis did the only thing they could: they prayed for his life and brought out their sacred relics, a nail from the True Cross, a spine from the holy crown of thorns, and the arm bone of St Simeon. Rigord tells us that they formed a procession and set off through the streets 'carrying with them the nail and the Lord's crown of thorns and the arm of Saint Simeon, with clergy and people pouring out tearful prayers'. The relics of saints were considered to have healing powers, so, followed by a crowd of weeping barefoot citizens, the monks took them to the palace. Once inside, the bishop of Paris approached Louis: 'The boy's stomach was touched all over by the nail and the crown of thorns. The arm was placed on it in the form of a cross, and he was liberated that very day from imminent danger.' Such was the grace of God in sparing the young prince's life, says Rigord, that 'on the same day clear air and weather was restored to all lands. For the Lord had long rained on the earth because of the sins of men.' It was also, apparently, the very same day that Philip was healed of his illness in the Holy Land, although this claim should be taken as symbolic rather than factual.

News of Louis's illness reached Acre, where it is possible that Richard deliberately told Philip that his son was dead in the hope of distressing him further. Once the city had fallen, there was still much to do in the Holy Land if Jerusalem was to be recaptured, but after the health of both France's king and its heir had been threatened (or, alternatively, using this as a convenient excuse) Philip decided that his own kingdom must come first. If he and Louis had both died it was anyone's guess as to who would take the throne, with the most likely scenario being a civil war between Philip's cousins and the husbands and sons of his sisters as they each sought the crown; this would not only damage the realm but also leave it vulnerable to attack from Richard and others. Philip had not worked so hard for so long to risk France descending into anarchy after his death. And so he set off home, much to the annoyance of Richard, who remained in the Holy Land, although he was destined never to reach Jerusalem. After a long journey across land and sea which must have taxed his health even further, Philip eventually reached Paris on a freezing

27 December 1191, to prostrate himself before the altar at St Denis and give fervent thanks to God for his safe return.

And what of the father–son reunion? It must have been very confusing for the four-year-old prince as he welcomed the returning king. Louis had not seen Philip since he was a toddler, and even if some shadowy memories remained, the man before him – sick, bald, prematurely aged – can have borne little resemblance to the father he remembered.

* * *

Louis continued to grow up in the palace; Philip resumed his duties, one of which was to ensure the succession by producing more heirs. Shortly before Louis's sixth birthday the prince received the news that he was to gain a new stepmother: Ingeborg, the eighteen-year-old sister of King Cnut VI of Denmark, reputed to be one of the most beautiful and the most pious women in Europe. The wedding took place on 14 August 1193, bride and groom having no common language and having met each other for the first time earlier that same day. And then, for reasons which have been inexplicable to generations of historians ever since, never mind to a small boy caught up in events, Philip repudiated Ingeborg the day after the wedding and sent her away to a convent. Louis was not to have a new mother after all. Many years of dispute were to follow, setting Philip variously against the king of Denmark, the pope, the clergy and people of France, and even his own loyal chroniclers, with Rigord describing the clergy who agreed to sanction the divorce as 'mute as dogs who did not know how to bark'. But Philip would never agree to live with Ingeborg as husband and wife again.

And so Louis remained an only child as he left the care of women and started his education. Most boys from his era, when they appear in contemporary writings, are depicted simplistically either as bellicose future warriors or as bookish future clerks, but – revealing not for the last time a personality which was complex and not easy to decipher – Louis seems to have enjoyed both scholarly and martial pursuits, and he had plenty of opportunity. Philip's own education had been cut short when he was crowned at the age of fourteen, taking over the reins of government during his father's last illness and then becoming sole king at fifteen; he was determined that Louis should have the complete education he missed out on, the best that the royal treasury could provide.

Paris, and northern France more generally, was a great centre of education and enlightenment. Many noble English boys were sent across the Channel (including, among others, the chroniclers Matthew Paris and Gerald of Wales during their youth) as the provision was better than anything which could be obtained in England. One of the most celebrated masters of the time, Amaury de Bène of the University of Paris, was engaged to teach Louis. We do not have any day-to-day details of Louis's schedule, but thanks to a wealth of surviving educational literature we do know that the curriculum in vogue at the time was wide-ranging. It included the liberal arts – the *trivium* of grammar, rhetoric and logic, and the *quadrivium* of arithmetic, music, astronomy and geometry – as well as lessons in good conduct, fine manners and morals. In theory, much was expected of a prince. Gerald of Wales's didactic text *On the Instruction of a Prince*, started during the 1190s and later to become influential across western Europe, noted that he should observe moderation, generosity, magnificence, justice and boldness, and also that he should be religious and devout.

The teachings of the Church were of great importance, but they may not have been a formal part of Louis's education: as Christian belief permeated every aspect of everyday life, 'religion' was probably not taught or emphasised as a separate subject, but rather was something which underpinned everything else. Of course, not all monarchs showed the same reverence for every facet of the Church's teachings (not when they had a war to fight or a wife they wanted to divorce, for example) but Louis showed himself, even at an early age, to be pious, and this would continue throughout his life. Hugh of Avalon, the eminent bishop of Lincoln (later to become St Hugh) visited Paris in 1200 and met the young prince, who listened to him with a gravity beyond his years. Possibly Louis may not have been quite as naturally shrewd or politically astute as his father, who had had to learn the hard way, but he did enjoy learning. This was all the more remarkable, says Gerald of Wales, because it is a rare quality in princes, who are often no more than 'crowned donkeys'.

Also in the year 1200, around the time of his thirteenth birthday in September, Louis was presented with a book called *Karolinus* by its author Giles of Paris, in which the great emperor Charlemagne was promoted as an exemplar for his young descendant. The book described how Charlemagne cultivated each of the four cardinal virtues – prudence, justice, temperance and courage – and how Louis could learn from this. Later, both Rigord and William the Breton would dedicate their works to Louis, recognising his love of letters.

The academic and moral facets of Louis's education were important, but of course he was going to be a king, not a cleric, so he also needed to learn the more martial skills. Henry Clément, the marshal of France, was appointed to oversee this area of Louis's training and was an exacting taskmaster; a small man himself, he was no doubt able to help Louis develop a style of combat which did not rely exclusively on size and strength. Again, surviving contemporary evidence means that we know what was considered to be the best way of training a boy destined for knighthood. Intense training should wait until puberty, but in early youth the basic skills such as riding, balance and coordination should be learned. Boys should start to become familiar with weapons by using wooden replicas, practising against posts and later against each other in mock combat. Louis enjoyed learning these knightly skills from an early age: when he was ten he wrote to his godfather Stephen de Tournai to ask him for a horse for his birthday (Stephen apparently agreed, but only on the condition that Louis did not use it as an excuse to neglect his studies). Despite being relatively small and slight Louis developed great skill in combat, which was to stand him in good stead in later life, when he became renowned for his enthusiasm for military campaigns. Not for nothing did he become known as Louis the Lion.

Knightly training also had a moral dimension. 'Chivalry' is a word which has changed greatly in meaning over the years; it originates from the French word *chevalerie*, meaning simply a body of knights or mounted warriors, and in its earliest incarnations it had none of the overtones of the distinctive and elaborate system of values which it would later gain. Put simply, in the twelfth century chivalry had very little to do with being polite to all men, gallant to all women or putting your cloak down over a puddle; the best description of it in this age and context is that it was a code which regulated the behaviour of knights *towards other knights*. Even the most cursory glance at contemporary events demonstrates that there was no particular requirement to behave respectfully towards commoners, women, non-Christians or heretics, as we shall see. However, there were by this stage some implicit rules regarding the keeping of one's word and the importance of companionship among knights, of being loyal to one's comrades, and this is a lesson which Louis took to heart, and which was later to have profound consequences for the kingdom of England.

In learning to be a knight Louis was not alone. It was the custom to gather together noble youths from the great houses into the royal household, so a number of companions of similar age were brought to Paris to be educated alongside him, among them Arthur, duke of Brittany and heir presumptive to the English throne; Louis's second cousins Robert and Peter de Dreux, sons of Robert II, count of Dreux, whose father had been a younger brother of Louis VII; and their cousin Guy de Châtillon, eldest son and heir of Walter III, count of St Pol. This gathering of noble boys served a dual purpose: not only would Louis have companions with whom he could practise his skills, but these boys would be the great lords of the realm when he was king, so they would develop a personal loyalty to him.

* * *

Meanwhile, events at court took a new turn. In 1196 King Philip married again, this time to Agnes, daughter of the duke of Merania in Bavaria (then part of the Holy Roman Empire), so Louis at last gained a new stepmother. The only problem was that the pope, Innocent III, had not recognised Philip's repudiation of and separation from Ingeborg, and he declared the new marriage bigamous. So when Agnes gave birth in 1198 to a daughter, Marie, and in 1200 to Philip, a long-awaited second son for the king (known throughout his life as Philip Hurepel for his wild hair), their legitimacy was widely called into question. Again, the chroniclers expressed their disapproval: William the Breton dares to refer to Agnes as a 'concubine' and Rigord saw the marriage as 'against the law and the will of God'. Eventually, with France under papal Interdict – the most severe punishment the Church could inflict, meaning that Mass could not be celebrated anywhere in the realm, and that the sacraments including weddings and burials in consecrated ground were forbidden to everyone – Philip caved in and sent Agnes away to a convent, where her death in 1201, in giving birth to a stillborn child, solved the question of bigamy. Much later, when as part of a negotiated settlement with the pope Philip would agree to restore Ingeborg to

23

her official position as queen – though he never accepted her back personally as his wife – Innocent agreed to legitimise Marie and Philip Hurepel. King Philip would never marry again, though he did father at least one illegitimate son, known as Peter Charlot, sometime between 1205 and 1209. Peter was tutored by William the Breton; destined for a career in the Church, he later became bishop of Noyon. As the eldest son of Philip's first and undisputed queen, Louis's position as heir to the French throne was not affected by the births of his much younger half-siblings, but the legitimisation of Philip Hurepel (albeit surrounded by murmurs that he would never be 'properly' legitimate, as there were questions over the validity of his parents' marriage at the time of his birth) meant that King Philip now had a second heir, which eased worries over the succession.

As Louis continued his scholarly pursuits and his chivalric training, his father began the momentous task of finding a bride for him. Matrimonial alliances were the best way of securing the ties between different houses and the control of lands, and Philip's inclination was to find a suitable granddaughter of Henry II and Eleanor of Aquitaine – and therefore niece of the current King Richard – of whom there were many. Some thought was given to Eleanor, daughter of Richard's deceased brother Geoffrey and sister to Arthur, the duke of Brittany, who was one of Louis's companions at court. But an ongoing conflict between Richard and Arthur made this match less attractive, so Philip turned his attentions to the daughters of Alfonso VIII of Castile (who was married to Richard's sister Eleanor) of whom three were of a suitable age. Negotiations began in early 1199 but were interrupted by Richard's sudden death in April at the siege of Châlus.

Richard's youngest brother John immediately claimed the throne of England, as his brother's heir, but this was challenged by Arthur and his supporters in Brittany, Anjou and Maine; Arthur's late father,

Geoffrey, had been John's elder brother, so if the laws of primogeniture were to be strictly interpreted then Arthur's claim was superior. However, primogeniture was not yet the exact science it would later become, and it was more open to interpretation about whether the younger son of a former king had a better claim to the throne than a grandson whose own father had never ruled – the question of *casus regis* (this related only to royal inheritance, not non-royal succession to other estates, which muddied the waters still further). Norman custom favoured the son and Angevin custom the grandson, thus setting the barons of Normandy and Anjou against each other; there was little point in looking to England for a precedent as the line of succession there had been bent and twisted almost out of all recognition over the preceding two hundred years. In general there was a preference for an adult man over a child, and consideration also needed to be given to the practicalities of the situation. In this particular case Eleanor of Aquitaine, John's mother, who was duchess of Aquitaine in her own right and therefore had many resources at her disposal, favoured her son over her grandson, which tipped matters in John's favour. Meanwhile, Arthur's claim was hampered by the inconvenient facts that he had never been to England and that he was twelve years old.

All of this provided Philip with an opportunity to profit, so he suspended the marriage negotiations and invaded Normandy. During the next few years he would switch his support from John to Arthur and back again depending on what was more politically convenient at the time.

A truce was declared in October 1199. John, by then in desperate need of peace with Philip, agreed to the marriage of one of his nieces with Louis, promising 30,000 marks of silver, the castle and lands of Gisors, the county of Evreux and those castles and lands which had been occupied by the French king at the time of Richard's death.

Philip agreed, and French representatives were dispatched to Castile, where they encountered the elderly Eleanor of Aquitaine, who had been enlisted by John to help with the marriage arrangements. She met the princesses and after careful consideration recommended Alfonso's third daughter Blanche as the future queen of France. The French ambassadors accepted her choice and returned to Philip with the news; Eleanor undertook to bring the girl north.

Further negotiations took place in early 1200 to arrange a more long-term peace between Philip and John, and a treaty was sealed at Le Goulet on 22 May. Louis, who had presumably been awaiting with some interest the outcome of the decision on his future life partner, was summoned, and he and Blanche were married the next day; they were both twelve. As we will see in later chapters, this was to be one of the most successful royal marriages of the Middle Ages; Blanche and Louis would form an effective partnership which would go from strength to strength. But neither of them could know that as, no doubt dazed by events, they returned to Paris to start their life together.

* * *

When Eleanor of Aquitaine had met her three granddaughters she held long conversations with them and considered their looks, personality and suitability for the demanding life ahead before arriving at a decision. Eleanor, of course, was something of an expert on the role of queen of France, having been Louis VII's first wife before their divorce and her subsequent marriage to Henry II of England. She knew that looks were important – no king would stand for an ugly bride – but also that more was needed. Berengaria, the eldest of the three sisters, was already betrothed to King Alfonso IX of León (her father's cousin) and so discounted from consideration, although one suspects that this might not have stopped Eleanor if she had really decided that Berengaria was her preferred candidate.

That left Urraca and Blanche, who was known in Castile as Bianca. We do not know exactly what Blanche looked like, but although she was born in what we would now call Spain, her ancestry meant that she may well have been blond; certainly the only surviving contemporary portrait of her has blue eyes. Whatever she looked like, Eleanor judged that Urraca was the more beautiful of the two, but she selected Blanche anyway. One Spanish chronicler put this down to her name: Bianca (meaning 'white') could easily be rendered into the more French Blanche, but Urraca would sound foreign however it was pronounced. However, given Eleanor's reputation as one of the shrewdest women of the Middle Ages, she may be credited with more imagination than to choose a future queen based merely on her name. She evidently saw something in Blanche.

And so, with no choice in the matter, which she would have known was the usual lot of the daughters of kings, Blanche was to leave her home. She must have been aware as she said goodbye to her parents that she would probably never see them again. Then came the journey through the mountain passes of the Pyrenees and northwards through France; their cavalcade was well guarded and not in particular danger of attack by brigands, but travelling in a slow, creaking, jolting cart for weeks on end was arduous. One of the stops they made on the way was at the abbey of Fontevrault, and it was here that Eleanor concluded that old age (she was in her late seventies) had at last got the better of her, so she decided to retire there. Blanche continued her journey into a foreign land with no family at all around her.

Due to the Interdict which was still in force over France the wedding could not take place in French territory, so the end point of Blanche's journey was Port-Mort just over the border in English-controlled Normandy. When Blanche arrived she may have been surprised to find that neither of the kings who had arranged the match was there: before letting his young son travel to English territory Philip, ever cautious, had demanded that John should give himself up as a hostage for Louis's safety, so both kings were in Paris. At Port-Mort were those nobles who had witnessed the treaty of Le Goulet, including the French counts of Dreux and Perche, and John's representative William Marshal; also the archbishop of Bordeaux, who was to preside over the ceremony; and of course Blanche's future husband.

When she first came face to face with Louis Blanche would have seen a slight, blond youth of about her own age. That was a reasonable start: numerous royal princesses were married off to men much older than themselves. Although many of these husbands were no doubt kind, they could also range from lecherous to distant, uncaring or downright cruel, and young girls had no right to reject them for these reasons; women, even royal ones, had very little power in their marriages and no real control over their husbands' behaviour or the way they were treated. The course of the rest of Blanche's life would be determined by Louis, and she had no doubt spent much of the journey praying that he would be kind.

The wedding was a quiet affair. There were no great feasts or celebrations afterwards: instead Blanche and her new husband travelled straight to Paris, where she met her father-in-law the king for the first time. Despite his intimidating status and fearsome political reputation, Philip was in his personal life something of a *bon viveur*, enjoying food, wine and good company, and there is no reason to suppose that he was not kind to his little daughter-in-law – she had, after all, been one of the means by which he had achieved his aims in the treaty so he had no cause to be anything other than favourably disposed to her. Indeed, Blanche actually found herself the first lady at court: she arrived after Agnes had been banished and while Ingeborg was still incarcerated in her convent; queen mother Adela, shocked at her son's marital behaviour, preferred to live away from the court. This may have enhanced Blanche's social position but it caused problems of its own as she had no older women of suitable rank on hand to whom she could turn if she needed help or advice in her new role.

At first Blanche struggled to adjust to life at the French court, as might any young girl uprooted from her home and large family and sent to live in a foreign environment, but she at least met with some sympathy, as one small incident which has come down to us illustrates. Some months after the wedding, Blanche was suffering from a bout of particular sadness and homesickness, and was crying inconsolably. This was during the visit of the saintly bishop Hugh of Lincoln to Paris, so, seeing his wife upset, the young Louis begged the bishop to go and see her. He did, and succeeded in offering her words of comfort which dried her tears. It must have been reassuring for Blanche not only to receive the prelate's visit, but also to know that Louis was considerate enough to have arranged it. Her loyalty to her new family grew.

A first test for Blanche occurred within a year of her wedding when King John and his queen made a state visit to the French court. As both Philip's daughter-in-law and John's niece Blanche could have been caught in the middle of their negotiations, but she came down squarely on the side of the Capetians, and according to the Anonymous of Béthune's *History of the Dukes of Normandy and the Kings of England* it was actually she who asked John to hand over the last areas of the Vexin which he still controlled. If John had hoped she would be his Plantagenet ally in the Capetian household, he was disappointed.

As Blanche and Louis grew older, it became apparent that they were well matched in both intellect and character. She was clever and literate: she enjoyed listening to poetry, and now had the means to employ jongleurs to recite the latest works to her and to compose new ones. She even wrote some of her own, and one poem of hers survives to this day. Blanche was also known to be very devout so she and Louis would have been able to share religious discussions and divine worship.

Together they headed a household which functioned almost entirely separately from the rest of the court. Blanche had companions as Louis did, daughters of the nobility, and they all formed a glittering company which drew to itself the noblest and brightest youth as well as the fashionable poets and writers of the day. A fragment of the royal household accounts for 1202–3 survives, and it details some of the clothes and fabrics which were bought for them: tunics, surcoats, an expensive dress; fabrics of wool, satin and brocade in different colours; expensive camlet imported from the east; the services of a tailor. The young couple were secure in their companions and well looked after. Paris at this time was an exciting place, home to somewhere in the region of 50,000 people and attracting not only scholars and poets but also artisans and craftsmen; during the first decade of the 1200s there was a thriving trade in books and book production, and building work was ongoing on the walls of the city, the tower of the Louvre and the great cathedral of Notre Dame. Louis and Blanche were at the centre of the city which was the central focus of much of Europe.

As time went by smaller children were also confided to the care of the prince and princess to be brought up in their household; Louis and Blanche were kind to his younger half-siblings Marie and Philip Hurepel, to Joan and Margaret, young orphan daughters of the late Count Baldwin IX of Flanders, and to little Theobald IV, posthumous son of the late Theobald III, count of Champagne. All of these young people, whether deliberately or inadvertently, would play a role in Louis's future.

Due to their tender ages at the time of their wedding, Louis and Blanche's marriage was not consummated straight away. And political as the match was, King Philip had a vested interest in keeping them in separate beds: the revenues from the fiefs which John had offered as a dowry would go directly to him until such time as the marriage was consummated. Whatever the reason, the delay gave Blanche some time in which to adjust to her new life without the added pressure of producing an heir, in which she was more fortunate than Louis's mother had been, and it also allowed her to develop physically without the strain of very early pregnancies. Other royal brides with older husbands were not always so lucky and there are various medieval examples of girls giving birth at thirteen or fourteen, to the detriment of their health. But as Louis was Philip's only undisputedly legitimate son, the demands of the succession meant that the pressure could not be delayed for too long. The right time arrived in due course, and in 1205, at the age of seventeen, Blanche found herself pregnant. She gave birth to a daughter who, sadly for the young couple, did not live long enough to be named. The one consolation was that no public condemnation came Blanche's way, and we may also imagine that Louis was sympathetic in private. Their marriage had started as political but there is no doubt that they developed strong bonds of affection, that they shared a mutual respect, and that after a time they genuinely cared for each other. Blanche was not to become pregnant again for another four years, but there were no moves for a divorce.

Meanwhile Louis went on with his knightly training, which was now in earnest. He moved from the wooden replicas of his boyhood to sharp steel weapons, and needed to train daily in order to become used to the weight of the armour which was worn at the time by those able to afford it. A full set of harness included a heavy gambeson made of layers of fabric, wadding and horsehair; a long-sleeved, knee-length mail hauberk made of riveted links; separate mail leggings known as chausses; a padded fabric arming cap under a mail hood or coif; mail mittens with leather palms; an iron or steel helmet; and a shield made of layers of wood and leather. Add in a lance and a side-arm such as a sword, axe or mace, and in total this could weigh in at about 100 lbs (45 kg); a man not used to wearing and carrying it would tire quickly and be of little use in battle. Louis's skills with sword and lance would need to be honed through constant practice with his companions, his horsemanship perfected.

All of this might have been enough for a man destined to be a simple knight, but Louis was to be a commander, a leader of men. He needed to learn about statecraft, and there could be no better example than his own father. Philip had masterminded France's relationship with England and other neighbours for most of his life, fighting when necessary, negotiating when expedient, and scheming constantly with a view to the long term. He had seen off two kings of England and now had a third almost where he wanted him. The whole background to Louis's youth was a situation where the borders of lands and kingdoms were fluid; an able ruler was ever alert to the opportunity to add to his lands, taking what he could whenever he could, by force or by diplomacy, and then defending his gains. Louis accompanied his father on a short campaign to Brittany in 1206 which would have added to his theoretical knowledge the practical experience of strategy, the deployment of troops and the logistics of a military campaign, all of which was useful experience for the future.

One important lesson to learn in the field of early thirteenth-century statecraft was that casualties were to be expected, even among those who were close friends or relatives. Louis's boyhood companion (and Blanche's cousin) Arthur of Brittany had continued his quest for the English throne even after Philip had recognised John's claim, this recognition being one of the conditions of Louis's marriage agreement. But Arthur had been captured by John's forces at the castle of Mirebeau in 1202, taken to Rouen and imprisoned, and disappeared in mysterious circumstances in April 1203, at the age of fifteen. He was widely rumoured to have been murdered, with the Minstrel of Reims even claiming that John carried out the murder personally. However, as the Minstrel depicts John as some kind of pantomime villain (he is variously 'the worst king who was ever born since the time of Herod', 'evil and cruel', 'a cowardly knight, perverse and traitorous' and a man who 'shamed his barons, and lay with their wives and their daughters by force, and took away their lands, and did such evil that God and everyone should hate him'), it may safely be assumed that John's personal involvement is an exaggeration. But Arthur was never seen again and there is little doubt that he was murdered. His sister Eleanor, another possible rival for the English throne, was taken by John and imprisoned in Corfe Castle in the south of England; she spent the remaining forty years of her life in captivity.

* * *

The accepted entry point for a youth of noble birth into manhood was the occasion of his knighting. Louis's ceremony took place at the royal castle of Compiègne, some 50 miles (80 km) north-east of Paris, on 17 May 1209, the great Church feast of Pentecost. Philip, as might be expected, fenced in the occasion with a number of conditions to which Louis had to agree before the knighting could go ahead. Chief among these were that he had to swear not to take into his service any knight or man who had not taken an oath of allegiance to Philip, and that he had to promise not to take part in any tournaments. This latter was not aimed at curtailing Louis's enjoyment of these martial events, but rather a recognition that tournaments were dangerous: they were not the elaborate individual jousts of later centuries but involved actual mass combat, and fatalities were common. Indeed, no less a personage than Geoffrey of Brittany, son of Henry II and father of Arthur, had been killed taking part in a tournament in 1186, leading to the eventual conflict over the English throne between John and Arthur. Philip was not willing to risk the Capetian succession in this way.

The conditions agreed, the ceremony could take place, and it was magnificent. The king himself presided, and in front of a large crowd he presented Louis with his sword and sword belt, the symbols of knighthood. His golden spurs were carried by the marshal Henry Clément who had trained him for so many years. A number of Louis's companions including the brothers Robert and Peter de Dreux were knighted alongside him, and there was a huge feast afterwards at which Louis was served each course by a different noble lord. It was, says William the Breton, such a dazzling assembly of the great men of the realm, with such an abundance of food and gifts, that nothing like it had ever been seen since.

At the time of Louis's knighting Blanche was some five months pregnant with the couple's second child. To great jubilation she gave birth on 9 September 1209 to a healthy son, who was named Philip; it was the first time since the accession of the Capetians in 987 that three generations of royal males had been alive together. France's future was safe, and Louis was a man of substance: a prince, a knight, a father.

He was now ready to take his place at the king's side.

CHAPTER TWO

FATHER AND SON

IF LOUIS THOUGHT that life would be straightforward now that he was, at twenty-one, considered of full age, he was mistaken. The problem was that his status as 'eldest son of the king' was not actually an official position with duties attached, and nobody knew quite how best to fit him into the existing governmental arrangements. There was no recent precedent for an adult heir to the throne: Louis's father and grandfather had both acceded when they were in their teens, and there had not been an adult heir for over a hundred years.

All previous Capetian eldest sons had been crowned and associated with the throne during their fathers' lifetimes. In turbulent times this practice of having a 'junior king' provided scope for a useful division of responsibilities, and it gave the heir a chance to learn the ropes before he became king on his own, on the assumption that he would later do the same for his own son; it also reduced the possibility of conflict over who would succeed to the throne next. However, Philip chose to break with tradition: he did not have Louis crowned and did not even suggest the possibility of such an event. Why? The chroniclers are silent on this point, but there are two main theories.

The first is that Philip now felt that the Capetian dynasty was so secure in its position that there was no need for such a precaution: when he died, nobody would challenge his son's right to inherit the throne. If Philip had suspected that his line was in any danger of being pushed aside, then surely he would have associated Louis with the throne in 1190 when he had departed on crusade, leaving a single two-year-old child as his heir – but he did not. Instead he left a testament which simply assumed that Louis would be accepted as king and which made arrangements for a regency should one be required. The second (and given what we know of the French king, eminently plausible) explanation is that Philip simply did not want to give up any part of the power and authority which was his. Since his illness in the Holy Land he had been afflicted by a paranoia which meant that he could not bring himself to trust anyone fully, not even his own son who had hitherto been entirely loyal and who showed no signs of disaffection.

Although Philip had experienced no problems in his relationship with Louis, there was abundant recent precedent for royal father–son conflict in the family of Henry II of England. The formal association of an heir with the throne was not a tradition in the Anglo-Norman royal family, but taking a leaf from the Capetian book Henry had crowned his eldest son (also called Henry and generally known as the Young King in order to distinguish him from his father) when the boy was fifteen; this had proved an unmitigated disaster. Young Henry technically had the same status as his father, and not unsurprisingly he wanted some of the power and the money which went with it, but Henry II refused to relinquish any authority. Young Henry rebelled openly against his father in 1173, and the consequent civil war came perilously close to resulting in Henry II losing his throne. Although they were later reconciled, young Henry rebelled again some years later, this time fighting against his brother Richard as well as his father and almost bringing the family to its knees. His death in 1183, at the age of twenty-eight, caused Henry II much grief but it probably saved the Plantagenet-controlled realms from greater peril.

Having witnessed all of this at close quarters – and, indeed, having supported various parties against others as part of his own long-term plan – Philip can have had no desire to replicate such strife in his own kingdom. Although generally considered a good king by his contemporaries he was not universally popular in France, and at about the same time that Louis attained his majority Philip was experiencing discontent from some of his nobles and most of his clergy over his continuing and increasingly cruel treatment of Ingeborg. Running out of excuses for keeping her incarcerated and not reinstating her to her rightful position, he was by now accusing her of sorcery, a very serious allegation. Agitated correspondence travelled back and forth from the royal court in Paris to the papal court in Rome, and there was some question over whether the discontent in France might possibly coalesce with Louis as its figurehead, to the detriment of his father. After all, Louis provided an opportunity for those who were unhappy with the king to turn away from Philip without being disloyal to the Capetians; suddenly all those prophecies about Louis heralding the start of a new dynasty due to his descent from Charlemagne started to surface again.

From the available evidence it would seem that there was no suggestion that Louis himself was fomenting discord or that he had any idea of taking up arms against his father or even challenging him judicially. He had no close interest in Ingeborg – she was a step-mother in name only and he is unlikely to have met her more than once or twice, if at all – and although his natural piety would have meant that he was unhappy with the Interdict and the conflict with the pope, he kept quiet and raised no hand or word against the king.

He also took no official part in government, as Philip and his closest adviser Guérin, bishop of Senlis, kept a firm hold on everything themselves.

In hindsight it would seem that Philip's caution was the correct course of action. If he really had no intention of delegating any authority to Louis, as seems the case, Louis was better off not being crowned as this would have raised unrealistic expectations. But still, in the light of previous practice it could certainly be considered a slight, if not an outright insult. As indeed were some of Philip's other acts towards his son in the years 1209 to 1212, all designed to lessen his influence and authority just at the time and age when Louis might have been expecting them to increase.

Take, for example, Louis's knighting ceremony, which we have already heard described by William the Breton. Lavish though it was, it had actually been put off until the latest possible time which would not be considered an affront. Twenty-one was considered a correct age for knighting, as it was also the official age of majority: lords who had inherited their estates as minors could legally take control of their own lands and affairs once they reached that age. However, this meant that for those of high rank it was also considered the latest age for entry into manhood – it would be an insult for a young count, duke or prince *not* to have been knighted after he turned twenty-one – and the higher the rank, the younger the acceptable age for the ceremony. Royal youths were often knighted much earlier, in their mid-teens, and Henry the Young King, Richard the Lionheart, King John, Arthur of Brittany, and indeed Philip Augustus himself had all received the accolade well before they reached the age of twenty, while Louis was actually only a few months away from his twenty-second birthday before his own ceremony took place. As someone who was so keen on chivalric pursuits he must have been impatient for knighthood, and there was only one person to blame for the delay.

Then there was the question of Artois. The county of Artois was Louis's maternal inheritance from the late Queen Isabelle, who had brought those lands into her marriage and would pass them down to her descendants. The normal custom at this time was for the eldest son in a family to be given the paternal inheritance, the lands which had been passed down through the family line, and for the second son to receive any supplementary gains which had been acquired by marriage or conquest. But Louis was Isabelle's only son, so he had been entitled to Artois since her death, even though his father was still alive. While he was a minor there was of course an excuse for Philip to keep the lands under his own control, but once Louis reached the age of majority he should by right and by custom have been named count of Artois. But Artois was a significant region in the north of France, fertile land bordering Flanders and reaching towards the Channel coast, and endowing Louis with it would mean that he had men and revenues of his own, thus giving him enough autonomy potentially to constitute a threat. However, postpone as he might the day when Louis was named count, Philip could not simply annex Artois to the royal domain, as that would be against feudal custom and might cause discontent in others who felt their own lands to be correspondingly less safe. So Philip steered a middle course, giving Louis some nominal legislative control over the lands – he could start to learn about governance – but without officially investing him as count of Artois.

Louis's treatment at the hands of his father while he was in his early twenties leads us naturally to wonder what he himself thought of his situation. Given all the apparent provocation and his own presumed ambition, why did he not rebel against the king? Louis is a shadowy figure in the chronicles between 1209 and 1212, seemingly passive, though he was undoubtedly still present at court, learning from his father and keeping up with his military training. We do know that he was devout, a strict and orthodox Catholic who would have held fast to the tenet of 'respect thy father', but further than that we cannot second-guess what he felt. However, we can judge him by his actions and the one undoubted fact is that, unlike the quarrelsome sons of Henry II, he did not rebel. Instead he accepted Philip's wishes and came to terms with him, living in some kind of harmony. What else could he have done? His choices were really only between acquiescence and outright rebellion, the consequences of which could have been disastrous. So he bided his time and acted with dignity, making the best of difficult circumstances. And it is, of course, possible that he was actually happy with his situation: although he wielded no real power, he benefited both from a settled court life where he could gain experience without having an enormous weight of responsibility on his shoulders, and from a settled home life with his wife and son and the other children in their care.

Philip and Louis were quite different from one another. For a start, they presented a physical contrast: in 1212, when Louis next comes to the fore in his own story, Philip was approaching fifty, ruddy, bald, corpulent and given to good living; while his son, in his mid-twenties, was blond, slim (some have even called him frail and sickly but his military exploits show he was not physically weak, as we shall discuss later), religious and chaste. They also presented a contrast in personality: Philip had always been ready to take up arms if he really needed to – France would not have been in the healthy position it currently enjoyed if he had shied away from military campaigns – but he was more given to political scheming, whereas Louis was more impulsive and liked nothing better than warrior-like pursuits. It may have been their very dissimilarity which saved their relationship: Philip might not have wanted to hand over any political power to his son, but he recognised a formidable warrior when he saw one, and this would shortly be to both their advantages. For there was trouble in France, trouble that was to foreshadow the next phase of the conflict against England.

* * *

For some years, the county of Flanders had been causing a problem. The previous count, Baldwin IX, had died in 1205 while on crusade, leaving two young daughters who were being brought up in Louis and Blanche's household. Before he left Flanders Baldwin had seized two towns, St Omer and Aire, which were actually part of the dowry of Isabelle of Hainaut, Louis's mother, and therefore part of the county of Artois to which Louis had in theory succeeded at her death. In January 1212 Baldwin's elder daughter Joan had been given in marriage to Ferrand, fourth son of the king of Portugal, who became count of Flanders in right of his wife. Ferrand promised to serve the French king faithfully, but he would not cede the two towns of St Omer and Aire. Rather than seeking a political solution Louis now acted decisively, if a little impetuously, taking matters into his own hands and riding with a host (including the counts of St Pol and Dreux and their sons Guy de Châtillon and the Dreux brothers) to Flanders. In a lightning military operation, he captured the towns. Louis did not seek to attack the rest of the county, but instead concluded a treaty with Ferrand in February which gave him St Omer and Aire, and the lands and fiefs which made up his mother's dowry, in return for promising not to claim anything else in Flanders.

If Philip and Louis had really been at loggerheads, and if Philip had seen this as a usurpation of royal power, he would no doubt have taken steps against his son, but in fact he agreed to recognise the treaty. He allowed Louis to increase his patronage among the nobles of Artois and to accept their homage – although the nobles also had to take an oath of loyalty directly to the king – and Louis began to issue his own charters in Artois. Meanwhile, the defeated and discomfited Ferrand turned his attentions to the other side of the Channel and began to make overtures of friendship to King John.

Louis found his standing in France improved, and in November 1212 he took Philip's place at an official meeting with Frederick of Hohenstaufen, claimant to the crown of the Holy Roman Empire. This vast and powerful realm comprised the land which is now variously eastern France, the Netherlands, Luxembourg, Germany, western Poland, Switzerland, Austria, Slovenia and northern Italy. It was therefore France's immediate neighbour to the east, and had been the scene of a bitter succession conflict for more than a decade. Holy Roman Emperor Henry VI had died in 1198 leaving only a four-year-old son, who had been overlooked in a two-way struggle for the crown between Henry's brother Philip of Swabia and Otto of Saxony, an ambitious representative of the rival Welf dynasty. After years of conflict it seemed that Otto had emerged the winner after he had Philip of Swabia assassinated in 1208 and subsequently married Beatrice, the eldest of Philip's four surviving daughters (she was barely into her teens at the time, and died of an unspecified illness just three weeks after the wedding). However, Otto enjoyed only a short period of ascendancy before a new claimant appeared on the scene: Frederick of Hohenstaufen, Henry VI's son now grown to young manhood. Frederick was supported by Philip Augustus, while King John backed Otto, who also happened to be his nephew as he was the son of John's elder sister Matilda and her late husband Henry, the duke of Saxony. John and Otto therefore formed a dangerous coalition with France sandwiched in the middle, so it was imperative that Philip's candidate for the throne be supported against them.

As Louis's first formal embassy on behalf of his father it was fortunately not too complex, for both parties were predisposed to want the support of the other. Louis accomplished his task without any problems, and a final treaty was sealed on 19 November 1212 in which

Frederick and Philip each promised that they would not make peace with either John or Otto, or with any of their allies. Louis's name did not actually appear on the document, but William the Breton makes it clear that it was he who conducted the negotiations.

* * *

Unusually, we are rather well informed about what Louis did during the next few months, as a fragment of his accounts survives that covers the period October 1212 to February 1213. From this document, no doubt considered dull in its time, we can open a small window on his life and peer through at his activities and priorities.

Just over half of the expenditure recorded in the fragment was spent in Artois: campaign expenses, payments to individuals, and works on the castle at Lens including payments to the master mason and carpenter. Louis's diplomatic side is revealed in payments to messengers for travelling with letters to the great men of the realm and to Blanche's father in Castile; he gave a present of money to one Henry, concierge of the royal palace on the Île de la Cité and no doubt a man who was well informed on the latest developments at court. Interestingly, there were also payments to two men of King John's, who were currently out of favour and banished across the Channel: Simon Langton (the brother of Stephen Langton, archbishop of Canterbury, also in exile at this time), and Robert de St Germain.

The accounts show Louis to be very much a noble lord of his time: there are expenses for hunting and hawking, for horses and military equipment, for squires and grooms. He also had his household to run, with payments made to cooks, bakers and clerks, and for food including expensive imports such as almonds and ginger; there was expenditure for the purchase and transport of wine.

Louis the family man is also revealed by his accounts. Blanche's principal residence was now at Lorrez-le-Bocage, 50 miles (80 km) south of Paris and therefore away from the dangers of disease which were prevalent in any large city; Louis's expenses show that he made frequent trips there, and that he paid for Blanche's ladies-in-waiting and servants. A Parisian doctor made several trips out to see Blanche during the winter of 1212–13, as she was with child. And, finally, Louis gave his little brother Philip Hurepel a gift of £10 when he came to visit – a substantial sum (enough, for example, to buy a very decent horse or a wardrobe of clothes) which the boy no doubt appreciated.

In January 1213 Blanche was confined at the royal castle at Lorrez-le-Bocage. Birthing customs had not changed since the time of Louis's own birth, and even if he was in the castle he would not have known until the news leaked out of the chamber that she had been delivered of twin boys.

Twins: the cause of the death of Louis's mother. Knowing as we do that he cared deeply for his wife, we can assume that he must have been frantic; and knowing as we do that medical science had not evolved into anything like its modern form, we can also be sure that he could do very little for her, other than to pay for the doctor and to pray. The two boys, who both died within days, are named in one lesser-known chronicle as John and Alfonso, but they made such a fleeting and tiny impression on life that none of the major writers mentions their names.

To have two sets of twins born in successive generations, when there had been none before in the French royal line, implies that it may have been Louis's mother who introduced a genetic predisposition; instances of twins appear regularly in the family tree thereafter, although none survived their first year until the fifteenth century and none reached adulthood until the eighteenth century. Had Louis's brothers or sons lived, there would have been repercussions for the order of succession: one twin, naturally, would have been born first, but there was a theory prevalent at the time that a twin born second had actually been conceived first and should therefore be considered the elder.

None of this would have been uppermost in Louis's mind as he gazed down at the tiny bodies and prayed for the souls of his sons. His natural grief is likely to have been tempered by the knowledge that the boys had lived long enough to be baptised, and that they would not therefore be denied eternal life in heaven. He would also have given thanks that Blanche had been spared; carefully nurtured back to health, she was pregnant again by the end of the year.

It was in February 1213, shortly after the babies' deaths, that Louis took a vow to join the Albigensian crusade against the Cathars in Languedoc, the southern region of France. Pope Innocent III had been calling for nearly a decade for the kings and lords of Christendom to eliminate the sect of Christians known as Cathars, whose beliefs were so different from the prevailing Catholic orthodoxy that they were considered heretics, heathens on a par with the Moors and Saracens. Catharism was a 'dualist' heresy, which meant that adherents believed in two deities: a good god who had created the spiritual realm, and an evil god who had created the physical world. Thus the physical world and everything in it including humans (and, by extension, Jesus Christ) was evil. Cathars recognised only one sacrament, the Consolamentum, which removed all sin and made the receiver a member of the Perfecti. The Perfecti were considered to be of the spiritual, rather than the physical, world, and among other restrictions they could not eat the flesh of animals or engage in sexual relationships or procreation. Therefore most Cathars were ordinary believers who sought the Consolamentum, if at all, only shortly before death. Those who were living Perfecti were considered exemplars and leaders.

The Catholic Church objected, unsurprisingly, to the depiction of Jesus Christ as evil, and also to other Cathar practices such as their rejection of marriage and the other sacraments, the equality of the sexes in religious leadership, and their belief in reincarnation. So divergent were Cathar beliefs from Catholic doctrine that the Church decided that such heretics were not to be forgiven and brought back into the fold; they were to be exterminated. Innocent had written to Philip Augustus as early as 1204 to urge him to 'remove this territory from the control of sectarian heretics; and then place it into the hands of true Catholics who will ... serve Our Lord in all faithfulness'. In 1208 the papal legate in the region had been murdered and Innocent had declared that the campaign to rid the world of Cathars was now a holy crusade. The call had been answered by many noblemen acting on their own accounts, but the kings of England, France and the Holy Roman Empire had variously been involved in wars and succession disputes or been under sentence of excommunication themselves and were therefore not eligible to participate. Equally their mutual suspicion meant that none was willing to leave his lands for fear that one of the others would attack while he was gone.

But here was Louis: a prince of impeccable Catholic credentials, enthusiastic about military activity, keen to ride and to fight in a holy cause, and with no particular lands or responsibilities to leave behind in other hands. What could be more suitable? He had to look after his own person, of course, but as he had a son of his own and a half-brother to act as back-up heirs, the situation for France was not as precarious as it had been previously. Philip allowed Louis to take the cross, and at an assembly in Paris in March 1213 plans were made for his departure. However, Louis's wish to fight on behalf of the Church to stamp out the Cathar heresy would have to wait, as the question of England had reared its head again.

* * *

King John, who as we will see in the next chapter was by this time troubled, excommunicated and with his kingship being contested, was forming an alliance. He and Otto of Saxony were joined by Ferrand, count of Flanders, and by another disaffected French nobleman, Renaud de Dammartin, count of Boulogne, who had borne a grudge against Philip Augustus since a judicial decision went against him some years previously and who had defected and done homage to John in 1212. The text of John's letter accepting Renaud's homage is illustrative in more ways than one: 'Know that we have accorded to our friend and liegeman Renaud de Dammartin, count of Boulogne, the assurance that we will not conclude without him either peace or truce with the king of France nor with his son Louis.' The specific mention of Louis's name indicates that, as far as John and Renaud were concerned, he was now considered a force in his own right.

William the Breton, who tells us of this letter, is admittedly not very keen on Renaud de Dammartin. He felt the count's betrayal of his king very deeply and heaps accusations upon him: Renaud persecutes his neighbours, says William; he dispossesses widows and orphans, gives himself up to debauchery and promenades his concubines in public, to the shame of his wife in whose right he holds his lands. The Minstrel of Reims goes even further, depicting Renaud engaging in a bout of unseemly and almost certainly fictional fisticuffs in the royal court itself. While we must allow for the Minstrel's dramatic licence and William's own chagrin, and not take all the accusations at face value, it seems clear that feelings were running deep in France over Renaud's defection to John.

King Philip, already in conflict with John and Otto, could not let lie the treachery of two of his own lords. It was at this time that he first formed an idea of invading England, possibly reckoning that attack was the best form of defence. At the same time, the spring of 1213, he finally agreed to reinstate Ingeborg to her rightful position as queen (although he did not consent to live with her as husband

and wife), thus becoming at a stroke the pope's new favourite son. Pope Innocent was still in conflict with John over John's refusal to accept the preferred papal candidate, Stephen Langton, as archbishop of Canterbury, and he eventually lost patience, declaring that John should be dispossessed of his crown, and appointing Philip as the man to carry out the sentence. In April Philip called a council of his nobles at Soissons, and stated his intention to conquer England and name Louis as its king.

Why did Philip not want the crown for himself? He was probably not all that interested in England, and may not have had any desire to cross the Channel himself, but it would make France more secure to have the neighbouring realm out of Plantagenet hands, and if Philip did not want the crown for himself then Louis, his faithful and obedient son, was clearly the next best choice. As one might expect, the offer was hedged around with conditions: Louis swore that if he were to become king of England he would make no claim on any French territory while Philip still lived, and he would demand from his English subjects that they would not seek to harm the king or the kingdom of France. For Philip the plan, if it succeeded, would be a win–win situation: his own kingdom would be safe from danger, the threat from England eliminated, and an outlet provided for Louis's martial ardour and political ambitions, without Philip having to give up anything which was his. For Louis the attractions were equally obvious: a chance for military glory and a kingdom of his own.

The date set for the gathering of the fleet was 10 May 1213, but due to the huge logistical operation required to collect and outfit the ships it did not actually happen until 22 May. At first glance the extra twelve days should not have made much of a difference, but the delay allowed two things to happen. Firstly there was good news for Philip and Louis: an experienced naval commander known as Eustace the

Monk, of whom we shall learn more later, deserted the English camp and sold his services, his knowledge and his wealth of maritime experience to the French. But the second occurrence was to turn all the French plans to dust.

Perhaps realising what very real danger he and his kingdom were in, John had been considering desperate measures and was already in contact with Pope Innocent to negotiate the question of ceding to him the whole of England and holding it as a papal fief. As the threat of invasion became more imminent, the arrangements were finalised: on 13 May 1213, just as the papal legate Pandulf Masca was sailing across the Channel, John had letters patent (that is, letters which were meant for public proclamation, not for private correspondence) drawn up which set out the terms, and on 15 May he officially placed England – and Ireland – under the pope's control.

The advantages of the deal for the papacy were clear: Innocent would gain more territory and influence, and the arrangement also allowed him to express his disapproval of Philip's plan to involve Louis in the campaign to the detriment of his vow to mount a crusade against the Albigensians. And the benefits to John were immediate: with England now a papal fief, Innocent could not countenance an attack on it by a hostile French king, so he cancelled the whole invasion and promptly threatened Philip with excommunication if he went ahead with it regardless. Philip, so newly reconciled with the pope after years of conflict, and statesman enough to recognise when he was outmanoeuvred, was not inclined to embroil himself in another quarrel so soon, so he accepted. But he was understandably furious. Roger of Wendover tells us: 'The French king was much enraged when he heard this, and said that he had already spent sixty thousand pounds in the equipment of his ships, and in providing food and arms, and that he had undertaken the said duty by command of our lord the pope.'

But stalking up and down swearing would serve little purpose; action was necessary. Philip might not be able to attack England, but he could take out his anger on those of his liegemen who had betrayed him. In order to adhere to the letter of the law he summoned Ferrand of Flanders to appear before him as his vassal – but gave him only one day to do so. When Ferrand unsurprisingly failed to show up, Philip launched an attack on his lands, 'destroying every place he came to by fire, and putting the inhabitants to the sword' according to Roger of Wendover, and authorised Louis to do the same. Louis, taking out frustrations of his own at the destruction of his chance of a crown, responded with alacrity, and Ferrand sent an appeal for aid to John.

Given England's position across the Channel from Normandy and the rest of mainland Europe, the Anglo-Norman kings had always maintained a small number of ships to convey them and their effects back and forth. But this was not a navy in the proper sense of the word, and when Henry II or Richard I required large numbers of ships for military purposes they had to hire or commandeer them. Richard, with his extensive programme of overseas travel, had a small number of ships built during his reign, but credit for the establishment of a proper navy must go to King John. His loss of Normandy meant that the Channel became his frontier, so armed ships were a necessity and by 1204 he had a fleet of forty-five galleys patrolling the east and south coasts. From then onwards ships were built and fitted out specifically for royal military use, and by 1213 John had around a hundred of them at his disposal. He responded to Ferrand's appeal by sending a fleet across the Channel.

On 30 May 1213 the English ships under William Longsword, earl of Salisbury (who, as an illegitimate son of Henry II, was John's half-brother) arrived at Damme, where they were fortunate enough to find the French invasion fleet at anchor, sparsely guarded as most of the men were engaged in Philip and Louis's raiding parties inland. Roger of Wendover takes up the tale:

> When the chiefs of the English army learned this, they flew to arms, fiercely attacked the fleet, and, soon defeating the crews, they cut the cables of three hundred of their ships loaded with corn, wine, flour, meat, arms and other stores, and sent them to sea to make for England; besides these they set fire to and burned a hundred or more which were aground.

Describing the same incident, the author of the *History of William Marshal* tells us of 'ships at sea burning and belching forth smoke, as if the very sea were on fire'.

Some of the English knights became overconfident and disembarked, mounted, to pursue the Frenchmen who were fleeing; however, Philip and Louis were not all that far away and they were able to launch a surprise counterattack. The English retreated to their ships and out to sea. Surveying the damage and calculating how risky it would be if more ships were to fall into English hands, Philip gave orders for the rest of his fleet to be burned. The ships were torched, flames visible for miles around and the stench of burning tar hanging in the air; and Louis watched as his plans to invade England turned to smoke and ashes.

* * *

Philip returned to Paris, leaving Louis in Flanders to continue taking revenge on Ferrand and his lands; through the summer and autumn of 1213 he captured, sacked and burned a number of towns. To modern eyes this may seem unpalatable, but the world of the thirteenth century was a very different place. The wealth and power of nobles were based on their lordship over lands or towns, and over the people who laboured in the fields or in urban industries. In order to hurt an opposing noble you had to damage his wealth-producing resources, as this would prevent him from raising the funds to equip a military force to fight against you. Therefore the ravaging of the countryside, the burning of crops, the killing of livestock and the sacking of towns were all acceptable methods of waging war, and, indeed, were more common than battles. But this meant that non-combatants were not safe: if you consider a peasant family to be not so much people in their own right as units of wealth-production for their lord, then by killing them you logically further deprive that lord of funds. Of course, this was not exactly fair for the peasants or townspeople who were considered little more than economic resources, who could lose their livelihoods or their lives through no fault of their own, but this was of little moment to the kings and nobles who were concentrating on other concerns. To them, acting in a way which we might consider cruel was not only acceptable, it was necessary: you had to be brutal when the occasion demanded it or you would not be respected and feared. So in burning the towns in the county of Flanders, Louis was acting very much as a man of his times. He did nearly get a taste of his own medicine at the town of Bailleul, however, when the fires set by his troops took hold so quickly that he and his companions were nearly burned, becoming trapped in the narrow streets before escaping at the last moment.

Campaigning was difficult in the winter due to the difficulty of finding food for men and fodder for horses. Louis took a break from his operations, and was in Paris in February 1214 when he heard the news that King John had disembarked at La Rochelle, a port in Poitou, intent on working with his allies to crush France once and for all. This was a threat to be taken seriously, so Philip and Louis called on all those who owed them military service, mustered their forces and rode south-west together; but then the catastrophic news reached them that the other part of the coalition – Otto, Ferrand and Renaud – were massing their forces further north. Surrounded on all sides, France was very much in danger of being crushed.

Fortunately Philip had what none of the other major players had: a grown son who could be entrusted with the command of an army. The king split his forces and took his share of the men back north, leaving Louis in charge of the southern campaign. Their armies divided largely along generational lines with Louis and his companions staying together and their fathers, including the count of Dreux and the count of St Pol, riding with Philip. But Louis had one wise old head in his camp – Henry Clément, the marshal, who had trained him as a boy.

Meanwhile, John was making a dangerous alliance with a powerful Poitevin noble, Hugh IX de Lusignan. For a number of years he had been John's enemy since John had taken Hugh's betrothed Isabelle of Angoulême and married her himself, but now in a strange twist John offered his daughter by Isabelle, Joan, in marriage to Hugh's son. Hugh decided to throw in his lot with the English king, and the betrothal took place on 25 May 1214 (Hugh junior was at this point in his mid-twenties; Joan was four), whereupon Hugh and many other Poitevin nobles joined John in the insurrection.

John's next move was to approach the well-fortified and strategically important city of Nantes, a port which straddled the River Loire and was the seat of the dukes of Brittany, and threaten it in an effort to force the new duke to submit to him. The succession of the dukedom of Brittany in recent years had been complicated. Constance, who had been duchess of Brittany in her own right, had remarried after the death of her husband Geoffrey, son of Henry II, in 1186 and had borne more children, so the murdered Arthur and the imprisoned Eleanor had three younger half-sisters. Due to her captive state Eleanor had been overlooked as Arthur's heir following his death, so the duchy passed to Alix, eldest of the three younger sisters, who had recently married; her husband therefore became duke of Brittany in right of his wife, and it was he with whom John attempted to negotiate. Unfortunately for John the husband in question was Peter de Dreux, Louis's cousin and boyhood companion.

Peter refused absolutely to surrender Nantes to the English king, despite the fact that any siege might endanger his twelve-year-old wife, and despite the fact that his elder brother Robert was at that time a prisoner in John's custody, having been captured during a skirmish, and was liable to be used as leverage. The taking of hostages of noble or knightly rank was a common feature of conflicts in the early thirteenth century: ostensibly this was because the 'brotherhood' of chivalry was international, so anyone of knightly rank or above was entitled to certain privileges, but of more practical import was the fact that it would be foolish to kill a nobleman if you could capture him and offer him up for ransom instead. Such hostages were normally treated reasonably well, but it was only two years since John had hanged twenty-eight sons of Welsh chieftains, many of them children, handed over to him by Prince Llewelyn of Wales, so Peter can have been under no illusions that his decision to remain loyal to Louis might cost his brother his life. His courage won him a reprieve, however, and John decided against a full-scale siege of Nantes and withdrew. Instead he headed back along the River Loire, taking Ancenis on 11 June and Angers on 17 June before turning his attention to the fortress of La-Roche-aux-Moines.

This was a castle which had been recently built by William des Roches, the seneschal (an officer appointed by the king to oversee justice and administration) of Anjou, in order to defend the route from Nantes to Le Mans. John arrived there on 19 June 1214 and demanded surrender, but the garrison refused. He brought in siege machinery and bombarded the castle for two weeks, even erecting a gallows outside the walls and threatening to hang the entire garrison, but still they held out.

Louis, meanwhile, was on the Breton border with his army when news of the siege at La-Roche-aux-Moines reached him. This presented him with a major dilemma. Should he ride towards John's forces and engage him, thus committing himself to a set-piece battle in which he risked all his troops? Or should he wait to see the outcome at La-Roche-aux-Moines and then seek to head John off elsewhere before he could march to join his allies in the north? Each course of action had its own particular disadvantages. Pitched battles were a rarity in the Middle Ages (the Capetians had not fought one since Philip's grandfather Louis VI engaged Henry I of England at Brémule in 1119, and even William the Conqueror fought only two in his lifetime) as they were a huge gamble – a commander risked everything on one throw of the dice, and external influences such as weather or luck could sway the outcome one way or the other. Warfare was therefore characterised more by ravaging and sieges than by battles. If Louis were to engage John he could risk his entire army, not to mention his own life. But if he did nothing John might subdue La-Roche-aux-Moines and then move on to the next castle, and before long find himself master of many of the major strongholds. His position would then be strengthened beyond challenge.

Louis was a warrior at heart so his decision, supported by Henry Clément, was to attack John's forces. He gave the order to advance and set off, 'as ardent as lightning', according to William the Breton, 'riding at the front of his cavalry squadrons, with every hour which delayed the onset of combat seeming long'.

At La-Roche-aux-Moines John heard that Louis's force was advancing towards him, and at first he welcomed the idea of a battle as he had a vastly superior number of men at his disposal (William the Breton puts it at triple the number Louis had with him). However, many of John's men were mercenaries, fighting for money and less willing to risk their lives in battle than they were to besiege a castle, and many of the others were Poitevin nobles who had defected to John's cause. Siding with the English might have seemed a good idea while the French monarchy was miles away, but when it came to a choice of actually taking up arms against the heir to the throne, the risks seemed too high and they wavered.

Unsure of how much of his army he could now rely on, and wary of being caught between the arriving force and a potential attack from the castle garrison sallying forth, John dropped the siege and fled, departing with such speed that he left behind his camp, most of his baggage, his siege machinery and many of his men. Roger of Wendover says that John 'retired in great annoyance from the siege', while William the Breton says he 'was vanquished by fear and thought of nothing but flight'; whatever the exact truth, John escaped, making such good time that he turned up some 70 miles (110 km) away only two days later, but much of his army had not yet crossed the river when Louis's host arrived. Many of John's men were killed, drowned or captured, and Louis seized much booty from the camp, collecting the armour, weapons and goods which had been abandoned.

Although there had been no battle as such, Louis's decisive action had annihilated the southern threat, meaning that Philip could deal with their enemies in the north without worrying about John's army suddenly appearing behind him. He too was persuaded that a pitched battle would settle the outcome, and he faced up to his enemies on 27 July 1214 at Bouvines, a village a few miles south-east of Lille. Among others he had with him Odo III, duke of Burgundy; Walter III de Châtillon, count of St Pol; Robert II, count of Dreux, and his brother Philip de Dreux, bishop of Beauvais; and Guérin, bishop of Senlis. Ranged against him were Otto, Renaud, Ferrand and William, the earl of Salisbury. The allies were confident – the Minstrel of Reims has them deciding even before the battle which bits of France they will award themselves after their victory – but despite a scare when he was unhorsed in the battle, the day belonged entirely to Philip. The battle was both bloody and claustrophobic, as some excerpts from the *Philippide*, William the Breton's eyewitness account, show:

> The combatants are engaging each other over the whole plain in such a close melee that those who are striking and those who are being struck are so close to each other that they barely have room to raise their arm to strike another blow.

> Lances are shattering, swords and daggers hit each other, combatants split each other's heads with their axes, and their lowered swords plunge into the bowels of horses.

> Loose horses are running here and there across the field, some giving out their last breaths, some with the entrails spilling out of their stomachs, some kneeling and falling to the ground ... there is hardly one place where you cannot see dead men and dying horses.

By the end of the day the allies were in disarray. Otto had fled the field; William of Salisbury had been taken prisoner after being bludgeoned to the ground, his helmet broken by the mace of the warlike bishop of Beauvais; Ferrand of Flanders and, after what even his enemies recognised as a heroic rearguard action, Renaud of Boulogne were captured.

The battle of Bouvines changed the course of medieval European history; it is as legendary in France as Agincourt is in England. But Philip's great victory would not have been possible without Louis's contribution in the south: it was father and son working in tandem that had defeated their massed enemies. Matthew Paris even goes so far as to say that 'the French rejoiced less in the victory at Bouvines than in the defeat inflicted on the king of England by Louis, because they hoped that in him they would have a valiant sovereign who would outshine his father'. While we must make allowances for Matthew's hindsight, it is clear that neither success would have been possible without the other.

While Philip was rejoicing in his victory, giving thanks to God and making arrangements for the detention of his prisoners, Louis stayed in Anjou until September, recapturing the castles taken by John and subduing resistance. Over the summer he suffered a loss when the gallant marshal Henry Clément died of a fever, possibly an after-effect of wounds sustained. He was much mourned, but his death did not halt Louis in his campaign: the twenty-six-year-old prince could take charge of his own army as an experienced and competent commander. Following his retreat and the defeat of his allies, John caused little trouble; 'Woe is me!', Roger of Wendover has him lament. 'Since I became reconciled to God, and submitted myself and my kingdoms to the Church of Rome, nothing has gone prosperously with me, and everything unlucky has happened to me.' John and Philip sealed a truce at Chinon on 18 September 1214, after which Louis was finally free to return to Paris and meet his new son Louis, who had been born in April.

The repercussions from the victories at La-Roche-aux-Moines and Bouvines were profound for all concerned. Otto abdicated in 1215, leaving Philip's ally Frederick of Hohenstaufen as Holy Roman Emperor Frederick II, and France free from fear of attack from that direction; Otto himself died in internal exile in 1218. The two French counts who had traitorously taken up arms against their rightful king were dragged away from Bouvines in chains and imprisoned. Ferrand remained in captivity until he was eventually released in 1227. Renaud was stripped of his lands and titles in favour of his twelve-year-old daughter Matilda, who, handily (and perhaps inevitably), was married to King Philip's thirteen-year-old son Philip Hurepel, who became count of Boulogne. Renaud was imprisoned in arduous conditions for thirteen years, chained to a heavy log and unable to take more than a pace in any direction. When Ferrand was eventually released and he was not, he finally gave up hope and committed suicide in 1227. Some months after Bouvines there was a slightly tardy exchange of prisoners, at which point Robert de Dreux was swapped for the earl of Salisbury, who was none too pleased that brother John had appeared in no hurry to pay his ransom.

John returned defeated to England with his reputation in tatters, to further conflict with a country full of barons who had refused to join him on the campaign anyway. Louis finally went to Languedoc to fight on behalf of the Church and to hone his formidable military skills even further. A year later, when the question of England arose again, the invitation to Louis to come over and take the crown from John came from the English barons themselves, and he was ready.

CHAPTER THREE

THE INVITATION

IN ORDER TO understand why the barons of England should take so radical a step as to seek to overthrow their king, and why their choice of replacement should be the son of the king of France, we must leave Louis for a while and spend some time with John.

John had never been a popular figure, suffering by comparison with his glamorous and chivalrous older brothers Henry, Richard and Geoffrey. This had not mattered too much while he was merely John Lackland, unlikely to rule any substantial territories, but it became a significant factor once he was king, and his behaviour did nothing to improve the situation.

John's initial success, capturing his rival Arthur and eliminating both the boy and any further resistance to his accession, proved to be the high point of his reign and the only time he could legitimately claim to be in control of the vast empire his father had left. After that his lands and reputation were gradually chipped away. In 1203–4 he proved no military match for Philip Augustus, who used the presumed murder of Arthur as an excuse to declare John's title of duke of Normandy (for which he owed homage to the French king) forfeit and to invade and capture Normandy. This was a huge blow to John's kingship and it lost him more than just land. Most of the earls and barons of England had ancestral homes in Normandy as well, as they were the direct descendants of those who had come to England with William the Conqueror; owning lands on both sides of the Channel was no problem when the same man was liege lord of both, but now that England belonged to John and Normandy to Philip, the barons had to choose between their two estates, keeping one and losing the other as they could not swear allegiance to two kings at once.

Only one lord successfully managed to retain his lands in both locations: the canny and not altogether scrupulous William Marshal, earl of Pembroke and Striguil. Initially a protégé of Eleanor of Aquitaine, Marshal had come to greater prominence in the 1170s as a tournament companion of Henry the Young King, and he went on to serve each of the Plantagenet kings in turn. He had been rewarded with the hand in marriage of the rich heiress Isabelle de Clare, more than twenty years his junior, which had endowed him with extensive lands and great wealth. Marshal had fought on John's side in Normandy and was then sent by John as an ambassador to Philip Augustus in 1204 to negotiate a truce; while he was in France he took the opportunity which the mission offered and paid homage directly to Philip for his holdings in Normandy. This did not please John, as Marshal would no longer be able to fight against Philip if Philip was his overlord. However, after a cool period which lasted several years Marshal returned to English royal favour and kept his lands in England as well. The other barons were not so fortunate and were forced into a direct choice: most of them chose England, meaning that their energies and their ambitions were now concentrated there.

This did nothing to halt John's troubles. As kings his father and brother had inspired loyalty and affection; John sought to rule by fear and insecurity. He would not put his trust in anyone who was not completely in his power, and he frequently took hostages (many of them children) from noble families to ensure their good behaviour, which did not endear him to the barons. He also kept his lords in a state of financial dependency, charging huge fees known as 'reliefs' to heirs in order to allow them to succeed when their fathers died, then holding the debt over their heads as a threat, knowing that if he ever called it in they would be bankrupt. For example, Geoffrey de Mandeville, earl of Essex, was forced to offer 20,000 marks (some £13,333, a mark as we will remember being 13s 4d or two-thirds of a pound) for the honour of marrying the heiress of Gloucester, John's ex-wife Isabelle, and succeeding to her lands – at a time when most earldoms raised an annual income of some £200 to £400. Matilda de Braose was asked for the frankly ludicrous sum of 50,000 marks for 'the king's grace' (which sounds suspiciously like protection money) when her total wealth amounted to 24 marks and a few gold pieces. Matilda and her family were harried, persecuted and eventually destroyed by John in a personal vendetta: John asked her and her husband William de Braose to hand over their sons as hostages, but Matilda made the mistake of saying in public that she would never hand her children over to a man who had murdered his nephew (William had been appointed by John as Arthur of Brittany's gaoler after his capture, and might be supposed to have had a great deal of inside information on what had happened to the boy). John immediately called in all the family's financial debts and confiscated William's estates in Devon and in Sussex. When they fled to Ireland and Wales he had them hunted down; Matilda and her eldest son William (a married man in his thirties, but as heir still subject to his father as head of the family) were captured and deliberately starved to death on John's order in 1210, while William senior made it to France only to die there, a broken man, a year later.

That this could happen to someone who had always stood high in John's favour meant that other barons became nervous and suspicious, wary of their own positions. But instead of providing any kind of reassurance John went in the opposite direction: his unwillingness to trust anyone who was not completely under his thumb meant that he relied more and more heavily on shipped-in mercenaries whose whole livelihoods rested on his whim, rather than on his less dependent barons. The English nobles hated and despised these 'foreigners', and the Barnwell annalist was convinced that one of the root causes of the desertion of John by his subjects was the favour he showed to 'aliens'.

John also provoked the Church. When the archbishop of Canterbury, Hubert Walter, died in 1205 the task of electing a successor fell, as was the custom, to the monks of Canterbury. One faction elected a fellow monk named Reginald as Hubert's successor, while another favoured the candidate proposed by John, his supporter John de Gray, bishop of Norwich. Both sides appealed to the pope, who, after some consideration, set aside both claims and appointed Stephen Langton, one of the foremost biblical and theological scholars of his time and a cosmopolitan figure who had studied in Paris and Rome. Pope Innocent consecrated Stephen as the archbishop of Canterbury in 1207 but John refused to recognise the appointment; he barred Stephen from entering England and Stephen was forced into exile. In March 1208 England was placed under Interdict and after his continuing refusal to accept the new archbishop John was excommunicated by the pope in 1209. The other bishops of England deserted him and soon only one remained: Peter des Roches, bishop of Winchester, one of John's foreign cronies who had only recently been appointed to that rich see.

The Interdict, of course, had the same strictures as those previously imposed on France, which we mentioned earlier. It affected everyone, not just the king: through no fault of their own the people of England were unable to attend Mass and were denied the sacraments, something of serious import at this time. Ralph of Coggeshall gives a flavour of their misery:

> Oh what a horrible and miserable spectacle it was to see in every city the sealed doors of the churches, Christians shut out from entry as though they were dogs, the cessation of divine office, the withholding of the sacrament of the body and blood of Our Lord, the people no longer flocking to the famous celebration of saints' days, the bodies of the dead not given to burial according to Christian rites, the stink infecting the air and the horrible sight filling with horror the minds of the living.

Ralph is perhaps being slightly overdramatic here, as there is evidence that some Church activities still proceeded despite the Interdict. The baptism of infants was permitted, and as long as they took place behind closed doors, with no bells, and not in the presence of any excommunicants, the regular rounds of services could continue in monasteries.

John's response to the religious crisis was to confiscate Church lands and incomes for his own benefit, which made his coffers swell but his popularity sink even further. In 1212 there was an unsuccessful plot to assassinate him, with one of the ringleaders being a lord named Robert Fitzwalter. Fitzwalter, a regular troublemaker with an over-inflated sense of his own importance, had been in dispute with John since the fall of Normandy a decade earlier (Fitzwalter had surrendered his castle of Vaudreuil there to the French without a fight, so John had refused to pay his ransom, meaning he had had to sell lands to raise the funds himself) and he now fled to France where he managed to convince many people that he was a martyr fleeing from the unjust rule of an excommunicate king. His whispers in the ear of Philip Augustus may have influenced Philip's plans to invade England in 1213.

As we have seen, Philip's plans were thwarted by the naval victory at Damme and by John ceding England as a papal fief, a decision which took many of the barons by surprise and which was not universally popular. Pope Innocent was at first not entirely convinced of John's sincerity and he sent his legate Pandulf to England to check that the offer was serious. It was, though it is likely that John's decision to cede the realm was a political move rather than being the result of some kind of religious conversion. Whatever the motivation, it worked: John gained immediate papal favour, his excommunication and the Interdict would in due course be lifted, and he was able to use the support of the pope in all his subsequent disputes with the barons.

Part of the agreement was that John would recognise Stephen Langton as archbishop of Canterbury, which he did. However, Stephen found his traditional archiepiscopal powers curbed: normally he would have been the pre-eminent churchman in England, but as it was now a papal fief it came under the jurisdiction of the papal legates, Pandulf and his colleagues who arrived later, Nicholas de Romanis and Guala Bicchieri. They were there to support the king in all matters on behalf of his new overlord the pope, but Langton was (perhaps understandably) less than wholehearted in his support for John and tried to mediate between him and the barons. He was later suspended from his position by Pandulf and in 1215 was summoned to Rome to explain himself, not to return to England for another three years.

Another item in the agreement with the pope was that John should reconcile himself with Robert Fitzwalter – still posing in exile as a heroic religious fugitive – who returned to England and began encouraging further discord.

John had little success in trying to persuade his barons to join with him to invade Poitou in 1214. They gave an array of excuses, positioning themselves variously as faux-moral (they could not in conscience follow John while he was still excommunicate), as poor (they had spent all their money preparing to defend England against the proposed invasion the previous year), or as legal sticklers (they were not bound by their oaths to serve overseas). Unwilling to have his invasion compromised by this display of his inability to command his own subjects, John hired mercenaries and made deals in Poitou, sending back demands to England that those who had not joined him should pay scutage – a tax whereby knights or nobles could 'buy out' their military commitments in cash – which were almost universally ignored. When John returned, defeated, in the autumn of 1214, he faced not only widespread lack of support but also further antagonism relating to his choice of regent during his absence: Peter des Roches, the foreign bishop of Winchester, whose rule had been unpopular.

A few words should be said here about the effect of the burgeoning conflict on those lower down the social scale. The earls and the great barons, those who controlled much of the land and with whom the king might expect to have some kind of personal relationship, made up only a tiny minority of England's population in the early thirteenth century: approximately a hundred out of a total of some four million. Below them were about a thousand knights (who controlled enough land to enable them to sustain a 'knightly' status – that is, one which gave them sufficient resources not just to live on, but also to train, mount and equip themselves and a retinue), and perhaps ten times as many minor landowners who held a manor or two which granted them some local importance. Allowing for the significant minority of men and women who were members of religious communities, this means that the remaining approximately 95 per cent of

England's population was engaged in agriculture or trade. Many of the actions of the king and the barons effectively passed these people by: goods still needed to be manufactured and sold, crops grown and harvested, and the weather watched carefully, regardless of who was on the throne or who controlled the land they lived on. But other events affected them and their families deeply. The Interdict meant that they were excluded from church services and their deceased loved ones could not be buried in consecrated ground; and a decade of rising inflation had seen the all-important price of wheat double, and hunger become widespread. But discontent was one thing; having the power and the resources to do something about it was another. Thus when the groundswell of feeling against King John turned to open rebellion, it was led not by the common people (who played very little part in the war other than as incidental victims, as we shall see) but by the barons.

The ringleaders were a group known as the Northerners, as their lands were mainly in the north of England. Among them was the ubiquitous Robert Fitzwalter, now claiming that John had tried to force himself upon Fitzwalter's daughter. Eustace de Vesci chimed in with an accusation against John concerning an attempted seduction of or attack on his wife, and further anti-John propaganda, now directed at him personally rather than at his kingship or administration, began to circulate. It is difficult to tell whether these rumours had any truth in them, but it is possible and even plausible. We have already heard some of the invective which the Minstrel of Reims pours out against John in this regard; but in his *History of the Dukes* another more sober and reliable chronicler, the Anonymous of Béthune, tells us of the king: 'He lusted after beautiful women and because of this he shamed the high men of the land, for which reason he was greatly hated.' It was not so much that John was unfaithful to his marriage vows – this was par for the course for a medieval king,

and John openly acknowledged half a dozen illegitimate children –
but that the barons felt that their own wives and daughters were not
safe. The Waverley annalist notes that the accusations against John
were starting to pile up: 'For some [John] had disinherited without
judgement of their peers; some he had condemned to a cruel death;
of others he had violated their wives and daughters; and so instead of
law there was tyrannical will.'

The combination of personal, political and financial motives
behind the rebellion makes it difficult to identify any one overarching
reason which pushed the barons over the edge – or even to identify a
coherent group of these barons, as loyalties fluctuated – but John
could evidently see the threat on the horizon as he strengthened the
garrisons of his royal castles with troops of mercenaries. In January
1215 the disaffected barons met John in London, and much was
made of the old coronation charter of Henry I – renowned as a just
king – in which he promised to uphold the ancient laws and liberties
of the realm and the rights of the nobles.

John procrastinated, and both sides appealed to Rome; John, of
course – following his decision to cede England as a papal fief – was
more likely to gain the pope's support, and he increased his chances
by taking the cross on the holy day of Ash Wednesday in March 1215.
It is likely that he had very little intention of ever going on crusade,
but by swearing the vows he was entitled to the special protection of
the Church. The barons did not wait for confirmation from Rome
that the pope supported John, but held another meeting in April.
Prominent among the nobles there were those with personal grudges
against John: Robert Fitzwalter, Eustace de Vesci and Geoffrey de
Mandeville. Saer de Quincy, the earl of Winchester, was also to the
fore: he was Fitzwalter's cousin and had been with him at the infa-
mous surrender of Vaudreuil castle in Normandy eleven years previously, which had weakened the English position before its collapse.

The barons sent an ultimatum to John, that he should abide by the Articles of the Barons, as the demands were now called; he refused. Rebellion turned to war, and Robert Fitzwalter, now styling himself rather grandiosely as 'Marshal of the Army of God' as a direct riposte to John's nominal status as a crusader, led a force which attacked the castles at Northampton and Bedford. What is particularly remarkable about the situation was the way in which the barons at this point started acting together. Previously they had been something of a disparate group, each looking out for his own interests while John sought to play them off against each other, so the fact that a large proportion of them were now united in this common cause points to the depth of feeling against the king. The revolt spread, and on 17 May 1215 the city of London opened its gates to the barons in support of their cause. The barons sent letters to all those still siding with John which, in the words of Roger of Wendover, told them to 'Abandon a king who was perjured and who warred against his barons, and together with them to stand firm and fight against the king for their rights and for peace.'

There were eruptions of pro-baronial violence in other areas of the country, and King Alexander in Scotland and Prince Llewelyn in Wales were poised to take advantage of the situation, threatening John on all sides. With his capital also under rebel control John had no choice but to agree to the barons' demands, and on 15 June 1215 he set his seal to the document known at the time as the Charter of Runnymede but more famous afterwards as Magna Carta. This document, which was copied and circulated around the country, is often portrayed now as a great charter of liberties, declaring freedom from tyranny and the rights of all, but equality for different classes (and sexes) was certainly not its original intention. Rather, the detail demonstrates what was important to the thirteenth-century noblemen who conceived it, with clauses such as fixing reliefs – the fees which heirs had to pay to inherit their lands and titles – at set amounts, ensuring that widows did not remarry without the consent of their overlords, and removing unpopular foreigners from high office. In effect it was a document concerned with short-term and immediate practical reforms which would protect the nobility against an auto-cratic king who did not abide by existing laws and customs. The authors did not trust John to keep to the terms of the charter of his own free will: there was to be a committee of twenty-five barons that would effectively oversee his actions. If the king did not abide by the terms, then (according to clause 61) the committee of barons could 'distrain and distress us in all ways possible, by taking castles, lands, possessions and in any other ways they can, until it has been put right in accordance with their judgement, saving our person and the persons of our queen and children'.

John appeared to submit to the will of his lords, but inwardly he seethed at the unprecedented challenge to his authority as God's anointed sovereign, and the chroniclers in England are in agreement that even after the sealing of the charter, the peace was uneasy. The Dunstable annalist emphasises the impermanence of it; Ralph of Coggeshall says that it was no more than a '*quasi-pax*'; and the Barnwell annalist tells of how John fortified royal castles and stayed near his own strong points. Matthew Paris tells us that John 'secretly prepared letters' and sent them to the foreign mercenaries holding his castles, ordering them to resupply and re-garrison in expectation of war, and adds: 'He then commenced gnashing his teeth, scowling with his eyes, and seizing sticks and limbs of trees, began to gnaw them, and after gnawing them to break them, and with increased extraordinary gestures to show the grief or rather the rage he felt.' While John's gestures of rage might be exaggerated, what is beyond doubt is that at the same time as he was promising to keep the provisions of the charter he was already sending messengers to the pope asking him to annul it.

Some of the barons were unhappy at making terms with John at all. They were suspicious of his seeming compliance and organised tournaments near London as an excuse to be near the capital and armed. The *History of the Dukes* tells us that in council with the king at Oxford in July 1215 a group of lords publicly insulted him by refusing to attend him in his chamber, where he was bedridden with an illness, meaning he had to be carried into their presence, whereupon they refused to stand when he entered. Once he had recovered, John sent to Aquitaine and Flanders for mercenaries.

A reply from Pope Innocent (in Rome) on the subject of Magna Carta was received. It was dated 24 August 1215, thus indicating that John must have written to him almost as soon as the charter was sealed, and that Innocent had lost no time in responding. Innocent did not mince his words:

An agreement which is not only shameful and base but also illegal and unjust ... we utterly reject and condemn this settlement, and under threat of excommunication we order that the king should not dare to observe it ... the charter, with all undertakings and guarantees, whether confirming it or resulting from it, we declare to be null and void of all validity for ever.

John rescinded the charter in September and the barons came to a final conclusion: if the king could not be controlled, he would have to be overthrown. Matthew Paris is once again a trifle exaggerated but nonetheless eloquent on the subject of their disappointment in the king and their despair:

Cursing the king's fickleness and infidelity they thus gave vent to their grief: 'Woe unto you, John, last of kings, detested one of the chiefs of England, disgrace to the English nobility! Alas for

England already devastated, and to be further ravaged! Alas! England, England, until now chief of provinces in all kinds of wealth, you are laid under tribute; subject not only to fire, famine and the sword, but to the rule of ignoble slaves and foreigners, than which no slavery can be worse. We read that many other kings and princes have contended even unto death for the liberty of their land which was in subjection; but you, John, of sad memory to future ages, have designed and made it your business to enslave your country which has been free from times of old … you have bound by a bond of perpetual slavery this noble land, which will never be freed from the servile shackle unless through the compassion of Him who may at some time deign to free us.'

Throughout this period of conflict in England, the barons looked across the Channel to the powerful and stable royal line in France. In marked contrast to the discontent, conflict and usurpations which had characterised the Anglo-Norman monarchy since 1066 (Gerald of Wales notes that the Plantagenets were 'princes who did not succeed one another in regular hereditary order but rather acquired violent domination through an inversion of order by killing and slaughtering their own'), the French had experienced over two hundred years of smooth successions from father to son. Philip Augustus had been on the throne for thirty-five years, and his five immediate predecessors had enjoyed reigns of between twenty-nine and forty-eight years each. He had an adult son, a younger son and two grandsons. The barons might be understandably wary of offering the throne to Philip himself (and besides, he was now fifty years old so possibly not a long-term prospect), but Louis was a younger man, a proven warrior, a prince with a reputation for being moral and just; he came from a dynasty which had a tradition of involving a council of nobles in its decision-making process; he had a claim via the blood of his wife, John's niece. And on a more practical level, with the might and resources of the French crown behind him, he was likely to be successful. This tipped the balance in his favour against other possible candidates such as King Alexander of Scotland (who was descended from the old Anglo-Saxon kings of England) who did not have the military might to back up a potential claim. And Louis being French had an additional advantage: many of John's mercenaries were from various regions of France, so having Louis at the head of the campaign might mean that John would be deprived of their services, as he had been in Poitou in 1214. Of further comfort to the barons was the fact that Louis, if and when he became king, would probably not reside in England permanently, thus giving them more scope for their own activities. This was not unusual as Henry II and his predecessors had spent much of their time on the Continent, so there was precedent for a cross-Channel king. All in all, he was the perfect choice. A party of barons headed by Saer de Quincy, the earl of Winchester, Henry de Bohun, the earl of Hereford, and Robert Fitzwalter sailed for France in September 1215.

September was the month in which John was expecting the arrival of the new mercenaries he had engaged from Aquitaine and Flanders; he headed to the Kent coast in anticipation. However, there were storms and heavy seas during that month and instead of the expected ships, waves of drowned corpses washed up on the shores along Kent and Suffolk.

While John was bemoaning his losses on the coast the barons decided to take advantage of his situation by capturing Rochester Castle, which would bar his route back to London. The castellan there had been loyal to John for many years but, perhaps seeing the writing on the wall, he opened the gates to the rebels. This irritated John, who moved to assault it; there would now be actual armed conflict on English soil between the king and his subjects. A line had been crossed.

The barons had garrisoned Rochester well: ninety-five knights and forty-five sergeants held it under the leadership of William d'Albini, an able commander. However, as they expected Rochester to hold until the delegation returned from France they had made no back-up plans for reinforcing it and had no second force ready to relieve a siege. John, on the other hand, was prepared for the long haul. He had siege machinery built and remained at Rochester for seven weeks, conducting the operations personally – the longest he had ever spent in one place since his accession to the throne sixteen years earlier. Roger of Wendover tells us: 'The siege was prolonged many days owing to the great bravery and boldness of the besieged, who hurled stone for stone, weapon for weapon, from the walls and ramparts on the enemy.' The keep resisted all attempts at assault so John turned to mining: a tunnel was dug under the wall, held up by wooden posts, then filled with flammable material including the fat of forty pigs which John sent for specially, and set alight. As the timbers burned and collapsed the roof of the mine caved in, bringing one of the four towers of the keep crashing down. The garrison, by this point starving and forced to eat their horses, retreated to the other half of the keep and resisted a little longer but eventually realised it could not hold out and surrendered on 30 November 1215. John's first inclination was to execute them all, but he was persuaded not to on the basis that similar treatment would then be meted out to royal garrisons by the barons. In the end only one man was hanged, a crossbowman who had previously been in John's service.

While John was at Rochester the survivors of his mercenary fleet finally arrived. John marshalled his forces and looked over the Channel, waiting for the invasion which was now inevitable.

* * *

While John was being humiliated by his barons, Louis had been in the south of France fulfilling his vow to crusade against the Cathar heretics. The crusade had been led for some time by the formidable military leader Simon de Montfort (not to be confused with his son and namesake who would later play a significant part in English history), and Louis took with him a force including Guy de Châtillon and his father the count of St Pol, and Philip de Dreux, bishop of Beauvais. Louis modestly took his position in the host as crusader rather than leader, assuring Simon that he would leave the command to him, and that he would not seek to seize for the crown any lands Simon captured. Louis's time in the south was to prove short before the autumn end of the campaigning season, when he returned to Paris to hear the news from England, but he was able to assist Simon in capturing the great city of Toulouse before he left. And his light touch paid eventual dividends: when Simon was later recognised officially by the pope as lord of many of the lands he had taken, he would come to Paris to do homage to King Philip for the duchy of Narbonne, the county of Toulouse and the viscounties of Béziers and Carcassonne, meaning that the French crown became direct overlord of these lands without too much effort; previously they had been subject to the duke of Aquitaine, a title held by the Plantagenets since Henry II's marriage to Eleanor of Aquitaine in 1152.

The opportunity for Louis to engage in a bigger and more glorious military campaign arose when the English delegation headed by Saer de Quincy, Henry de Bohun and Robert Fitzwalter arrived at the royal court in Paris. Without beating around the bush they declared that the barons of England had sworn never to hold their lands from John; they paid homage to Louis for them and offered him the crown of England if he would consent to come and take it.

What prince would not jump at the chance of chasing such a glittering prize? Louis, as might be expected, was raring to go; Philip, unsurprisingly, was more circumspect. The king's suspicions were aroused when a letter from England arrived shortly after the delegation, saying that the barons there had made their peace with John and that the embassy needed therefore to be cancelled. Despite their protestations of innocence, Philip accused the men before him of treachery and demanded twenty-four noble hostages before he would discuss the matter further. Twenty-four sons of the nobility were duly sent for and arrived in France to be lodged in some comfort at Compiègne; the letter turned out to have been forged by John's agents.

Louis, without waiting on the niceties, immediately agreed to support the baronial cause, and he sent a first contingent of 140 knights across the Channel in December 1215 to join the barons holding London, and another fleet of twenty ships in January 1216. Their first and presumably unintended effect on the war was the loss of a key ally: during a tournament which was organised as part of a joint military training exercise, Geoffrey de Mandeville, earl of Essex and Gloucester, did not arm himself properly and was killed by a wound to the stomach inflicted accidentally by a French knight.

Events were moving a little too fast for Philip, who liked to make sure he had all bases covered and every possible justification for his actions before he embarked on any new endeavour. The situation presented him with something of a dilemma: if Louis were to lose, then the reputation of the French crown, which Philip had been building and consolidating for so many years, would be soiled. John might end up in a stronger position and therefore want to attempt to regain his continental possessions, leaving Philip with another war to fight. On the other hand, if Louis were to be victorious he would make immense gains in power and influence and, as a king, would be the equal of his father and no longer subject to his control, with everything that implied in the light of Henry II's conflicts with his son Henry the Young King, still fresh in Philip's memory. But when would Philip ever again get such a chance to overthrow the Plantagenets once and for all? And however powerful Louis might eventually become, better him on the English throne than John. Philip agreed in principle to have the judicial case heard for Louis's claim to the English crown, and a council of the French nobles was summoned.

In the meantime John had not attempted a siege of London, which would be difficult – although, had he tried and succeeded, he might have won the war outright before it really started. Instead he launched devastating raids into the lands of the rebel barons in the northern counties, killing and burning as he went. The revolt against him began to stutter; the troops Louis had sent over so far were of some help to the barons but they were not enough to turn the tide. Louis needed to go in person, which meant that he had to persuade the nobility of France of the justness of his claim.

The Assembly of Melun, as it came to be known, was held between 23 and 25 April 1216. King Philip presided but did not take an active part for either side (interposing his view only where his own interests were affected) while a council of French nobles listened to Louis and his advisers arguing against the papal legate Guala Bicchieri, who did everything he could to prevent the expedition.

Louis was impetuous and eager to get the talking over and done with so he could move forward with his military preparations. Nevertheless, he needed at least a fig leaf of justification so he had a team of legal advisers (including Simon Langton and Robert de St Germain, who, as we have seen, had been among his retainers for some time) draw up an argument for him. Meanwhile a third English churchman, Elias of Dereham, was in Rome to plead on his behalf.

The discussion went back and forth as Louis ('looking upon the legate with a scowling brow', according to Roger of Wendover) and his advisers made their case. In summary his arguments were on three grounds: that John had lost his right to the English throne, which was now vacant; that Louis was the legitimate heir to that throne; and that the papacy had no right to intervene in the matter.

From the available evidence it would seem that Louis was better at fighting than he was at talking, and not all of his points were entirely convincing. His case that John had vacated the throne was in three parts: firstly, that John had rebelled against his brother Richard and attempted to seize the crown while Richard was away on crusade, for which he had been condemned as a traitor and therefore forfeited his right to the throne; secondly, that John had murdered his nephew Arthur and had been condemned in a French court by the judgment of the king and of his peers, therefore forfeiting all his possessions; and, thirdly, that John had reneged on his oath to uphold the rights and customs of the English Church and nobility. He had not consulted them about his decision to hand the entire kingdom over as a papal fief; he had done away with good customs and introduced bad ones; he had attacked the lands of his own barons. For this reason he was not fit to rule and the barons were entitled to elect a successor.

The first two of these arguments do not stand up to much scrutiny. Following John's attempted seizure of the throne from Richard the brothers had been reconciled and Richard had later designated John as his successor. As to the murder of Arthur, Philip might have exercised his right to strip John of his duchy of Normandy (although he appears to have done this unilaterally, as there are no official records of any formal 'court' being convened to condemn John at the time) but he could not depose him as king of England, as this was a separate title even though it was held by the same man. The third accusation was more serious. As with all kings since William the Conqueror, John had sworn at his coronation to preserve peace and protect the Church, to maintain good laws and abolish bad, to dispense justice to all. If there was any doubt that he had broken this oath, then his subsequent revocation of the charter, which in itself formed a genuine peace treaty and reiterated in different words and more detail the coronation oath, sealed this accusation. Effectively (and as other, later kings of England would find), a king could only rule if his nobles allowed him to.

Assuming that Louis succeeded in convincing the assembly that the throne of England was now empty, he now needed to demonstrate that he was the man to fill the vacancy. The papal legate Guala argued that if John were to be deposed then the new king should be his eight-year-old son, Henry (John also had a second son and three daughters). This, of course, did not suit the barons: the two young boys were in their father's power and little Henry would be ruled by his father as some kind of puppet, therefore making very little change to the status quo. So Louis and his advisers argued that in forfeiting his right to the throne John had also forfeited the rights for his heirs – a tenuous claim which went against normal practice. We may recall at this point that as recently as two years previously Philip Augustus had succeeded in bringing the county of Boulogne under royal control by disinheriting the treacherous Renaud de Dammartin in favour of his daughter, who was married to Philip's son Philip Hurepel.

If the claims of John's children were to be ignored then the rest of the family tree needs to be examined. Interestingly, one fact which does not seem to have been put forward at any point by Louis or his advisers was that Louis was a direct descendant of William the Conqueror: his paternal grandmother, queen mother Adela, was the granddaughter of her namesake Adela of Blois, who was William's daughter (and also, as it happened, the mother of King Stephen of England). Perhaps this relationship had become less readily apparent in the 130 or so years since the Conqueror's death, or perhaps it was considered less relevant after such a passage of time. As it was, the arguments relating to heredity were centred on the family of Henry II.

Four sons of Henry II and Eleanor of Aquitaine had lived to adulthood, two of whom (Henry the Young King and Richard the Lionheart) had died childless. Other than John's children the only surviving descendant in the male line was the unfortunate Eleanor of Brittany, daughter of John's elder brother Geoffrey (and therefore with a better claim to the throne than John himself if primogeniture were to be observed strictly), who was living out her life in close confinement at John's order. Henry II and Eleanor also had three daughters, who were by now all dead: Matilda, Eleanor and Joanna. Matilda was the mother of Otto, the erstwhile Holy Roman Emperor who had been defeated at Bouvines; Otto himself had a living older brother, Henry. Eleanor was the mother of Louis's wife Blanche, and it was from her that he derived his hereditary claim. The youngest sister, Joanna, had been married to Raymond VI, count of Toulouse, and there was one surviving son to the marriage, also named Raymond, who was in his teens.

As Joanna had been the youngest sister the claims of her descendants could safely be ignored and, besides, her widower and son were embroiled in the wars in the south of France and busy trying to get their county back from Simon de Montfort. The imprisoned Eleanor of Brittany does not seem to have been mentioned by anyone, her captive status rendering her ineligible. She was thirty-two and unmarried, so in theory a claim could have been raised by anyone who could break her out of John's custody and marry her. Louis cut this off by declaring rather speciously that as Geoffrey Plantagenet had been dead since before John's 'condemnation' in 1203, he could not transmit a right which he had never possessed. The same argument was also made against the children of Matilda, who had died in 1189, so they were pushed out of the queue as well. Her sons were in any case not in a position to mount any claim to the English throne: Henry had extensive lands in Germany and had no interest outside the borders of the empire; Otto was still licking his wounds after Bouvines and would not be able to raise an army. Henry and Otto had also had a younger brother William and a sister Matilda, both now deceased but with one surviving son each: William's was a small child located deep in Germany, while Matilda's was the French count of Perche, who was not about to advance a counterclaim against that of his liege lord.

That left John's middle sister, Eleanor, who was Blanche's mother. Of course, a further complication here was that Blanche had two living older sisters: Berengaria, queen of León (a realm neighbouring Castile and covering what is now north-western Spain and northern Portugal), and Urraca, now queen of Portugal (then comprising the southern two-thirds of its current area). The increasingly desperate Guala pointed out that if Louis's previous arguments were correct, then King Alfonso of León had first call on the English throne. Louis countered this by saying in all innocence that if Alfonso wanted to raise a campaign to claim the crown then he would do everything he could to support him; he would have known that this was very unlikely, as Berengaria had separated from her husband on the grounds of consanguinity and was now living back in Castile as regent for the new king there, her eleven-year-old brother Henry.

To us it may seem as though Louis was simply erasing at will from the succession anyone who stood in his way. However, we must consider this in the context of the early thirteenth century. As we have already noted, at the time there was a certain fluidity to the principles of primogeniture in favour of the interests and practicalities of the moment, with an adult male heir being much preferred even if he had less of a hereditary claim. There would be little point in the monarch being someone who was not vigorous enough, powerful enough, and backed by enough resources to win the campaign and keep the crown – that would simply be a recipe for ongoing disputes and wars such as those which had marred the Holy Roman Empire for the best part of two decades. All that was really needed was a blood claim and enough resources to back it up. If William the Conqueror could invade in 1066, kill the existing king and take the throne, and if his grandson Stephen could sail to England in 1135, usurp the direct heir Matilda and be crowned in her stead, then why could not Louis do the same?

Louis also made the valid point that he could claim the throne by right of election. The barons had invited and accepted him; if they acclaimed him king and he was crowned, then who would gainsay him? Again, this has parallels with King Stephen, who, although feeling entitled to trample over the rights of his cousin, was the son of the youngest of William the Conqueror's five daughters and had at the time of his coronation at least one and possibly two living older brothers; therefore he could not justifiably claim to be king by heredi- tary right. This may have been on Louis's mind all along, and there is a hint, in a letter he sent to the Abbey of St Augustine in Canterbury in May 1216, that John's coronation in 1199 had actually been by virtue of election and not by right of succession – he had after all pushed past the two nearer heirs, Arthur of Brittany and his sister Eleanor – thus lending legitimacy to Louis's claim that he could do the same.

The momentum seemed to be going Louis's way, but Guala still had what he thought was a trump card to play: John had taken the cross and so his lands were under the protection of the Church and could not be attacked; and England was in any case a papal fief held by John from the pope. Louis had an answer to this, too: he had made no peace or truce with John since his (supposed) condemna- tion in 1203, so John's crusading vow of 1215 did not protect him in this instance; also, John had attacked his lands in Artois in 1213 so

Louis had the right of reprisal; and, finally, as John did not legally possess the crown of England, he was not entitled to cede the kingdom as a papal fief so the agreement was void.

Looking at Louis's claim as a whole it is evident that very few of his individual points would stand on their own. However, when put together they provided him at least with the semblance of a legitimate claim to the throne, and the momentum was with him: he had a blood claim via his wife, he was keen and he had the resources to mount and sustain a campaign. But Guala had one last ace up his sleeve: his influence over King Philip. Philip, let us not forget, had only recently been reconciled with the pope after the years of conflict, excommunication and Interdict occasioned by his treatment of Ingeborg. He did not want to endanger his papal relations now and Guala played on this, demanding that he forbid his son from invading England under pain of excommunication.

At this point Louis lost his temper, partly at the threat to his father but mainly at being treated like a minor of no account. He was twenty-eight and a seasoned warrior and leader, not a boy to be sent to bed with no supper. The crown had been offered to him, not to Philip. He declared that Philip was of course his overlord for his lands in France, but that he could have no say in his rights to the throne of England. According to Roger of Wendover his reply was firm as he appealed to the council:

'I therefore throw myself on the decision of my peers, as to whether you ought to hinder me from seeking my rights, and especially a right in which you cannot afford me justice. I therefore ask of you not to obstruct my purpose of seeking my rights, because, for the inheritance of my wife I will, if necessary, contend even unto death.' And with these words Louis retired from the conference with his followers.

Philip Augustus was not a man to fall for melodramatic cloak-swirling, but this did leave him in a quandary. His subsequent actions are open to interpretation: he announced that he would not support Louis in his campaign; he would not forbid him to go, but he would not prevent him either. Whether he genuinely opposed Louis but felt that his jurisdiction did not extend to England, whether he was afraid of a further excommunication, whether he simply did not want to underwrite what might be a losing cause, or whether he actually supported Louis but wanted to appease the pope, we cannot know. William the Breton, loyal to Philip, says quite definitively that Philip refused to support his son so as not to offend the pope (having already noted specifically that Louis sent the first contingent of 140 knights 'against the will of his father'). But it does seem plausible that Philip's official washing of hands masked a more covert personal support that he may have conveyed to his son behind closed doors. In his *Chronicle of the Kings of France* the Anonymous of Béthune says that 'his father publicly made it appear as though he did not want to be involved because of the truce he had granted [i.e. reconciliation with the pope]; but privately, it was believed that he had advised him'. The last word on the subject shall go to the Minstrel of Reims, who depicts a heated conversation between father and son ending thus: '"By the lance of St James," said the king, "do whatever you like, but you will never succeed, as the English are traitors and felons, and they will never keep their word to you."' It is ironic that this most maligned and least reliable of chroniclers should be the one proved right in the end.

One last point to note on this subject is that Innocent, too, may have been playing a double game. He let his legate rant against Louis and Philip, threatening excommunication, but made no moves to do so himself and made no personal announcement on the subject. Guala left the French court in something of a huff after the assembly and headed for England, with a warning from Philip ringing in his ears that he was assured safe conduct while he was on French soil, but that the king was not to be blamed if Guala should just happen to fall prey to pirates on the sea.

* * *

Louis was now free to make his preparations for invasion. A fleet of some 800 ships began to assemble at Wissant, Gravelines, Boulogne and Calais and troops were sent there as they were raised. Louis was able to call up from his own lands those who owed him military service, but he would need more men than this. As Philip was not officially supporting him he could not call on anyone who owed service to the French crown, so he needed to recruit privately. In some quarters he met with little success. One of the greatest land-owners in France was Odo III, the duke of Burgundy, but as he was making his own preparations to go to the Holy Land he refused to engage personally and would agree only to a loan of 1,000 marks; he would not live long enough to be repaid, dying on his journey east. Another great lord was the count of Champagne; this was Theobald IV who was at the time still a minor (having been born posthumously to the previous count in 1201 and then placed in the household of Louis and Blanche, as we saw earlier) so the decisions were made by his mother, Blanche of Champagne, the dowager countess. She also refused to supply men or funds on the pretext that she could not sanction an attack on a crusader (meaning John, although as we have noted he had never been within a thousand miles of the Holy Land). Some of Louis's men got overexcited and paid her a personal call while she was sitting down to a meal, scaring her so much that she fled the table. King Philip was angry when he heard of the incident and demanded that the men be put in prison, to which Louis agreed.

In truth Louis did not need to go to such lengths, as other nobles were flocking to his banner. His friends were there, of course, including the Dreux brothers – although Peter was tied up with immediate responsibilities in Brittany and agreed to sail at a later date – the counts of Bar and St Pol, and Simon Langton. Others who had a taste for adventure or a grudge against John volunteered: William des Roches, William des Barres and William the count of Holland. Another who joined Louis, possibly with an eye to the main chance, was Hervé de Donzy, the count of Nevers, Auxerre and Tonnere, who as a senior nobleman would be Louis's second-in-command. Hervé was something of a slippery character (the author of the *History of William Marshal* goes so far as to call him 'an arrogant and vicious man') who was not constant in his loyalties. He had supported the French against the English in Normandy in 1203–4 and had been in French service on the Albigensian crusade in 1208, although he had gone home after forty days, the exact period of service which he owed. But by 1214 he had wavered; he fought against King Philip at Bouvines. In contrast to other traitorous lords, Hervé had somehow inveigled his way back into royal favour afterwards; this may have had something to do with the fact that his only son died in 1214 so he was left with one daughter, Agnes, who became his sole heiress and who thus represented a chance to annex Hervé's three counties to the royal domain. She was now betrothed to Louis's elder son Philip, so if Hervé played his cards right and stayed in royal favour he could expect that in due course his daughter would be queen consort and his grandson would one day be king.

Between them, the lords brought some 1,200 knights, a large force for the time. None of the chroniclers gives a precise figure for the number of non-knightly soldiers who made up the rest of the host, but judging by what we know of early thirteenth-century armies, and by the number of ships, it would be reasonable to assume that there were about two to three times as many again.

The final figure of note in Louis's company was the sea captain and commander of the fleet, Eustace the Monk. Eustace, a colourful figure and one of the few non-royal, non-knightly, non-saintly men to have an entire medieval text written about him (the *Romance of Eustace the Monk*), had at one time been committed to the cloister by his family, hence his nickname. But he fled the monastery and eventually became a maritime mercenary operating in the Channel from a base on the island of Sark. He began selling his services to John in 1205 and attacked the Normandy coast for him in an attempt to regain the duchy; although he did not conquer the land he did destroy many French ships. With a free-and-easy attitude towards loyalty and honesty he also raided English towns, but as without him John did not have the naval strength he needed, this was conveniently overlooked. However, Eustace had a long-standing enmity with Renaud de Dammartin, so when Renaud entered into alliance with John in 1212 and demanded that John rid himself of his pirate, Eustace offered his services to Philip instead. He had been in French service ever since, raiding English towns and ships, and was now appointed admiral of Louis's fleet. His ship was to be the flagship on which Louis and his chief adviser Simon Langton travelled.

Once the fleet and the army were assembled, Louis was ready to embark upon his greatest adventure yet. We may imagine his feelings of excitement and pride: it was 150 years since William the Conqueror had set sail for England, and Louis intended to emulate him and to return to France a victorious king. As this first wave of the invasion was military in character he would not be bringing his wife and family with him just yet. He bade farewell to Blanche, who was expecting another child, and accepted the blessings of French prelates against the dangers of the sea voyage, which had proved fatal for John's fleet of mercenaries only a few months before.

It was 20 May 1216, the auspicious feast of Pentecost and the seventh anniversary of his knighting ceremony, when Louis embarked on Eustace's ship; the tide was right in the late evening so they led the way out of the harbour and into the open sea as darkness began to fall. But despite the blessings, despite Louis's prayers and despite the air of optimism, God did not immediately show approval. As the ships reached open water the winds rose and a huge and violent storm blew across the Channel, scattering the fleet, jeopardising the campaign and putting Louis's life in danger.

CHAPTER FOUR

KING OF ENGLAND?

THE STORM RAGED all night, and Louis's flagship was tossed on the waves like a toy. All those on board were hurled backwards and forwards, up and down, belongings and effects tumbling round them as they sought to quell their heaving stomachs and listened to the howling wind and the sounds of the terrified horses in the hold below. Did Louis think his last hour had come? Did he pray for deliverance as another wave crashed over the ship and threatened to engulf it? If he did then his prayers were answered, for as night gave way to day the sea became calmer, and as the sun rose on the morning of 21 May 1216 he was in sight of English shores.

Just seven ships of the fleet had managed to stay together, and they anchored at Stonor on what was then the Isle of Thanet. Trusting that the rest of his army would soon catch up, Louis was not to be dissuaded from making his way on to land to set foot in the kingdom he was claiming. He was the first to wade ashore, watched by his men and by a crowd of curious locals who had gathered once the ships had been sighted. From this gathering there emerged a priest; Louis approached him and kissed the crucifix he was holding

– whether in relief or in triumph we cannot know – before planting his lance in the ground. He was on English soil and he meant to make it his.

Louis's confidence in his fleet was not misplaced, as during the course of that day and the next more and more of his ships arrived. It soon became apparent that almost all of them had survived, and they mustered at Sandwich, which was then a major port.

Meanwhile, John had hurried towards the coast to see the size of the invading army for himself. His own plans had been thrown into disarray by the storm. He had assembled a fleet of his own which was meant to have sailed to Calais, blocking Louis's exit and therefore stopping him from crossing the Channel, but the conditions had prevented his ships putting to sea. Now he watched as more and more of the enemy arrived, their masts forming a forest around the port, and he needed to make a decision. He had a host with him: should he attack now, while the French were still seasick and before they had a secure foothold on land, risking everything in a great pitched battle in the hope that he could drive them back into the sea? Or should he make a strategic withdrawal until he could muster more forces, and then challenge Louis on a ground of his own choosing?

John must have had at the back of his mind the knowledge of what had happened to another English king who had given battle against invaders from France as soon as they had arrived: Harold and the flower of his men had been slaughtered at Hastings 150 years before, leaving the kingdom wide open. And Harold's men had been loyal to him personally, whereas a large number of the troops John had at his command were foreign mercenaries, many of them Poitevins, who might well turn against him if they were forced to fight against the French king's son. The advice of the experienced William Marshal, on whom John now relied to an increasing extent, was that battle should not be attempted at this stage. But the decision was the king's to make, and he needed to determine his course of action quickly. What would he do? The Anonymous of Béthune gives us two slightly different takes on John's feelings, telling us in his *History of the Dukes* that he 'lost heart' as he rode up and down trying to decide, while noting in the *Chronicle of the Kings of France* that he 'did not dare' engage Louis. William the Breton, never a fan of John, says that although he had an army three times the size of Louis's he abandoned his camp, and 'forgetting his promise and his royal pride, preferred to flee rather than fight'. Roger of Wendover is more measured: 'He did not venture to attack Louis on his landing, lest in the battle they [John's troops] might all leave him and go over to the side of Louis; he therefore chose to retreat for a time, rather than to give battle on an uncertainty.'

By this point John must really have felt as though he were walking on shifting sands. Here he was, a king supposedly on home ground, and not only were men who had once sworn fealty to him lining up to support the invader, but he could not even trust the troops he did have with him, as they had merely sold their swords to the highest bidder. The *History of William Marshal*, perhaps unsurprisingly, is critical of those who served John for financial gain rather than out of loyalty:

> I should inform you at this point that, when the king ran out of resources, very few of the men stayed with him who were there for his money; they went on their way with their booty in hand. However, the Marshal at least, a man of loyal and noble heart, stayed with him in hard and difficult circumstances.

Whatever was going through John's troubled mind, his ultimate decision was not to engage Louis, and he withdrew first to Dover and thence to Guildford and Winchester. And in so doing, he lost the initiative in the war straight away. Louis was able to establish a beachhead unopposed, and his men disembarked with their horses and equipment, set up camp, and took control of the port of Sandwich on 23 May. Aware of the dangers of leaving an enemy fleet behind him as he looked to move further inland, Louis captured John's ships and sent them, with his own, back across the Channel, thus denying himself an escape route if things should go wrong. He had burned his bridges: there was to be no going back.

Given that he had not been able to claim victory in a pitched battle immediately, and that his opponent lived to fight another day, Louis set about doing what any good commander would do in the circumstances: subduing the local area and giving himself a secure foothold from which to launch further attacks. His troops spread out through Kent and took control of lands and supplies.

The major stronghold in the region was Dover Castle, a huge fortress which had been strengthened by John's father, Henry II, until it was one of the showpiece castles of Europe. Matthew Paris called it 'the key to England', and so it was, for while it was held against him Louis could never quite consider himself safe. We have already noted that sieges were more common at this time than battles, and this was because the tactical importance of castles was such that leaving one in enemy hands could derail an entire campaign. A well-fortified castle could be held by a relatively small number of men who could cause a disproportionately large amount of trouble. The area they controlled was not, as might be supposed, limited to a bowshot's length from the walls; rather it was a day's ride in any direction. A garrison could make a sortie, launching devastating raids for miles around, and then retreat back behind their walls and towers to rest in safety before they attacked again.

It was therefore imperative that Louis take Dover as soon as possible, but John had left it in the trustworthy hands of Hubert de Burgh, his justiciar (the highest administrative officer in the kingdom), and Hubert was safely ensconced behind the thick walls with a garrison of knights and sergeants and plenty of supplies. A siege would take a long time. And it was equally imperative that Louis meet the barons who had been waiting for him for six months, and that he make his way to London. Wasting no time agonising over a decision, he opted to leave Dover for another day, and set off immediately along the road to London.

From Sandwich he rode to Canterbury, which surrendered without a fight as soon as the inhabitants saw him coming. One of those in England's ecclesiastical capital was the papal legate Guala, based at the cathedral, who fled westwards to join John at Winchester and then solemnly inflicted the gravest penalty the Church had at its disposal, as Roger of Wendover describes: 'The legate then convoked all the bishops, abbots and clergy whom he could muster, and, amidst the ringing of bells, and with lighted tapers, excommunicated by name the said Louis, with all his accomplices and abettors.' Louis, unaware at first of the dread sentence, arrived at Rochester on 25 May. The barons who had been holding London against John now left the capital and came to meet him at Rochester: Robert Fitzwalter; Hugh Bigod, earl of Norfolk; Saer de Quincy, earl of Winchester; William de Mandeville, the new earl of Essex; Robert de Vere, earl of Oxford; and even William Marshal the younger, eldest son and heir of the earl of Pembroke who remained loyal to John. This might seem something of a shock, but it is possible that Marshal senior, ever the best guardian of his own interests (and in a situation not dissimilar to that of Philip Augustus and his support or lack thereof for Louis), might not have been all that upset by his son's defection as it gave the family a foot in both camps, which could be exploited whoever emerged the victor. These barons and their compatriots and their men did homage to Louis as their king, the rightful occupier of the throne they claimed as vacant due to John's misdeeds. Their combined forces were too much for the garrison of the shattered castle at Rochester, not yet properly rebuilt after John's long siege there the previous year, and it surrendered to Louis on 30 May 1216.

All the momentum of the campaign so far was with Louis. While John skulked in Winchester, Louis had taken swift control of the south-east and now had something like half the barons of England with him. More were to arrive: as the lords of the land heard of his success they realised that if they wanted to be on the winning side they had better declare themselves before it was too late. The rumblings of discontent about John had been circulating for years, as had the rumours of a projected invasion from France, but now that Louis was here, now that the unthinkable had happened, now that a French prince of the house of Capet was actually on English soil, it was time to take sides. Once Louis had been crowned and had taken possession of the whole realm, they reasoned, he would look least favourably on those who had taken longest to come over to him.

Riding at the head of his men, Louis entered London in triumph on 2 June 1216. London at this time was not quite as populous as Paris – a reasonable estimate would be that it was home to about 40,000 people – but it was unquestionably the premier city in England. The only city mentioned by name in Magna Carta, it was many times larger than any of its nearest rivals such as Winchester, Lincoln, Norwich, York or Bristol. Its nearby suburb of Westminster was home to the exchequer and a number of large and luxurious residences such as Westminster Hall. London controlled trade routes thanks to its road and river links, and was also very defensible, dominated by the great Tower and surrounded by high stone walls. The people of London saw themselves as members of a kind of semi-independent commune within England, and they had certain rights and liberties freeing them from tolls and guaranteeing free trade; they also had the right to elect their own mayor.

As we have seen, the Londoners had been in alliance with the barons since the spring of 1215, and now they opened their gates for Louis. He was cheered in the streets by the crowds, the citizens no doubt eager for an end to the civil war that had disrupted life and trade for far too long. They would be glad to have anyone on the throne who could call a halt to the conflict and enable a return to normal life; that he was a man with a reputation for being both just and devout no doubt helped, as did the fact that his blond youthful good looks made him appear to advantage as he rode through the throng accepting their acclamation. That he was French appeared to bother them not at all; after all, England's previous kings and their lords had their roots across the Channel, and French was the language of the court anyway. That his resources meant he could bring a swift peace to the realm was uppermost in their minds; he represented a new hope.

The canons of St Paul's welcomed Louis with a solemn procession in the cathedral. Louis swore on the holy gospels that he would restore to his new vassals all their rightful inheritances and good laws. He installed himself in the palace of Westminster, and wrote to King Alexander of Scotland and then to all the barons who had not yet done homage to him, instructing them either to do so or to leave the kingdom. The mayor of London and the leading citizens swore their faith to him.

Louis considered himself, *de facto*, the king of England.

* * *

But, of course, there is more to being a king than considering yourself one. How did Louis act, now that he was in this favourable position? How would he seek to govern?

Given that – according to his own justification – Louis was claiming the throne by right, he did not see England as a 'conquered' country. Thus he would need to find a way of establishing an admin-istration which recognised this situation and which integrated in positions of authority those who had accompanied him from France with those who had invited him to England. Of course, at this point he did not have the whole realm under his control, so creating and running all the complex machinery of a proper government would be difficult to achieve until he was more firmly established. But some steps could be taken to set up the bare bones of an administration: he named Simon Langton his chancellor, and also called on the services of two other men who were members of his expedition, Guy d'Athies – who had been a member of his administrative household in France – and the French chamberlain Ours de la Chapelle.

A priority in a war-torn land was the establishment of a system of justice, and here Louis made some headway, appointing men to hear legal cases in those areas where he held sway. He also made grants of land to various followers, thus indicating that he felt he had the right to do so. One charter which has survived was dated 21 November 1216; in it Louis grants the manor of Grimsby to one William of Huntingfield. The first six names on the witness list are the earl of Winchester (Saer de Quincy), Robert Fitzwalter, Ours the chamber-lain, the viscount of Melun, Simon Langton and Guy d'Athies – a mixture of English barons and French household members.

One very interesting point about this charter is that although Louis clearly gives himself the authority to determine who should hold the manor of Grimsby, he does not style himself in it as 'king of England'. Instead, he is described as 'Ludovicus domini regis Francie primogenitus', or 'Louis, eldest son of the lord king of France'. The seal, made of green wax and depicting Louis armed and on horse-back, is now broken, but from the remaining lettering around the outside it is just about possible to extrapolate that a similar form of wording is used: 'Sigill[um Lud]ovici p[rimogeniti regis Franci]e'.

This nomenclature which Louis used about himself is a point to which we will return later.

Other aspects of Louis's proto-government were not so well organised. His financial situation was irregular; he tried to impose some order by insisting on tributes from Essex, Norfolk and Suffolk, but he did not have the systems in place to enforce payments except on an ad hoc basis. Louis did not mint his own coins: the Empress Matilda had done so during her abortive attempt to claim the English crown some eight decades previously, as a mark of her implied and asserted status of monarch, but Louis's administration was not in a position to organise such an undertaking. Indeed, his government was very much improvised, and could hardly be anything else. Before he could embed it properly, he needed to work on gaining control of the rest of England.

Before Louis could take many further steps in this direction, however, catastrophic news arrived. In order to form a successful regime he would need to have a good working relationship with the Church, but it was either during his ride to London or shortly after he arrived that the news reached him that he was under sentence of excommunication from the papal legate. He would have known that this was a possibility for some time, since the threat had been made previously by Guala, but for a lifelong devoted Catholic it still must have come as something of a shock. Louis had lived his life according to the rules of the Church, and now the Church had expelled him from its community, decreeing that he was outcast, that divine services could not be said in his presence, and that he could not even enter a place of worship. If he were to die while excommunicate he would go straight to hell where he would burn for eternity.

Why did he not give up his campaign in order to make immediate peace with the Church? The answer appears to lie in a combination of factors. Firstly, although it was a fearsome punishment for any devout person, by this stage it has to be said that excommunication might have been losing some part of its shock value simply by over-use. Philip Augustus had been excommunicate for a number of years, as had John. Pope Innocent had not hesitated to welcome either of them straight back into the fold as soon as they had made their peace, or as soon as it suited the papacy. Louis had not seen his father visited with any form of divine retribution while he was outside of the Church.

A second reason is that Louis, with his chivalric background, had been brought up to keep his word. He refused to renege on a promise, as Roger of Wendover tells us: 'He had given his oath to the barons of England that he would come to their assistance, and therefore, he would rather be excommunicated by the pope for a time than incur the charge of falsehood.' Louis was being put in what must have been, to him, an impossible situation: disobey the Church on one hand, or break his word on the other. The two lay in the balance, but what tipped the scales was surely that his desire to be king of England was overwhelming: he was a powerful, intelligent and energetic man who had been brought up to rule, and there was nothing on the horizon for him in France for many years, King Philip still being in the best of health and unwilling to relinquish any of his responsibilities. Therefore Louis's chivalric ideals, the martial side of his character and the chance to campaign won out against his religious faith.

However, his determination to ignore the excommunication did not mean he had to deny his religion entirely, for the final factor in the equation, and the one which he proclaimed most publicly, was that the excommunication had been performed by the legate, not by the pope in person, and that the Holy Father would no doubt see fit to rescind the penalty once the facts were explained to him. Simon Langton, Louis's chancellor in England and a man of the cloth himself, released a statement saying that Louis believed the pope to have been misinformed by his subordinates and that he had sent word to him to clarify matters; he gave orders to the clergy that while they awaited a definitive answer from the pope himself, the excommunication should be ignored. He and Elias of Dereham preached Louis's cause loudly in the churches of London, and made it known that the archbishop of Canterbury was in Rome seeking to lift the sentence. The archbishop was of course Simon's exiled brother Stephen Langton, whose interests would be much better served by having Louis on the throne rather than John, so he could be counted on to do everything in his power to help.

None of Louis's secular supporters, presumably of varying degrees of devoutness themselves, chose to desert his cause due to his excommunication – they preferred pragmatism and to follow the prince of France who had proved himself a leader rather than a prince of the Church who knew nothing of war or campaigning. Most of the clergy of London, too, chose to obey the present chancellor rather than the absent legate, and in the end only five churches observed the excommunication protocol and denied Louis entry. Unfortunately one of these was Westminster Abbey, the place where English kings were crowned, so Louis's coronation could not take place immediately. Louis appears to have taken this with equanimity: he was in no particular hurry. He saw himself as the *de facto* king of England, John having been declared deposed and having voluntarily abandoned his crown when he fled from the invading forces and away from the centre of government.

Was there also a touch of arrogance at work here? At this point, Louis was in a very favourable position, and he was no doubt confident that matters would proceed according to plan. Barons were flocking to his side as each week went by, and there did not seem to be any concerted resistance effort; so all in all he could feel that there was plenty of time for him to worry about his coronation once he had the whole realm firmly under his control. Also, proclaim as he might that his excommunication was mistaken, Louis knew that his opponents could use it against him to claim that his coronation was not valid, and it would be better if there were no doubts about the legitimacy of the ceremony in future. It could be delayed until both Westminster Abbey and the archbishop of Canterbury were available.

Although Louis did not know it yet, this was to be the biggest mistake of his life.

* * *

Meanwhile, Louis's messengers had reached Pope Innocent in Rome in May, and the Holy Father was presented with a dilemma. Louis had defied the legate he had sent to the Assembly of Melun and had invaded England despite Guala's objections, a direct challenge to papal authority. Moreover, his opponent was John, Innocent's vassal, and the realm invaded was a papal fief. This called for Innocent to intervene. On the other hand, Louis was known to be a good son of the Church who would not act against its interests – and as the certain future king of France, as well as the potential king of England, he would be a figure of immense power and influence in the years to come. He was also Innocent's best hope for a swift resolution to the Albigensian crusade. The pope noted to the messengers:

> If your lord Louis is conquered, in his harm the Church of Rome is harmed, and we consider an injury to him as one to ourselves; we always indulged the hope, and we indulge it now, that he would be in all its times of need the arm, in oppression the solace, and in persecution the refuge of the Church of Rome.

The result was that he officially resolved nothing, and Louis's messengers were left to kick their heels in Rome as they waited for an answer. This apparent indecision and prevarication seem uncharacteristic of the canny Innocent, so it is possible that he was waiting for more news about the progress of the invasion, and which side was more likely to win, before he officially declared support for one 'king' or the other.

So Louis, in London during the first week of June 1216, received neither confirmation of his excommunication nor news of its overturn. He could not let the lack of religious news halt the momentum of his military campaign, however. His allies in other parts of the kingdom were acting in his interests – the excitable teenage King Alexander of Scotland was besieging Carlisle, and there were outbreaks of pro-Louis conflict in Wales – but they could not be expected to continue if Louis were to remain entrenched in London. John had fled but he was still at large in the west of the country, so the next priority must be to capture him before he could muster his remaining resources, while also taking charge of wider territories. Louis therefore divided his forces into three: he left a garrison within London's walls in order to defend the city, and sent a second force under Robert Fitzwalter to subdue the eastern counties. He himself rode for Winchester in order to engage John, in an effort to put a swift end to the war.

This is where all Louis's years of training and of education in the knightly arts paid off. Thanks to the hard work of his youth he was fit and strong, able to bear the weight of his armour, the long days in the saddle and the discomforts of campaign life with ease. Apart from four days in London he had been on the move almost constantly since his arrival in England, and this was imperative in thirteenth-century warfare. To sit still was to become stagnated and lose momentum; an army needed to be fast and sharp, with a leader who could plan ahead, but who could also react to unexpected events as they happened.

There was a string of castles in Louis's path to Winchester which would need to be captured in order to secure the territory behind him as he went. A day after leaving London his force arrived at Reigate, owned by William de Warenne, earl of Surrey (referred to in most contemporary documents simply as earl Warenne). Warenne had hitherto been a staunch supporter of John, who was his cousin, but Louis encountered no resistance at Reigate and entered it unopposed. Warenne had not declared for him, but evidently he was not prepared to stand in his way, either. Louis then took Guildford, advanced on Farnham and had barely set up a siege before the garrison surrendered. The country was falling into his hands exactly as planned, and it was not until he reached Winchester on 14 June 1216 that he encountered the first real resistance.

As Louis and his army approached the great city, they saw smoke and flames reaching into the sky. John had fled again, further west to Corfe Castle, and as he left he had ordered the suburbs of Winchester to be burned to the ground. The primary purpose of this was to deny the oncoming force shelter and resources, regardless of the fates of those people who lived and worked there. We have already noted that this was a tactic used frequently in the early thirteenth century, but in the normal course of events it would be an invader destroying enemy territory, or a lord razing a town which had defied him; that John was prepared to take this course of action on home ground, against a city which was not standing against him, demonstrates his desperation.

The war was to have profound consequences for many of the common people of England, who suffered all the ills of it without reaping any of the benefits. Most of them were undoubtedly more interested in their own crops or livelihoods than in who sat upon the throne, a social level which was so distant from their own experience that it could barely be imagined. But the people and even the clergy were powerless, as Matthew Paris describes:

God permitted a war in England ... the father strove to confound the son, the brother his brother, the citizen his co-citizen and the relative his relative, by seizing, exterminating, burning, despoiling, disinheriting, torturing and destroying. Not even the Church was strong enough to protect those fleeing to her. The religious were trodden underfoot more than anyone and became a prey for warmongers.

Later he notes the indiscriminate nature of the destruction, with commoners being at the mercy of both sides: 'The war got worse ... first the barons who supported [Louis], and then the royalists, extorted sums of money on every side ... everything lay open to arson and everyone to slaughter, arrest, incarceration and being clapped into irons.'

In Winchester the wooden buildings with their thatched roofs caught light all too easily after John's order, and the fire spread rapidly; by the time Louis arrived almost half the city was a smoking ruin. Still standing, however, were Winchester's two castles: the larger royal stronghold and a smaller one belonging to the bishop of Winchester, which was currently in the hands of a young man named Oliver Fitzroy, one of John's illegitimate sons. The castles could not be left behind with enemy garrisons inside while Louis pursued John. Equally, it would not be a good idea to besiege just one of them, as the men in the other could sally forth and attack the host from the rear. Therefore Louis divided his forces once more: Robert de Béthune would take some of the army and attack the smaller castle, while Louis would deal with the larger, royal one. His army occupied what was left of the city, the inhabitants presumably too shell-shocked and worried about their own lives and livelihoods to put up much resistance.

It is tempting to think of thirteenth-century armies as being made up of knights and squires, but in reality these were the minority in any host. Louis also had with him many footsoldiers, known as sergeants – more useful than mounted combatants in a city or in a siege situation – and engineers. These men built and set up siege machinery around the castle: the *History of the Dukes* mentions two types of stone-throwing machine called petraries (which worked by balance and traction, with men pulling down on ropes on one side of a large lever in order to throw missiles from the end which was forced upwards) and mangonels, which used the torsion of twisted ropes to produce the same ballistic effect. These machines bombarded the royal castle every day for two weeks, causing fear, danger and an unknown number of deaths and injuries to those inside. The garrison was allowed to send a message to John asking for aid, but when it became clear that none would be forthcoming the defenders surrendered, as did those inside the bishop's castle. Louis allowed all the men from both strongholds to withdraw unharmed, and he replaced them with his own followers, giving the royal castle to Hervé de Donzy, the count of Nevers, to hold in his name. He now had Winchester fully under control and could pursue John again.

* * *

John, meanwhile, was still on the defensive, moving from Corfe even further into the West Country. He had with him a commander named Falkes de Bréauté, a rare example at this time of a man from lower down the social scale risen to a high position, who would play an important part later in the war. His origins are obscure but it was probable that he was the illegitimate son of a Norman knight; he was originally not well off but on entering John's service he performed loyally, was knighted and rose to prominence. The *History of the Dukes* tells us that 'this Falkes had been a poor sergeant; he was the son of a knight from Normandy, but he served the king so well and knew his business so well that he became one of the richest men in

England'. Together with Falkes and his other remaining supporters John set about doing really the only thing which he could: refortifying and supplying those castles which were left to him. The south-west was still mainly under his control: he laid in good supplies of knights, provisions and arms in the castles of Wallingford, Corfe, Wareham, Bristol and Devizes. The south-east and much of the Midlands had already fallen into Louis's hands, although there were some small pockets of resistance on John's behalf. Hubert de Burgh was still safely at Dover; Windsor Castle held for John, and in Sussex, Roger of Wendover tells us, there was

> A young man named William, [who] refusing to make his fealty to Louis, collected a company of a thousand bowmen, and taking to the woods and forests with which that part of the country abounded, he continued to harass the French during the whole war, and slew many thousands of them.

It has been suggested that this William of Kensham, or 'Willikin of the Weald' as he became known, lurking in the forests with his bowmen and waging a guerrilla-style war, may be the origin of Robin Hood stories.

But other than these isolated examples of support things looked bleak indeed for John. William earl Warenne, who had given a hint of his intentions when he chose not to defend Reigate against the coalition of invaders and barons, submitted to Louis, as did two other earls who had previously seemed staunch supporters of John: William d'Aubigny, earl of Arundel, and William de Forz, earl of Aumale. Each brought with him not only the prestige of their rank, but also many hundreds of knights and men and a number of important castles. A major coup was scored by Louis soon afterwards when John's own half-brother William Longsword, earl of Salisbury, also defected. Salisbury had become increasingly disillusioned with John following the latter's apparently deliberate delaying of a ransom payment following Salisbury's capture at the battle of Bouvines two years previously; according to William the Breton, a rumour was even circulating that John had procrastinated so he could seduce Salisbury's young wife in his absence. Whether this was true or not, his brother's change of allegiance must have seemed to John like the last straw. Of those of the highest rank in England the only men to remain loyal to him were William Marshal, earl of Pembroke; Ranulf de Blundeville, earl of Chester; William de Ferrers, earl of Derby; and Hubert de Burgh the justiciar.

* * *

Louis, never resting, continued to expand his domain by pushing his campaign further along the south coast. He took Portchester, again confiding it to the count of Nevers, the father of his son's intended bride, before moving inland and encountering unexpectedly stiff resistance at the small and not terribly defensible castle of Odiham. The garrison there held off and held up his army for a whole week before agreeing to surrender ... at which point just thirteen men marched out, three knights and ten soldiers. In honour of their bravery they were permitted not only to leave unharmed, but also to take their horses and armour with them, an unusual concession. And if there was a lesson to be learned about how a very few men could have a disproportionate effect on a campaign as long as they were behind castle walls, Louis learned it.

It was while Louis was at Odiham that the castellan of Marlborough, who had previously held out for John, came to him and offered him the castle and the town. Louis accepted and gave them into the keeping of Robert de Dreux, although this was disputed by William Marshal the younger, who felt that they should have gone to him; he had also previously complained about being overlooked for the position of marshal of Louis's army. This foreshadowed what would become a growing problem for Louis: there would effectively be two claimants for every stronghold, town or piece of land that he captured. He would have to tread a fine line to balance the wishes and ambitions of those who had volunteered to come with him from France – and who must therefore be rewarded for their loyalty and service – with those of the English barons who had invited him over and who did not expect to end up being disinherited. Fortunately Louis had plenty of practical experience of compromise, and in this particular case Marshal junior was offered Worcester instead, after the sheriff there offered to surrender, so he rode off to occupy the town. However, Worcester was just a step too far westwards and out of Louis's safe zone, and it was shortly retaken by forces loyal to John, under the command of Ranulf, earl of Chester, and Falkes de Bréauté, who was fast becoming John's enforcer of choice.

Realising that chasing the fugitive ex-king deeper and deeper into the west was proving fruitless, and that he needed to consolidate before stretching his forces further, Louis turned and headed back to London, reaching the capital later in July to be greeted by news both religious and military. Word had sped to English shores from Rome, but it did not concern Louis's excommunication: instead he heard that Innocent III was dead. This was news of significance for all Christendom: Innocent had been one of the most powerful and influential popes of the Middle Ages, ascending the throne while still in his thirties and reigning for eighteen years during which he had lobbied unceasingly for crusades to recover the Holy Land, fought against heresy in Italy and southern France, presided over the fourth Lateran Council which reformed many aspects of the Church, and established and extended papal power in secular affairs – as witnessed by his unhesitating willingness to excommunicate kings and impose Interdict on their realms. Following his death, fears of a schism and of heretical advances led to a very swift election, and the new pope had already been named as Honorius III. He was known to be a less severe and forceful man than Innocent, so Louis is likely to have considered his election as good news.

The military reports were also good: the force which Louis had sent to the eastern counties under the command of Robert Fitzwalter was having success in Essex, Norfolk and Suffolk. The great city of Norwich had been occupied; Lynn was attacked and many inhabitants taken prisoner for ransom in order to raise money for the campaign. Things were also going well further north: Gilbert de Gant, another baronial adherent of Louis, had taken control of the city and county of Lincoln, although the castle, with its separate defences, was holding out. It was held by an elderly lady, Nicola de la Haye, who had bought a truce; de Gant was therefore able to return to Louis with more money for his campaign and with the captured ceremonial sword of Lincoln. As a reward he was named earl of Lincoln.

Further north still, Eustace de Vesci had been killed at the siege of Barnard's Castle, but Louis's allies had made inroads into Yorkshire and had taken the all-important city of York, while King Alexander of Scotland was still besieging Carlisle and ravaging Northumbria. 'All these provinces', says Roger of Wendover, 'were subdued and swore allegiance to Louis.'

Now that he had large swathes of territory under his control, Louis's next task was to crush the pockets of resistance in the south that were still causing trouble, which meant that he had to turn his attention to the great castles holding out against him. Once again the best idea was to split his forces in order to make a simultaneous attack, so he sent Robert de Dreux and Hervé the count of Nevers to Windsor while he rode for the great fortress of Dover.

Louis arrived in front of Dover Castle on 25 July 1216. It was an impressive sight and a daunting prospect: huge and well fortified, it had been much enlarged and improved by Henry II and now comprised a stone keep – 100 feet (30 metres) square and with walls up to 20 feet (6 metres) thick – in its own compound, surrounded by curtain walls broken only by a great twin-towered gatehouse at the north-western tip of the castle enclosure, which was itself protected by a wooden barbican, an additional defensible structure erected in front of it. Inside, Hubert de Burgh had some 140 knights (many of them Flemish or Poitevin), a greater number of sergeants, plenty of weapons and an ample store of supplies. The castle was set high on a hill overlooking the town, which gave the defenders even more of an advantage. To capture it would take a huge investment of time, troops and resources.

Thanks to a remarkably detailed and almost certainly eyewitness account in the *History of the Dukes*, we are very well informed about the progress of the siege of Dover. When Louis arrived he spent several days with his army billeted in or camping around the town, reconnoitring and planning. Louis accommodated himself in a priory rather than in the tented encampment; he needed a campaign head-quarters, and he no doubt thought that he might as well lodge in some comfort as nobody was going anywhere for a while. Then he divided his forces, one part remaining in the town to one side of the fortress and the other moving to the hill in front of the castle gate-house, which gave him the advantage of higher ground and from where he was able to direct siege operations. Petraries and mangonels were set up to bombard the walls and the gate, but the machines which had succeeded at Winchester and Odiham would be insufficient at Dover.

Before he had set off for the coast Louis had sent a messenger back to France to ask his father for help, and this help duly arrived in the shape of large-scale siege machinery. Philip sent over a device known as *Malvoisin* or 'Evil Neighbour', which was probably the first appearance of a trebuchet on English soil. A trebuchet acted in a similar way to a petrary, in that it used balance in order to throw stones. However, instead of using traction – men pulling down on ropes in order to fling the other arm of the lever in the air – it used a counterweight. A long wooden beam was pivoted near to one end; the longer side of the beam ended in a sling, in which the projectile was placed, and the shorter end held a large weight, generally a container filled with earth or rocks. A team of men would haul down the sling end in order to lift the counterweight into the air, at which point the beam was fixed and held in place. A stone or other missile was loaded into the sling, and then the beam was released: the counterweight came crashing down and the missile was flung into the air. The advantage of the heavy counterweight was that the trebuchet could throw much bigger stones over a much greater distance than either traction or torsion machines.

Despite what must have been his satisfaction with his new engine of war, Louis did not rely on this alone. His troops were already blockading the landward side of the castle; now his ships, after unloading their cargo, secured the sea outside Dover so the castle was completely cut off from outside aid and could not be either reinforced or reprovisioned.

Louis's first point of attack was the gatehouse and barbican to the north of the castle enclosure. As well as his stone-throwing machinery he also had his men build a wattle siege-tower (a device which put the besiegers on the same level as the defenders on the wall, meaning they could shoot arrows across at them; alternatively it could be filled with men and then moved closer to the wall, so the besiegers would not need to try and scale it by ladder, which left them open to attack or bombardment from above) and he also set men, under cover of a protective moveable device known as a 'cat', to undermine the walls. As had been demonstrated at Rochester the previous year, mining was an effective strategy, but it was a very slow process as the attackers were only able to use pickaxes and other hand tools against the gigantic stones and their foundations.

The siege was by no means one-sided. While Louis was directing these operations from the field north of the castle, the garrison made frequent sorties, charging out on horseback to kill and wound the attackers in hand-to-hand combat. Louis's men repulsed them but were unable to inflict many casualties in return as the defenders could retreat back behind their walls. Those inside were also able to use their crossbowmen as snipers, picking off anyone foolish enough to bring himself into range without adequate protection. Louis, who had no doubt been told in his youth of the agonising end of Richard the Lionheart from blood poisoning following a wound inflicted by a crossbow at a siege, was not harmed, although he probably wore his mail armour almost permanently.

The weeks went by, and gradually men began to trickle away from Louis's force. The count of Holland had taken the cross and now decided that the time was right for his pilgrimage to the Holy Land; some knights felt that their obligatory period of military service was up; some mercenaries thought they were not being paid enough; others were killed by the frequent sorties of the defenders. Committed to staying in one place, Louis for the first time began to lose the initiative in the war, and with it his temper. Roger of Wendover notes that he was 'greatly enraged and swore he would not leave the place until the castle was taken and all the garrison hung'.

In the middle of August there was a breakthrough when Louis's knights made a direct and bloody attack on the barbican which protected the main gate, and were able to capture it; the *History of the Dukes* tells us that Peter de Craon, who had defended the barbican so well for many weeks, was killed in the attack along with other men. However, although the besiegers were one step closer they were still confronted with the double-towered gatehouse; and, even if they could batter their way through that, the defenders could regroup further by taking refuge in the keep. A long campaign was still on the cards.

Additional good news reached Louis at Dover at about this time when he heard that King Alexander of Scotland had finally taken the town of Carlisle (although, in what was becoming a theme, the castle was still holding out), and that he was on his way south to do homage to Louis. Louis left the siege long enough to go and meet the young king at Canterbury, and then, in what may have been a pointed gesture to Hubert de Burgh and others, he had Alexander accompany him back to Dover to give homage in public for the lands he held in England. Roger of Wendover tells us that 'Alexander . . . did homage to him for the right which he ought to hold from the king of the English.' As with the charter we mentioned earlier, which demonstrated Louis's conviction that he had the authority to grant lands in England, this event indicates that Louis believed himself entitled to receive this homage. The occasion no doubt also gave him further confidence: he already had much of the nobility of England on his side and might consider himself the *de facto* king, but this was the solemn recognition of his claimed status, in public, by a crowned monarch. And the situation certainly attested to Louis's control over large parts of England: Alexander had been able to march with his men some 400 miles (640 km), all the way to the south coast, without encountering any resistance.

After the ceremony Alexander made his way back north, again managing to travel the length of the country without incident. Louis continued with the siege, and was heartened by further reinforcements from France: Peter de Dreux, who had left his obligations in Brittany

1 A nineteenth-century portrait of Louis. The artist appears to have paid close attention to contemporary descriptions of his appearance.

2 Louis, as a young boy, surrounded by the four cardinal virtues of Prudence, Justice, Temperance and Fortitude, is presented with a copy of the *Karolinus* by its author Giles of Paris.

3 King John (left) fights in France while Louis (right) marches on La-Roche-aux-Moines in 1214.

4 Replica mail constructed according to a thirteenth-century pattern. Each link is joined to four others, two above and two below, and rows of solid links alternate with rows of riveted links. A full set of harness made of such mail, as worn by Louis and others who could afford it, would be heavy but flexible.

5 Louis arrives in England, in an image sketched by Matthew Paris in the manuscript of his *Chronica Majora*.

6 Dover Castle. The stronghold was heavily fortified during the reign of Henry II, and was an imposing structure by the time of Louis's attempt to besiege it in 1216.

7 The north wall of Dover Castle, at the place where Louis and his men made a breakthrough and breached the wall, only to be pushed back before they could force their way farther inside.

8 The opposite end of the castle spectrum: the remains of the small keep at Odiham Castle in Hampshire, where Louis's army was held up for a week by a garrison of just thirteen men.

9 A charter issued by Louis in 1216 while he was in England, in which he grants the manor of Grimsby to William of Huntingfield. The first five words of the charter are the abbreviated Latin for *Ludovicus domini regis Francie primogenitus*, or 'Louis, eldest son of the lord king of France' – Louis was not at this point attempting to style himself as king of England.

10 Louis needed to effect repairs to many of the castles he captured. This image of Guédelon in France (where a castle is currently being constructed using only the tools and techniques of the thirteenth century) shows stone blocks and wooden scaffolding which match the descriptions of Louis's repairs to Winchester in 1217.

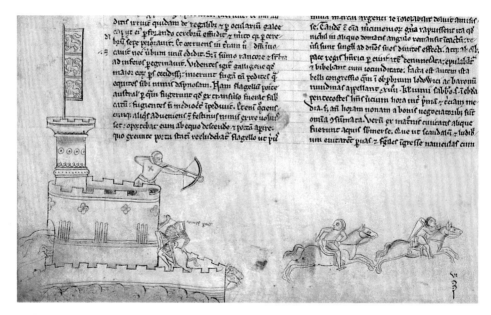

11 The battle of Lincoln, 1217, from an image in Matthew Paris's *Chronica Majora*. Note the crossbowman in the castle, the French fleeing from the city and the count of Perche being stabbed in the eye.

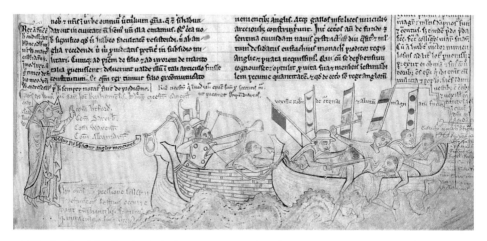

12 The battle of Sandwich, 1217, from an image in Matthew Paris's *Chronica Majora*. The English archers shoot pots full of blinding lime across at the French, and (on the right) Eustace the Monk is beheaded. The scene is observed by those lords and prelates who remain on land.

13 Louis and Blanche are crowned king and queen of France, in an illustration dating from the mid-fourteenth century.

14 Louis's seal as king of France shows him crowned, enthroned and holding a sceptre.

15 A French silver *denier* of Louis VIII. The inscriptions on the obverse and reverse read LVDOVICVS REX ('King Louis') and TVRONVS CIVI, indicating that the coin was minted in Tours.

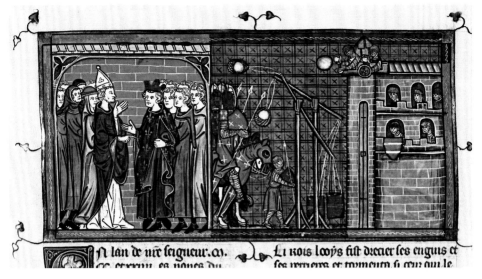

16 The siege of La Rochelle, 1224, with the royal army's counterweight trebuchets in action. A crowned Louis receives the submission of the town.

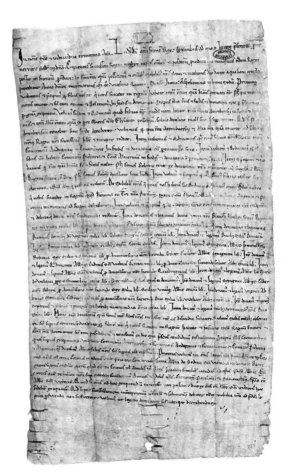

17 Louis's testament of 1225, in which he stipulates which of his lands will be left to which of his children.

18 The wide river Rhône at Avignon presented a formidable obstacle during the Albigensian crusade. The medieval bridge pictured (the Pont Saint-Bénézet) was built later in the thirteenth century to replace the one destroyed on the same site during Louis's siege of the city in 1226.

19 A mounted and crowned Louis receives the submission of Avignon from its citizens at the end of the three-month siege.

ous devons avoir en memoire
les fais et les contenances de
noz devanciers et nous devons
remurer es enciennes escriptures
quilz parlent des preudõmes et leurs
vies si côme fut saint loys qui se contint

20 A composite image from the fifteenth century shows the events of 1226: the siege of Avignon (left), the death of Louis VIII at Montpensier (centre) and the crowning of Louis IX (right).

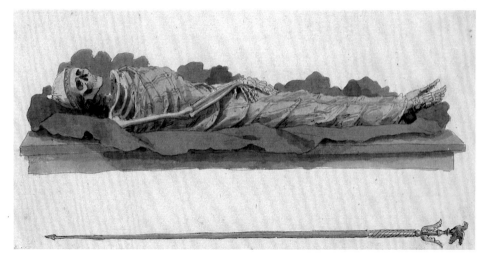

21 Following the exhumation of the royal tombs at St Denis in 1793, the archaeologist Alexandre Lenoir was able to make this sketch of Louis's corpse before it was tossed into the 'Capetian ditch' along with many others. The body was still wrapped in the hide in which it had been transported to Paris.

TROISIEME DYNASTIE.

	Morts en
HUGUES CAPET.	997 57
ROBERT, Fils de Hugues Capet.	1031 61
CONSTANCE D'ARLES, 2.e femme du Roi Robert, Fils du Roi Hugues Capet.	1032
HENRI 1.er	1060
ROBERT, Fils du Roi Henri 1.er	1060
LOUIS VI. (le Gros)	1137
PHILIPPE} Fils aîné du Roi Louis VI.	1131
CONSTANCE de Castille, 2.e femme du Roi Louis VII.	1160
PHILIPPE, surnommé Dagobert, Fils du Roi Louis VIII.	1221
PHILIPPE II. (Auguste)	1223 58
LOUIS VIII. (le Lion)	1226 39
PHILIPPE, C. de Boulogne, Fils de Philippe Auguste et d'Agnès sa 3.e femme.	1233
BLANCHE, Fille du Roi S.t Louis.	1243
JEAN, Fils du Roi S.t Louis.	1247
LOUIS de France, Fils du Roi S.t Louis.	1259
MARGUERITTE, 10.e Fille du Roi S.t Louis, 1.re femme de Jean I.er D. de Brabant.	1269
JEAN, dit TRISTAN de Damiette, Fils du Roi S.t Louis.	1270
LOUIS IX. (Saint Louis.)	1270 5.
ISABELLE d'Aragon, 1.re femme du Roi Philippe le Hardi, Fils du Roi S.t Louis.	1271 2
ALPHONSE, Comte de Poitiers, Fils du Roi Louis VIII.	1271
LOUIS et PHILIPPE} tous deux Fils de Pierre d'Alençon, Fils du Roi S.t Louis.	
LOUIS, Fils aîné de Philippe le Hardi et d'Isabelle d'Aragon.	1276
PHILIPPE III. (le Hardi.)	1285

22 When the royal remains were re-interred following the restoration of the French monarchy they were all entombed together, with plaques erected to list the individuals. Here Louis's name appears on a Capetian plaque, preceded by his father Philip Augustus and followed by his half-brother Philip Hurepel.

in order to come to the aid of his cousin and companion, and Thomas, the young count of Perche. Perche was a rising star of the French nobility: he had succeeded to his title in 1202 at the age of seven after the death of his father, had fought for King Philip at Bouvines while still in his teens, and now at twenty-one was building a reputation for deeds of arms and chivalry. In an example of how inextricably the men on both sides of the conflict were linked, Perche was a kinsman of John's most faithful supporter, William Marshal (his great-grandmother and Marshal's mother were sisters); he also had a tenuous claim to the English throne himself as his maternal grandmother was John's sister Matilda, but he supported Louis wholeheartedly.

Both nobles had brought knights and men with them, which would help the cause, but the news also came across the Channel that the new pope, Honorius, had confirmed Louis's sentence of excommunication. It was a bitter blow, but Louis was by now in far too deep to back out from claiming the crown of England even if he had been so inclined. He would push on: once he had subdued the country, captured John and been crowned he would have the leisure to talk properly to the pope, not to mention the power to influence him.

In the meantime, as August turned into September, Dover still needed to be subdued. The miners had been continuing their slow and painstaking work, and now came the breakthrough: one of the towers of the gatehouse was brought crashing down, and Louis and his knights could charge into the breach.

This is what the knights had been waiting for. Trained since boyhood to engage in hand-to-hand combat, they detested having to kick their heels at a siege while miners and engineers held sway. Now they had the chance to throw themselves at the enemy in person, to take out their frustration at the long siege, to hack with their swords and their axes into armour and flesh. But the defenders were just as frustrated, just as fierce, and even more desperate – after all, had

Louis not threatened to hang them all once the castle was taken? The normal policy at the time was that if a garrison surrendered they would be allowed to leave unharmed, but that if a castle had to be taken by storm then those inside were liable to be executed. After irritating Louis and thwarting his plans for so many weeks they were unlikely to be treated with clemency if defeated, so they fought back with all their might, filling the gap in the wall with men. Slowly but surely they repulsed the attack, holding the line, pushing the besiegers back and keeping them out long enough for running repairs to be made to the breach, which was shored up with timbers taken from buildings inside the compound. The barricade held. Dover still stood.

The stalemate could not be allowed to go on forever. Force had not worked; starving the garrison out would take too long and Louis needed to be on the move. To stand still for too long, as he well knew, was to lose momentum. Louis agreed a truce with Hubert de Burgh, and his army withdrew from the siege on 14 October 1216.

* * *

While Louis had been stuck at Dover, Robert de Dreux and the count of Nevers were making little progress at Windsor. 'They were there a long time,' says the *History of the Dukes*, tersely, 'without achieving much.' Windsor was held by an experienced commander who had with him sixty knights, and Robert did not have anything like the power of the siege machinery which was being deployed at Dover, or the number of men which would be required to compensate for this and overrun the castle by sheer force of numbers. And, meanwhile, John was finally on the move.

Bolstered by the knowledge that Louis was still at Dover, John emerged from his safe ground in the west of England, leaving Cirencester on 2 September 1216 and reaching Reading four days later. He then moved to within striking distance of Windsor, but yet again he avoided a pitched battle: he sent forward his archers to loose their arrows on the besiegers and a small skirmish ensued, but no sooner had the besiegers readied themselves for a full-scale battle than John's forces melted away, as he once more lived up (or down) to his nickname of 'Softsword'. Instead of risking himself in an engagement John turned to a favourite tactic, ravaging and burning his way through lands held by the barons supporting Louis, extorting money on the way and reaching Cambridge on 16 September. The besiegers of Windsor, still making little headway, left the castle in order to follow John; it was harvest time so the damage he was doing to crops would have serious repercussions. Roger of Wendover notes that 'the cruel destruction which he caused among the houses and crops of the said barons afforded a pitiable spectacle to all who saw it', and Matthew Paris also deplores his actions:

Meanwhile, the lieutenants of Falkes [de Bréauté] who was the captain of all those abominable soldiers who were mercilessly plundering ... having thrown many other citizens into chains, they either took them away or, having devised tortures for their minds, impoverished them to a state of starvation ... everywhere there was misery and lamentation; everywhere was the sound of wailing.

The sound of wailing, the smell of burning, and the sight of hungry men, women and children followed John everywhere as he spent the rest of September ravaging Norfolk and Suffolk and heading towards Lincoln. Louis's men could not catch him and force him into an engagement as he continued his technique of battle avoidance, preferring instead to deny his enemy economic resources by murdering the defenceless. Monasteries and abbeys were not safe from his men either; but as the clergy and people begged for deliverance from the cruelties of the man who had been their king, little did they know that their prayers were about to be answered.

In early October 1216 John laid waste to a great tract of land through Grimsby, Louth, Boston and Spalding before stopping at Lynn where he was well received and given lavish gifts; possibly in genuine welcome, or possibly as protection money to bribe him not to destroy the town. The citizens also hosted a feast for him and it was here that he first began to fall ill. Our sources vary on the exact cause – dysentery, food poisoning, or sickness caused by exhaustion or gluttony – but he managed to get himself back on the road on 11 October. He crossed the Wash, and it was somewhere during this crossing that his baggage train suffered some kind of accident resulting in the loss of his belongings. Roger of Wendover gives the most dramatic account:

> He lost all his carts, waggons, and baggage horses, together with his money, costly vessels, and everything which he had a particular regard for; for the land opened in the middle of the water and caused whirlpools which sucked in everything, as well as men and horses, so that no-one escaped to tell the king of the misfortune. He himself narrowly escaped.

Roger is almost certainly exaggerating here, for if the situation had been as serious as he describes it would have been mentioned in more detail by other sources. The *History of William Marshal* mentions 'terrible misfortune', but only in relation to John's illness; Ralph of Coggeshall writes more calmly that a mishap befell part of the baggage train when some packhorses were mired in quicksand 'because they had hastily and incautiously set out before the tide had receded', resulting in the loss of some household effects. He adds that some members of the household were also sucked in, but does not say how many or give any names.

It was a superstitious age. To the sick John, crippled by stomach pains, deserted by most of his barons, pursued by the stench of burning crops and houses, the loss of his belongings must have seemed the final sign that God had abandoned his cause. His kingdom was gone, his health was gone, his hope was gone. As he staggered his way to Swinesford Abbey and Sleaford, he felt his mortality: he wrote to the new pope asking him to protect his heir. By the time he reached Newark Castle on 18 October 1216 he could no longer sit in his saddle and was having to be carried on a litter. He made a hurried will: his desire to bequeath goods to 'make satisfaction to God and Holy Church for the wrongs I have done them' and to 'distribute alms to the poor and to religious houses for the salvation of my soul' was a ploy used by many dying kings who had done as they liked in life but now feared that their sins would catch up with them when they were face to face with the Almighty. Once the executors were named – among them the papal legate Guala, William Marshal the earl of Pembroke, Ranulf the earl of Chester and Falkes de Bréauté – John whispered his final confession to the hastily summoned abbot of Croxton, and gave himself over to the agonies in his stomach and the torments of his mind.

* * *

Louis had left Dover after the truce was agreed on 14 October; within days he was back in his stronghold of London, planning his next move. The quickest way for news to travel in 1216 was on horse-back, a fast messenger aided by good conditions and changes of mount being able to make perhaps 40 miles (65 km) a day. A journey from Newark to London on muddy roads during the shortened autumn daylight hours would take three or four days, so it was likely to have been on or around 22 October that the momentous news reached Louis at the palace of Westminster: John was dead.

———◆◗◖◗◆———

CHAPTER FIVE

THE TIDE TURNS

King John reigned for eighteen years, five months and five days, during which time he caused many disturbances and entered on many useless labours in the world, and at length departed this life in a great agony of mind, possessed of no territory, yea, not even being his own master. (Matthew Paris)

He was generous and liberal to foreigners but a despoiler of his own people. Since he trusted more in foreigners than in them, he was abandoned before the end by his own people, and in his own end he was little mourned. (Barnwell annalist)

THESE EPITAPHS ARE among the more balanced of the thirteenth-century verdicts on John and his reign. John has been called many things over the centuries, both by chroniclers and by historians: tyrant, murderer, oppressor and adulterer among them. As it happens, none of these were particularly detrimental characteristics for a medieval king: many monarchs considered to be great exhibited one or more of these behaviours, and being genial, universally popular and

well liked was more often than not counterproductive in the circumstances. But alas for John, he was also lacking in those qualities which
would have impressed his contemporaries and made him an effective
thirteenth-century ruler. He did have significant skills as an adminis-
trator, but even here he was let down by his small-mindedness and
suspicion, his unreliability and unpredictability, and his lack of trust
in his nobles. He was not a great warrior like his brother, or a great
leader like his father; he did not seem to inspire loyalty in the way
they did. This is not to say that Henry II or Richard I were perfect
kings either: Henry ruled a huge empire but did not really foster any
sense of unity among the diverse parts of it, which set his successors
up for trouble; and Richard, had he lived longer, might well have
faced some sort of revolt from his barons over the enormous financial
exactions he forced out of them in order to pay for his crusading
fervour. But they were both effective in ways John was not, and the
main point must be this: power in the early thirteenth century was
gained, held, displayed and transmitted through the possession and
retention of land, and in this John was a failure. In 1199 he inherited
England, Normandy, Anjou, Maine, Touraine and all of Aquitaine, as
well as a claim to Ireland; in 1216 he left only England and the Poitou
and Gascony parts of Aquitaine, none of which was actually under
his complete control.

With London in Louis's hands there was no question of John
being interred at Westminster Abbey (which was not, at this stage,
the official royal mausoleum it later became); instead his remains
were embalmed by the abbot of Croxton and taken by a troop of
his mercenaries to Worcester cathedral, to lie near the shrine of
St Wulfstan.

Once Louis had had the chance to take in the momentous news,
he was faced with a range of options for immediate action. After
spending the last several months outside the walls of Dover Castle,

the subduing of the great fortress was naturally still in the forefront of his mind: he sent word to Hubert de Burgh to surrender it now that John was dead, but Hubert refused on the grounds that he now served John's sons and daughters. Hubert's declaration of support for John's heirs was matched by four other important and influential men who would form the backbone of the continuing resistance to Louis: William Marshal, earl of Pembroke; Ranulf de Blundeville, earl of Chester; Peter des Roches, bishop of Winchester; and the papal legate Guala. They were supported by Falkes de Bréauté: as John's favourite he could have found his position in jeopardy now that his patron was gone, but the cause could not afford to do without his military skills or the string of vital castles which he held in the Midlands.

John left five legitimate children: Henry, who had just turned nine; Richard, seven; Joan, six; Isabelle, two; and baby Eleanor. Joan was in France being brought up by the Lusignan family following her betrothal to Hugh the younger which had been negotiated as part of John's campaign in Poitou two years earlier; the others were being kept safe in the west of England, out of Louis's reach for now. Henry, who was at the royal stronghold of Devizes along with his mother, Queen Isabelle, was hurriedly summoned by John's remaining supporters who needed him as the figurehead for their cause; they declared him king. Their declaration was based on the principle of hereditary succession rather than on election by the barons, as this is where Henry had a stronger claim than Louis. There was of course no way the boy could be taken to Westminster for a coronation as London held firmly for Louis, and in any case there was no archbishop of Canterbury in the country (archbishops of Canterbury had enjoyed the exclusive right to conduct coronation ceremonies in England since the issue of the papal bull *Quanto majorem* by Pope Alexander III in 1171). Indeed, there was not even a crown as it had been lost during John's last days, either during the baggage incident in the Wash or possibly stolen after his death as his possessions were looted.

However, it was vital to the cause of the resistance that they should have a crowned king, or at least the appearance of one, so a hasty ceremony was arranged at Gloucester cathedral on 28 October 1216, just ten days after John's death. Little Henry, a solemn child, was met outside the town by William Marshal and an armed escort; he gave a short speech placing himself in the care of God and the Marshal, and then burst into tears.

Once they were safely inside the town of Gloucester, Henry, dressed in 'child-sized robes of state', was dubbed a knight by William Marshal and gave homage to Guala for England, reiterating the realm's status as a papal fief. He was carried to the cathedral, where Guala sang a Mass and Peter des Roches 'crowned' him with a lady's circlet provided by his mother. As part of the ceremony Roger of Wendover tells us that Henry

> Swore on the holy gospels and other relics of the saints that he
> would observe honour, peace and reverence towards God and the
> holy Church . . . he also swore that he would show strict justice to
> the people entrusted to his care, and would abolish all bad laws
> and customs . . . and would observe those that were good, and
> cause them to be observed by all.

All of this, of course, was merely symbolic; as we have already seen, Louis had postponed his own coronation as it would only be above dispute if carried out in Westminster Abbey by the archbishop of Canterbury, and the same applied to any other candidate to the throne. But Henry's temporary ceremony overseen by a papal legate, when added to his status as the eldest son of the previous anointed king, provided the semblance of legitimacy and gave weight to his cause.

Henry's age meant that he could not, and would not be expected to, rule in person. This was the first accession of a minor since the Conquest, so there was no Anglo-Norman precedent; Henry's supporters needed to make some swift and practical arrangements. William Marshal was named as regent – that is, he would rule on Henry's behalf and would technically be king in all but name. The *History of William Marshal* is unsurprisingly full of the details: we are told that at first Marshal tried to refuse due to his age (he was around seventy) and his modesty; but after being persuaded, encouraged and begged at length by the other men he agreed. The text tells us of the stirring speech he then made, which, while probably embellished, gives a flavour of the heightened emotions of the time:

> 'By God's lance!', said the earl . . . 'if all the world deserted the young boy except me, do you know what I would do? I would carry him on my shoulders and walk with him thus, with his legs astride, I would be with him and never let him down, from island to island, from land to land, even if I had to beg for my daily bread.'

The only one of Henry's supporters who was not entirely comfortable with the arrangement was the earl of Chester, who, as Marshal's equal in rank, wealth and land ownership, felt that he should have been given more of a share of the power. He was also considerably younger and more vigorous, being in his mid-forties. In the event he had to be content with a more supporting role, but the first seeds of what would later become discord had been sown. The others divided up a number of responsibilities: Marshal would be in control of the military campaign to put Henry on the throne; Peter des Roches would take personal custody and tutorship of the boy; Hubert de Burgh would return to the south-east to continue the defence there.

But the real mastermind of the outfit would be the papal legate Guala. Playing on his role as the pope's representative in a realm subject to the papacy, he wielded great power both behind the scenes and unabashedly to the fore: his seal appears on a number of official acts from around this time and it precedes that of the Marshal as regent. Guala was in effect almost an absolute ruler: Pope Innocent had ordered all English magnates to submit to him 'humbly and devotedly' and had given him full power to act in his name in England, to do whatever he thought best without appeal.

One person who played no role in the new regime, when she might have expected (or been expected) to, was Henry's mother, Isabelle of Angoulême. Other recent queens dowager such as Eleanor of Aquitaine in England or Adela of Champagne in France had been major political figures in their time but Isabelle was not prominent in the support of her son. Isabelle's experiences as John's wife have been the subject of much speculation which we will not explore here, but much can be inferred from her actions after his death: staying in England only long enough to see her son installed with his protectors, she left him and her younger children, returned to France, and, as far as we can tell from her surviving charters and other evidence, never mentioned John's name again. In one of the more bizarre marital arrangements of the Middle Ages she married in 1220 Hugh X de Lusignan (the younger), who was betrothed to her daughter Joan and who was the son of her own original intended husband, Hugh IX the elder. 'This caused much talk,' says the Anonymous of Béthune's *History of the Dukes*, succinctly. Joan was later palmed off on King Alexander of Scotland, whom she married in 1221 when he was twenty-three and she was ten. Isabelle and Hugh went on to have nine children within the next twelve years, a number of whom later came to their half-brother Henry's court and became the unpopular foreigners of their own day. Isabelle had very little contact with her children by John and did not see her eldest son again until he was an adult; Henry was left to the care of his regent, his tutor and his council.

* * *

In all the euphoria and emotion surrounding the 'coronation' of Henry it might have been possible for his supporters to forget for a while that there was actually another claimant to the throne in England: a grown man, a warrior and leader in charge of his own army, to whom most of the barons (almost three-quarters of them by this stage) had sworn allegiance, who was currently in the capital and who had more than half the country under his direct control.

We might imagine that the death of Louis's chief antagonist would leave the field clear for him, resulting in an immediate land-slide victory of the sort enjoyed by his predecessor William the Conqueror after the death of Harold. But the lingering support for John's children meant that this was not the case, and the war would go on. In Louis's favour was the fact that, given Henry's age, long years of minority beckoned which would inevitably invite more conflict and there were many in the kingdom who might prefer the strong man who could take charge now rather than the promise of a boy with arguably more hereditary right (depending on your point of view of John's deposition), who would not rule in his own stead for another decade or so. On the other hand, the prospect of a lengthy minority offered more scope for personal gain, something never far from the minds of the individual barons. The immediate result of John's death was therefore an uneasy stalemate, and there were no major defections one way or the other during the autumn and winter of 1216.

Both sides used the breathing space to regroup and take stock of their situation. Geographically, England was split along a line which ran more or less from north to south; Louis was in control of the east, while Henry's camp held territory and a number of royal castles in the west, and William Marshal's own lands were in south Wales, which made that area secure. Moreover, the Henricians retained control of three major strongholds situated in Louis-controlled areas: Dover, Windsor, and Corfe, home to the royal treasury. Thanks to the truce which Louis had agreed there in October, Hubert de Burgh was finally able to leave Dover, and he travelled to Bristol for a first meeting of Henry's council in November. The council used the opportunity provided by John's death to send letters to all the opposing barons offering them amnesty and restoration of their lands if they would swear fealty to Henry. This produced only one defection of note before the end of the year: William d'Albini, last seen defending Rochester against John in late 1215 and having been in John's custody since the castle's eventual surrender, decided to throw in the towel and pay homage to Henry. He raised the considerable sum of 6,000 marks to pay for his ransom and was released.

On 12 November 1216, Henry's council reissued Magna Carta. This had little immediate concrete effect, but it acted as a sign that his regime would abide by the concessions which had been wrung from John, without reneging upon them in the way John had done. This astonishing U-turn – they would agree to something John had gone to war to prevent – demonstrates the weakness of their overall position at this point: they might not have been clutching at straws quite yet, but their fingers were definitely slipping. There is no evidence to suggest that Louis would reconfirm Magna Carta, and indeed it is difficult to see how or why he would have accepted the throne of England if his rule were to be hedged and restrained in this way. Therefore this announcement by the regent and the legate effectively pulled out one of the props from under Louis's campaign, politically if not militarily. If Henry and his regent would abide by the charter then those barons who supported Louis could not claim that their support for the charter was their principal reason for doing so.

Louis needed to think and to plan his next steps. John's death had not resulted in his overall victory: the campaign and the crown still needed to be won, and to do that he would need to regain some momentum. But as he remained in London working on his immediate plans – having moved his base to the more securely fortified Tower – the garrison with whom he had made a truce at Dover finally emerged from behind their walls; they burned the buildings he had erected in front of the castle, and then ravaged the countryside for miles around, both to replenish their own stores in anticipation of a further siege, and to deny Louis's troops any sustenance when they should come again. The 'key to England' would not turn in his favour.

Politically Louis could do little against the propaganda being issued by Henry's council. But he still had the upper hand militarily, so his next move would capitalise on this: he would seek to capture more and more of the smaller castles being held against him, tipping the balance of power further his way, before returning to crack the larger nuts. He went on to prove that he was still the master of this strategy as a series of fortifications proved no match for him and his troops. On the same day that Henry's council was reissuing Magna Carta Louis began a siege of Hertford Castle, which had been much strengthened during the reign of Richard the Lionheart. It was defended stoutly against him for more than three weeks, during which time he was able to deal with some administrative matters – it was here that he drew up and sealed the charter we mentioned earlier granting Grimsby to William of Huntingfield – but his tactics and machines eventually proved too much for the garrison, and they surrendered after twenty-five days. As had been the case with his previous victories, Louis kept his word and allowed the defenders to march out unharmed on 6 December 1216.

On taking charge of the castle, Louis was presented with the same dilemma which had dogged all his previous captures: into whose custody should it be given? The natural claimant in this particular case was Robert Fitzwalter, to whom Hertford had previously belonged, but according to Roger of Wendover the French argued that it should go to one of them as a spoil of war; they had, after all, followed Louis on campaign in the natural expectation of gain. This situation, as we have noted previously, was inevitable, but Louis had until now managed it gracefully and avoided any major disputes among his followers. He has been accused in some quarters of favouring his French supporters (Roger of Wendover in particular giving this as a reason why some of his English barons later chose to desert him), but in fact the evidence would suggest that he was even-handed, balancing the rights and demands of both halves of his force even though they were to all intents and purposes incompatible. Since arriving on English soil and being proclaimed king by his supporters he had set up an administration, headed by Simon Langton as chancellor, which had functioned simultaneously with his military manoeuvres; his previous hard-won lordship of and administrative experience in Artois were finally proving useful. Louis had adapted well to English forms of government, seeking to keep existing practices where possible and upholding ancient customs and liberties – as we mentioned earlier, he did not see England as a 'conquered' country on which foreign customs should be imposed, but rather one to which he had succeeded through entitlement. Changes were necessary in some areas, though, as he sought to enforce order on those territories under his control which were in varying states of chaos due to the flight of previous lords and officers of the law; he established in post interim officers of justice and administration while retaining the previous system of sheriffs in each county.

Louis recognised that English towns had their own urban communities and customs which would not be suited to the imposition of French-style governance, so he respected the right of burgesses to have a hand in their own self-determination. In the capital he paid particular attention to the mayor and citizens of London and did not seek to overthrow or interfere in their affairs; trade could continue as normal. The Londoners, who could be fickle if and when their interest dictated, remained loyal to him for now.

* * *

Part of the arrangement of the surrender of Hertford was that Louis would also receive Berkhamstead Castle, some 28 miles (45 km) away, so he wasted no further time and moved there on 7 December 1216. However, when he arrived he found that the garrison commander had renounced the agreement made at Hertford and would not open the gates, so despite the worsening weather Louis would have to set up a siege there as well. His siege engines, weighing several tons each and dragged in pieces on carts through the muddy and rutted roads, would need to be reassembled. The troops, strung out back along the road from Hertford, were arriving slowly and piecemeal, and the garrison took advantage of this: they made a sortie before the besiegers were properly organised, capturing baggage and supplies and inflicting casualties. Louis, cold, frustrated and undoubtedly beginning to tire, had his machines rebuilt and they 'kept up a destructive shower of stones' (Roger of Wendover) until the castle surrendered on 20 December. Despite the resistance he had encountered and the men he had lost, Louis once more allowed the garrison to leave with their lives, their horses and their armour.

Campaigning was difficult in the winter. Food and fodder were hard to come by, especially in the large quantities needed by an army and its horses; the short hours of daylight meant that travel was limited to a very few miles a day; the state of the roads prevented the easy movement of baggage carts and other heavy items; and men were more likely to succumb to illness and disease. The Church also frowned upon fighting taking place during its great holy feasts, so when a message reached Louis on 20 December from William Marshal, in which the regent proposed a general truce over Christmas and until 13 January, Louis accepted.

It took Louis several days to travel the 35 or so miles (55 km) back to his base at the Tower of London, breaking his journey at the abbey at St Albans where he became irritated by the abbot's refusal to pay homage to him, apparently – according to Roger of Wendover – threatening to burn the abbey and the town before being appeased by a gift of 80 marks from the 'dreadfully threatened' abbot. As the likelihood of Louis inflicting violence on either a religious institution or on a man of the Church is slim, we may choose to take Roger's version of events with a pinch of salt.

Louis was able to catch a few days' rest in London over Christmas and the New Year, but he set out on the road again as soon as the truce was concluded, this time to the east. The cities (but not the castles) of Ely and Lincoln had been taken by his men before the truce, and now he headed for Cambridge, where he took the castle by late January 1217 without too much trouble. He was still there when word came from William Marshal, who was at that point in Oxford, that he would like to arrange another truce – that is, a complete cessation of hostilities by both parties – until the end of April. Louis agreed, with the canny proviso of the handover of more castles in order to buy his agreement: Colchester, Orford, Norwich and Hedingham were surrendered without him having to lift a finger. His military conquest of England was still moving in the right direction, keeping many of the barons in his camp or at least on the fence, untempted by Marshal's offers and blandishments. Roger of

Wendover points out that their pride may have been a factor, too: 'On the other hand, it seemed a disgrace for them to return to their allegiance to a king whom they had renounced, lest they should be like dogs returning to their vomit.' Despite Louis's progress, however, the major strongholds were still a thorn in his side. Ominously, before the four agreed castles were handed over to his men, their stores were transferred to Dover.

* * *

During the winter many letters were sent back and forth to Rome on behalf of both sides. Those of Louis were less well received: Honorius was keen to retain England as a papal fief and he wanted to exercise control over it. In a letter of 6 December 1216 he noted the papacy's dominion over England and said that the Holy See would not be compared to the shepherd who fled and left his sheep at the first sign of the wolf. He sent messages of support to Henry and to Guala, renewing the latter's ecclesiastical powers and authorising him to annul the oaths of the barons to Louis and to suspend any members of the English clergy who refused to support Henry. Honorius also sent the abbots of Cîteaux and Clairvaux (two of the greatest monasteries in Europe and the motherhouses of the Cistercian order) directly to Philip Augustus to persuade him to order his son to cease his campaign.

Guala, no doubt disappointed that Marshal's letters and offers to the barons had thus far had little success, responded enthusiastically to the confirmation of his powers in order to revive Henry's flagging cause. In the pope's name he decreed that Henry's campaign to take the throne was now a crusade (Louis still being under sentence of excommunication) and he instructed Henry's forces to wear white crosses. This again pulled the rug out from under Louis's feet, as the Barnwell annalist observes: 'Those who once called themselves the army of God, and boasted that they fought for the liberties of the Church and the kingdom, were now reputed to be the sons of Belial and compared to infidels.' Under intense pressure, eleven of the twelve bishops who had sided with Louis went over to Henry, the exception being the bishop of Ely.

However, Henry was broke. This was a very dangerous position to be in during a campaign: if troops were not paid they were liable to slip away or to change allegiance. Guala squeezed as much as he could out of the Church in England, becoming slightly less popular with the clergy as a result, and William Marshal sanctioned more ravaging of the countryside, which also did little to promote their cause with the ordinary people. The beleaguered abbey and town of St Albans were threatened again, this time by Falkes de Bréauté and his men who extorted more protection money from the abbot. Falkes then embarked on a vicious tour of the wider region, taking clergy and civilians prisoner and extorting ransoms as he went. If this state of affairs were to continue then the general population would care less and less about who was on the throne; they just wanted peace.

Unfortunately, Louis's own finances were such that he was unable to push for the final conquest; he had the upper hand but did not have enough troops to force the decisive victories which he needed for overall and overwhelming control. Years of stalemate beckoned which could leave much of the realm burned, unprofitable and unin-habitable. If Louis was going to win the war he needed to do it soon, which meant that he needed more men and more money. Unlike Guala he did not have the option of levying a tax on the Church, and for reasons which no chronicler specifies he chose not to embark on a ravaging campaign. Either he did not wish to antagonise the population further or he felt that the possibilities for gain were exhausted. No, there was only one place he could drum up the level of extra support he needed. It was a momentous decision which could swing the fate of England either way, but it had to be done: while the truce was still in force, Louis would go back to France.

Louis's supporters were, not unnaturally, dismayed by this. Roger of Wendover comments rather gloatingly that Louis would never again enjoy the same level of goodwill with the English barons, while the Barnwell annalist tells us that Louis swore a solemn oath to them that he would return before the truce expired. After offering this reassurance he gathered his close companions and a troop of men, and set off for Rye on the coast.

Louis's journey to France was not to be as straightforward as he hoped; indeed, it came close to being a total disaster. During the autumn, while he had been north of London, Hubert de Burgh had been active in the south coast area and the Cinque Ports (Dover, Sandwich, Hastings, Hythe and Romney) were no longer fully under Louis's control. Now, in February 1217, ships under the command of Philip d'Albini – nephew of William d'Albini, now, as we have seen, in the Henrician fold – were blockading the associated port of Rye, while the castle there was held in Henry's name. Not having enough troops with him to force a siege of Rye, Louis bypassed the town and rode instead for nearby Winchelsea, there to wait while he sent messages to his allies in an attempt to have ships sent to him there.

The people of Winchelsea, forewarned of the arrival of the host, had fled. Louis's men could find little to eat in the already devastated areas and his losses mounted. The Anonymous of Béthune notes in his *Chronicle of the Kings of France* that as they went the people had burned their mills behind them, so that Louis's men had to find corn and try to grind it by hand; they were reduced to eating nuts and began to starve. Meanwhile, William of Kensham and his guerrilla force had burned the bridges between Louis's position and London and were blocking the route, so Louis could not send men back to the capital to summon help. He was trapped. What could he do?

At this point the *History of the Dukes* takes up the story. Instead of trying to get a large force through to the capital, potentially losing many of his troops and leaving himself isolated on the coast, Louis sent individual men on foot to try and slip through the cordon and make it to London, to ask his barons there for help 'as he was in a great deal of trouble and surrounded by the English'. Some of these lone messengers succeeded in their task, and a relief force was sent out; avoiding the direct route blocked by William of Kensham, it instead travelled via Canterbury to Romney, on the other side of Rye from Louis's position at Winchelsea, and managed to send a message across the Channel to Boulogne.

We will recall at this point that when Louis had landed on the English coast the previous May, he had sent his fleet back to France; a large number of the ships were still moored together at Calais and at the ready. A fleet of some 200 ships was organised within a short space of time, and it set sail. Most of them went straight to Dover, with a harbour big enough to hold them, where the castle was still in Hubert de Burgh's hands but Louis's men controlled the port. One ship, however, that captained by Eustace the Monk, managed to evade the English fleet at Rye 'thanks to the hardiness of his sailors' and sail direct to Winchelsea to give Louis the news. There they were forced to wait for another two starving weeks (Louis and all who were with him were in great distress, says the *Chronicle of the Kings of France*) as the winter storms of a cold February made it too dangerous for the French fleet to sail around from Dover.

The English fleet knew by now that the French would be attempting to sail around past them as soon as the weather permitted, so a naval engagement loomed. During the two-week hiatus Eustace the Monk and his men spent their time constructing a 'castle' on their ship, in order to make it bigger than any in the English fleet and therefore to give them the advantage of height in any potential engagement (missiles or arrows shot downwards being much more effective than those aimed upwards), while Louis had two petraries built on the shore.

The sentries posted by the French, however, proved to be less than efficient and one night a group of English soldiers raided and were able to destroy the modified ship. Louis, says the *History of the Dukes*, was furious and hauled Adam, the viscount of Melun, before him to explain why the security had been so slack. The viscount apparently replied (either bravely or foolhardily, if Louis were really as angry as portrayed) that his men were so hungry that they could not stand watch properly, and that he doubted that there were even four knights in the host who were in a fit state to do so. Louis, says the *History*, retorted that in that case he would stand guard himself. Clearly he was not about to let his English conquest end here in ignominy if he could help it, however hungry he was.

Eventually the weather subsided and the French ships were able to sail out from Dover. In order to reach Winchelsea they had to pass the English fleet at Rye; Philip d'Albini's ships left their blockade of the port to sail out into open water to engage them. The potential battle turned into an anti-climax; a combination of over-ambition and contrary winds saw some of the English ships run into others, causing enough chaos and confusion for the French to slip round them. They arrived in Winchelsea without loss and just in time for the starving men there.

Louis now found himself with some 3,000 troops at his disposal, more than enough to mount an attack on the castle at Rye to secure it ahead of his projected return in a few weeks; they marched and the garrison fled. Louis entered the castle and was able to seize the stores of provisions to feed his men. Then he was finally able to take ship for France, sailing at the end of February 1217.

As he landed back on home shores and saddled up for the ride to Paris, Louis would have been aware that this was not exactly the victorious homecoming he had envisaged. Admittedly, he had not been beaten and was not returning in disgrace, but it was not exactly a victory parade either. All he could hope for was that Philip would be able to supply him with enough men and resources to go back and finish the job properly.

He was to be disappointed.

Louis spent some eight weeks in France, during which time Philip ostentatiously refused to offer him any money or troops or even to discuss the English campaign. William the Breton is quite clear on what he sees as the reason for this: 'King Philip, fearing excommunication, gave no aid to his son ... like the most Christian man he was, he would not speak with him.' Philip, indeed, was busy protesting his loyalty to the papacy; in a letter of 21 April 1217 Honorius thanked him for his sentiments.

It would appear, however, that the double game which Philip may have been playing when the invasion was first planned was still continuing. He did not offer any troops, but nor did he stop Louis from raising them himself. He may not have been entirely straight with the pope, either: Honorius wrote to him urging him to recall his son, but Philip managed not to receive the letter until after Louis had left the court again and then was able to reply sorrowfully that he had not been able to speak to his son about the matter.

And so it was left to Louis to find more willing men himself. Again he was unable to raise the royal banner to claim service from those who owed it to the crown; he had to resort to personal exhortation. Most of those who were likely to support him most wholeheartedly were already doing so, so his additional gains were few.

It might have been tempting, at this point, for Louis just to give it all up. It was almost a year since his first invasion and the euphoria of his early gains; since then he had been bogged down in sieges and resistance, and the current state of affairs – particularly given that new recruits had not exactly flocked to his banner – indicated that this was going to continue for some time. Meanwhile his wife and family were in France, where he could be enjoying court life while reconciled with the Church and planning further campaigns in the south against the Cathars. But he would not give up. With dogged determination he embarked from Calais on 22 April 1217 with both Dreux brothers, the count of Perche, the viscount of Melun, some 140 additional knights and a troop of mercenaries, to finish what he had started.

* * *

Of course, Louis's trip to France had been something of a gamble and the situation had, as might have been anticipated, deteriorated during his absence. Without him there to hold everything together in person and to act as surety for the cause, the earls of Salisbury, Arundel and Warenne, along with William Marshal junior, had taken advantage of the situation to desert his cause for Henry's. These were the men who had been notable waverers anyway, and Louis still had the core of his baronial force, but it marked a symbolic shift, setting a precedent for others to follow, as well as losing him men and resources.

Meanwhile Guala had been scuttling round in his attempts to whip up a crusading fervour against Louis, doing all that he could to suppress the oaths that the barons had sworn to him and announcing that anyone who opposed Henry was 'an enemy of God and the Church'. And most seriously of all, despite the moralising tone of the Henrician camp, who claimed to have God on their side, they had during Louis's absence broken the terms of the truce, launching attacks behind his back and against their sworn word.

William Marshal is often held up as a paragon of chivalry, but as we saw in an earlier chapter, 'chivalry' was not quite the same concept in the early thirteenth century as it later became. Marshal needed to adopt a win-at-all-costs attitude, and he did. Nevertheless, breaking an agreed truce in an age when a man's word was his bond was no light undertaking, and could seriously affect the chances of another being granted in future, so we find that the author of the *History of William Marshal* feels he has to offer justification. Keen that his hero should not be seen to break his word or to act in an unknightly manner, he is insistent that Louis broke the truce first, although he does not say how or why other than to imply that Louis's decision to travel to France was against the temporary peace in some way:

> Then Louis decided to return to France. Once the Marshal saw and knew that Louis had no intention of keeping the truce, indeed that he had broken it, he said: 'He can know this for a fact, that it will never be kept by our side. We shall never ask him for anything, there will be no further bargaining, and it will be every man for himself.'

It was with this rather thin justification that Falkes de Bréauté was allowed to attack and take Ely and Philip d'Albini Rochester, as well as destroying the castles of Chichester and Portchester; Marshal himself, together with his son and with William Longsword, earl of Salisbury, assailed Farnham and Odiham. In retaliation, the French and barons based in London and awaiting Louis's return sent a further force to Lincoln, where they already held the city, to make another attempt on the castle.

Louis would not have been aware of all the details as he sailed towards Dover on 22 April 1217, thankfully in calmer weather than when he had first arrived a year earlier, but as he approached English shores he saw the town there on fire – it had been attacked by a force led by William of Kensham and John's illegitimate son Oliver – so he realised he might be heading into an ambush and switched course for Sandwich. He landed there the following day and went straight for Dover overland. However, news soon reached him that Winchester, Southampton, Marlborough and Mountsorrel (in Leicestershire) were all under siege from Henry's forces.

Louis faced a battle on many fronts. Militarily and strategically he was more than a match for the Henrician faction, especially now that he was back in the country to lead his campaign personally from the front, with a refreshed force (albeit a modestly sized one) of re-inforcements. He had the energy, the determination and the skill to start all over again if he needed to. But politically his ground had shifted enormously in the half a year since John's death, and this was to prove a huge factor in the campaign.

Contradictory as it may seem, the death of John was actually one of the worst things that could have happened to Louis. When he first invaded he had been the saviour, the just and Christian prince from overseas who would liberate England from the evil tyrant and ensure peace and the rights of the nobles. But now, without any particular change in the military situation, his position had shifted and he could be depicted by William Marshal, Guala and other adherents of young Henry as the foreign bully-boy who had invaded and was seeking to take the crown from an innocent and defenceless child.

Marshal and particularly Guala made the most of the propaganda value of this: the barons' complaints had supposedly been against John personally, not against his whole dynasty, so now that John was gone, why substitute him with a foreign prince? Why not return to the fold of the boy king who accepted their charter and who promised a clean slate, a new beginning? The proclamation of a crusade by the legate exacerbated Louis's problems: he had been put more or less in the same position as the Cathars against whom he had been fighting in the Church's name, and that must have hurt.

Again, the temptation arose to turn round and go back to France, especially when more of the English nobles started to slip away from him. But Louis was not about to give up so easily on the oaths he had sworn or on a conquest he had planned and started to execute, and which could still be completed. As far as he was concerned he was the king, having been elected and acclaimed by the nobles of England; Henry was the usurper, the son of a man who had dispossessed not only himself but his heirs as well. This was going to be difficult, but the prize would be worth it.

And unknown to William Marshal and the rest of the Henrician party, Louis had a secret weapon: his wife.

CHAPTER SIX

FIGHTING BACK

Blanche had not been idle during Louis's campaign in England. Firstly, she attended to the principal duty of a future queen consort: in September 1216 she gave birth to a third son, Robert, who joined seven-year-old Philip and two-year-old Louis in guaranteeing the royal line of succession. But the job of a royal or noble wife at this time was not only to provide heirs, important as this was: it was to support her husband in all matters, including running his estates and organising his finances in his absence, and, where necessary, raising money and troops for him.

Louis's return to France in the spring of 1217 must have both pleased and dismayed Blanche. On the one hand, she was able to see her husband for the first time in nearly a year, and to show off the new addition to the family; but on the other hand she expected and wanted Louis to succeed in his quest for the English crown, so to see him return without it would have been disappointing. Being an intelligent woman who had been brought up in two royal courts, she was no doubt also reasonably well versed in the basics of military strategy and would have grasped immediately the implications of King

Philip's refusal to offer further financial support or even to speak to his son on the matter.

Once Louis returned to England in April 1217, Blanche took personal control of the back-up campaign in France. She was no wilting flower, remaining at home and writing begging letters: she saddled up and spent the late spring and summer riding through Artois, visiting the various lords and towns there in order to drum up money and men from those who owed allegiance to Louis. The sudden personal appearance in their midst of a determined liege lady and future queen, and the force of her exhortations, were too much for most of her targets and in time Blanche was able to raise enough to equip a further fleet. And not content with her gains in Artois, she was also brave enough to face down the king himself.

The bare fact of the situation is that Blanche somehow succeeded where Louis and his other supporters had failed, and persuaded Philip to hand over some of the contents of his royal treasury. However, the details of how she achieved this vary according to the points of view of different chroniclers. William the Breton's fairly terse account does not actually mention Blanche by name: he says merely that a new army was assembled. The Anonymous of Béthune's *History of the Dukes* is similarly brief but does note that the troops were raised by 'my lady Blanche, wife of Louis ... to send them to England to help her lord'. Roger of Wendover is more explicit: 'The king was afraid to give assistance to his excommunicated son, as he had been often severely rebuked by the pope for granting his consent. He laid the burden of the business on the wife of Louis, who was not slow in fulfilling the duty imposed on her.' But this does not really tell us how, with all the odds stacked against her, Blanche could have succeeded in persuading Philip – all-powerful king for the last thirty-seven years and one of the most authoritative figures in Europe – to go against all his protestations to date and to part with his gold. The answer lies in a combination of the force of Blanche's personality and the depth of her devotion to her husband. This is neatly illustrated in an entertaining scene from the Minstrel of Reims (never afraid to overdramatise when the situation calls for it) in which he depicts Blanche marching into the throne room and asking the king bluntly whether he is prepared to let his son and heir die in a foreign country while he sits by and does nothing. When Philip remains unmoved by this, Blanche declares dramatically that she has no choice and that she will pawn her three sons – his heirs – to anyone who will give her enough money to support her husband. And on that note, she storms out. 'When the king saw her leave,' says the Minstrel with unusual understatement, 'he knew that she meant what she said.' Philip calls her back and tells her that she can have as much of his treasure as she needs, to do with as she wills.

In the end, then, honour was satisfied all round. Philip managed to stay on the right side of the pope – just – as he could claim that he was not giving any money to Louis, but only to Blanche, and that it was up to her to decide what to do with it. In turn, Blanche received the funds she needed to raise and equip a force and a fleet. Her willingness to risk papal displeasure in so doing was a testament to her relationship with Louis: it would have been all too easy for her to sit in her apartments, secure in her position as the mother of the heirs to the throne, and await the outcome of the campaign from a distance. Some royal wives, subject to arranged marriages and without any particular attachment to their husbands, might have done just that. But the commitment to each other which Louis and Blanche had shown since their earliest days together as children was as strong as ever, and she would not give up on his cause while there was any chance that she could do something about it.

* * *

Blanche's recruitment drive would, of course, take some time, and she was busy with her campaign all through the spring and early summer. Meanwhile, as we have seen, Louis landed at Dover in April 1217 to the news that Winchester, Southampton, Marlborough and Mountsorrel castles were all under siege from Henry's forces, the regent having broken the truce while he was away. 'The Marshal heard about Louis's return,' says the *History of William Marshal*, 'and he was not one bit pleased when he did.' No doubt he had been hoping that Louis's temporary strategic withdrawal back over the Channel was a precursor to a full-scale retreat, and that he would not return, but here was the prince again: reinforced, furious and prepared to reconquer the ground he had taken once already.

Louis hit the ground running. He now needed to fight on several fronts, so he deployed his troops accordingly, dividing his army as he done to great effect on previous occasions. He himself would storm across the south of England, while a second force commanded by Saer de Quincy, Robert Fitzwalter and Thomas the count of Perche would head northwards towards Mountsorrel. Dover Castle, looming behind him still, would have to wait; Louis arranged another truce with Hubert de Burgh, who was safely installed once more behind the great walls, and set off.

Determined not to have to cover the same ground a third time, Louis now adopted more ruthless tactics. Burning Sandwich behind him as a punishment for defecting to Henry's camp in his absence, he and his force rode through Canterbury, Malling (where he met his chancellor Simon Langton for an update on events during his absence in France) and Guildford, where he was reinforced by troops from the garrison he had left in London during his absence. He reached Farnham by 27 April, only four days after landing back on English soil, but thanks to the lightning nature of his operation so far his baggage train could not keep up and had only just reached

Guildford. This means that he was without his heavy siege machinery; nonetheless, he managed to take the outer bailey of Farnham, although the keep held out against him.

At this point Louis received word that although Mountsorrel was still holding (and, it was hoped, would continue to do so until the force commanded by Saer de Quincy got there), Winchester, Southampton and Marlborough had all fallen. Louis needed to be in several places at once; he took the decision to leave Farnham and ride immediately for Winchester, as he could not allow such a major city or its two castles to be refortified against him. There was also the tantalising prospect of a great prize: William Marshal was there and had young Henry with him, and if Louis could capture the boy then the war would be over once and for all. Capturing or killing the regent would also put a serious dent in the Henrician camp, so all was to play for. Louis made off at speed.

It would appear that the threat of an angry and determined Louis appearing over the horizon was enough to effect a change of heart in William Marshal. Instead of garrisoning Winchester he chose to flee from it (burning it behind him, much to the dismay of the luckless citizens who had been rebuilding following John's decision to fire the city the previous year) as he withdrew to Marlborough. Under the circumstances this was probably a wise decision; given Louis's record of military successes, the mood he was probably in, and the damage which had been inflicted on the royal castle at Winchester as Marshal had besieged it, staying to put up a fight was a risk not worth taking.

And so Louis arrived once more at Winchester to find it a smoking ruin, just as he had done the previous year. This time he needed to make sure he could hold on to the city more permanently, which was not likely with the royal castle in ruins and all but indefensible (the *History of the Dukes* tells us that 'a large part of the wall had been knocked down by miners'), so he oversaw some speedy repairs. This is where having engineers in his ranks as well as knights and sergeants paid off: he was able to organise everything very quickly and efficiently. The two sources that mention the rebuilding of the castle give differing accounts of how this was carried out: the *History of the Dukes* says that 'he had great timbers of oak put in all the holes in the wall', while the *History of William Marshal* seems to imply something more permanent:

> Within a period of a very few days he had rebuilt the tower and the high walls magnificently, with stone and lime, and had restored all the fallen masonry and repaired the damage to the walls to the point where they were fine and solid, just as if they were completely new.

These accounts are not necessarily contradictory, as the wooden timbers put into the holes in the wall which the Anonymous mentions might well have been scaffolding allowing masons access to repair the stonework. Louis must have given his orders for the rebuilding and the re-garrisoning quickly, as he remained in Winchester only from 30 April to 4 May, the feast of the Ascension. At that point he left Hervé the count of Nevers in charge and rode back to London in triumph. He had regained the whole of the south in a whirlwind two weeks, and with it the favourable military position he had enjoyed the previous year; the fate of England was still very much in the balance.

* * *

While Louis was reconquering the south Saer de Quincy was riding northwards to Mountsorrel in Leicestershire, together with Robert Fitzwalter and Thomas, the young count of Perche. De Quincy was particularly keen to relieve the siege as the castle there actually belonged to him along with the surrounding lands and associated revenues. It was being defended for him and for Louis by one Henry de Braybrooke, along with ten knights and an unspecified number of sergeants, 'who courageously returned stone for stone and weapon for weapon on their assailants', according to Roger of Wendover. But the attacking force was a numerous and high-profile one led by the earl of Chester, the earl of Derby, the earl of Aumale and others, including Falkes de Bréauté, so the defenders were hard pressed.

Roger of Wendover is scathing on the subject of de Quincy's force as he moved north: the 'wicked French freebooters and robbers' are 'the refuse and scum of that country', he says, and they pillage towns on their way. However, it was clearly more than de Quincy's reputation was worth to break Louis's word – Roger notes specifically that the abbey of St Albans escaped any attack as Louis had accepted a sum of money previously from the abbot to ensure its safety.

As de Quincy and his host of seventy knights and other men neared Mountsorrel, the earl of Chester sent out scouts, who reported back to him. According to the *History of William Marshal*:

> Once they heard tell of the mighty army that was making every effort to attack them, in order to do them harm and capture them, they did not dare stand their ground and meet them, for, given the huge force they faced, they thought that Louis in person was among them, and that is why they left.

Louis's name cast a long shadow in England in 1217; it had already caused William Marshal to retreat from Winchester and now, in the expectation of Louis's presence, Chester destroyed his siege machinery and retired to Nottingham. Mountsorrel was relieved without further bloodshed.

As Saer de Quincy, Robert Fitzwalter and the count of Perche basked in their success, they were contacted by one Hugh d'Arras, who was part of the force led by Gilbert de Gant that had been besieging Lincoln Castle for some time in Louis's name. The city of Lincoln had fallen into their hands some months ago, but the castle, with its separate defences, was holding out. Gilbert de Gant was now of the opinion that the castle would fall if they could make one final push with an increased force. He asked de Quincy to bring his army to Lincoln.

Lincoln Castle was being held by Nicola de la Haye, one of the most remarkable women of the thirteenth century. She had inherited the castellanship of Lincoln in 1169 on the death of her father (she had no brothers), and was now, in 1217, in her mid-sixties. Twice widowed, she had always been actively involved in her own affairs even when her husbands were alive; in 1191 she had personally commanded the defending force when Lincoln was besieged for a month during a conflict between King Richard and the then Prince John (she and her husband were supporters of John, even then). She was still the castellan in 1216 and, as we have seen, had staved off the first approach by the invaders by purchasing a truce from Gilbert de Gant when he attempted to occupy the city.

When King John had visited Lincoln later in 1216 Nicola made a show of presenting him with the keys to the castle, explaining that she was too old and could not endure the burden any longer, but John responded by entreating her to keep it in his name. One of his last acts that autumn had been to appoint Nicola to the position of sheriff of Lincolnshire: the appointment of a woman to a shrievalty was unprecedented and shows the high regard which John had for her capabilities in a time of war. It is true to say that many of the male candidates who might have been eligible for the position were actually siding with the French against him, but no doubt he could have found a man to act as sheriff if he had really wanted to. Indeed, Nicola's son had by then reached adulthood, but it was his mother and not he who was appointed.

Nicola's son Richard de Camville died in March 1217 but this did not stop her from carrying out her duties; even after the town fell – the citizens being unprepared and untrained to defend it – she and her garrison staved off every attempt on the castle as it was bombarded from the south and east by siege machinery all through March, April and early May. She refused all requests to surrender.

But by early May the garrison were exhausted and hungry, so Gilbert de Gant felt that his time had come. Saer de Quincy, Robert Fitzwalter and the count of Perche agreed, and their force moved off to join those already at Lincoln. Even without Louis's auspicious personal presence they felt confident that the castle could be taken.

* * *

Louis had reached London, but there was to be no rest. While Louis's attention had been centred further westwards, Hubert de Burgh had taken advantage of his absence to break the truce at Dover: as more of Louis's reinforcements had arrived in the port Hubert had launched an unexpected and violent sortie from the castle and killed many of them, taking others prisoner.

This was not to be borne. Louis had been in London only two nights, no doubt glad of the opportunity for him and his men and horses to rest after the speed of their campaign across the south, but with no hesitation he donned his armour once more and marched his troops to the coast. Dover had been a thorn in his side for too long, and he was now determined that whatever it took he would stay there until it was captured and under his control once and for all. He arrived there on 12 May 1217 and settled in for the long haul.

Establishing the camp for a siege which was expected to last several weeks or even months was a very different proposition to setting up a short-term or overnight camp; it was a complex logistical operation that needed to be carefully planned. We have already seen that Louis transported his dismantled siege machinery around the country with him, and that the engines would be rebuilt at a suitable distance from the walls by a team of engineers, but this was only one of many aspects of the siege which needed to be organised.

Firstly, the basic needs of the men and their animals needed to be catered for. The lords, knights and troops all needed somewhere to sleep so shelters of differing size and quality were erected, calculated to be situated outside the range of any arrows or other missiles which might be shot from inside the castle. These might vary from luxuriously appointed tents with beds, hangings and furniture for those who could afford them, down to basic bivouac-style shelters for those lower down the social scale. Some suitable point would be designated as the command centre which housed the leader of the host and served as a place for meetings; we do not know whether in this case Louis used the priory building as he had before or whether he lodged in a tent, but he would certainly have travelled with the appropriate equipment for a man of his rank.

Next, everyone needed to be fed. A supply of clean water was essential, as was adequate provisioning. An army would carry a reasonable quantity of victuals with it, but it would be impossible to transport enough for everyone in the host for several weeks, so the troops would use the resources of the surrounding area, either by foraging and requisitioning (in friendly territory) or by stealing and ravaging (in enemy lands). This needed to be kept up on an almost daily basis, which meant that the longer a siege continued, the wider the area which had to be covered to find food, or the siege would fail. The dangers of a castle running out of food and being starved into submission are evident, but if the fortification was well provisioned, as Dover was at this time, the besiegers could well starve before the besieged. Food would be cooked and shared by small groups of men from each household (each lord being expected to feed and provide for his own men), with the nobles again benefiting from the best of the available resources.

Another very important consideration was sanitation; disease could sweep through a camp otherwise, causing large numbers of casualties. For this purpose latrine trenches would be dug behind the lines. Also behind the main encampment would be an area for the host's animals: warhorses, riding horses, packhorses, oxen for pulling baggage carts, and also any livestock which the army had brought with it or procured. They needed picketing, feeding and cleaning out on a daily basis, with regular exercise for the horses if the siege was prolonged. There may also have been ancillary facilities such as for washing or caring for the wounded. Not everyone in the host was a combatant; the nobles would have brought squires, servants, cooks and grooms with them, and of course any long-term siege camp would have attracted hangers-on, including entrepreneurs with merchandise to sell, and camp followers. In this case the French had been away from their homes for over a year and in addition to the inevitable casual liaisons some of the lords had taken mistresses. Louis was not one of them: despite having the suggestion put to him, he steadfastly remained faithful to his wife.

Life in a siege camp is likely to have been characterised by nervousness and boredom punctuated by short periods of frenetic and dangerous activity. Each part of the host had its part to play, but the knights were out of action while the miners and engineers were at work, and vice versa. Only a full-on assault would involve most of the army at once. In the meantime guards needed to be posted constantly against the possibility of sorties from inside the castle, and to look out for the danger of a relief army arriving from the rear. Becoming trapped between two enemy forces would be a very dangerous position.

A siege would often start with delegations going back and forth with offers and counter-offers, but in this case Louis was already aware that Hubert de Burgh would not agree terms or surrender lightly, so he set up his siege machinery and his mighty trebuchet straight away. The trebuchet did its work, causing damage to the castle, but Louis did not have a sufficient number of men with him to risk an all-out assault: the loss of the portion of his army sent north with Saer de Quincy, and the necessity of leaving a garrison in London, had depleted his forces. Much as he and his knights would have preferred the excitement and energy of hand-to-hand fighting, Louis was an experienced commander and he knew there was no point in launching an assault which would be easily beaten back by the well-armed and well-provisioned defenders and which would cost him many casualties.

His hope for a swift resolution to the siege now resided in the groups of reinforcements being sent across the Channel: a small fleet of forty ships was even now nearing the English shore. But, as the *History of the Dukes* tells us, the sea was heavy and the wind was great and against them, so they were blown back out to sea without being able to dock and unload their troops and supplies. It was another two days before they could make a further attempt to land at Dover, two days which gave Henry's supporters time to prepare: when Louis's fleet approached again it was ambushed by eighty ships under the command of Philip d'Albini.

The captains of Louis's ships were not all of the same calibre or the same opinion on the best course of action: thirteen of them turned about and sailed back to Calais, while the other twenty-seven manoeuvred themselves into a tight formation in an attempt to force their way through the much bigger English fleet and drive through to the safety of the harbour. As we saw earlier, one of John's few successes had been the building and equipping of a proper navy, and this now paid off. The *History of the Dukes* tells us that twenty of the English ships were large and fully equipped for combat; in conjunction with three times as many smaller vessels, they were a fearsome proposition. Miraculously, nineteen of the French ships managed to get through and reach the port to discharge their men on to dry land; the other eight were captured, their sailors and the sergeants they carried being immediately put to death while the knights were thrown into holds to be kept for ransom.

And so Louis was reinforced by less than half of the fleet which had set out, but the worst news was that there would be no more: Philip d'Albini stationed his ships at sea just outside the port of Dover to ensure that no further reinforcements or supplies could reach Louis from the sea. Until Blanche could send a larger fleet which might stand some chance of breaking through, Louis would have to sink or swim with whatever resources he possessed already.

As the stakes in the war were raised, mercy became more of an unaffordable luxury, and in retaliation for the blockade of his fleet and the loss of his men Louis had no hesitation in using his military superiority on land. He sent troops to burn Hythe and Romney to the ground, which they did despite some resistance from William of Kensham and his men, still waging their guerrilla war. With the wasted and therefore safer area of land around him Louis dug in at Dover, determined this time to grind the castle and its defenders into submission whatever the cost.

* * *

On the same day Louis was setting up his engines at Dover, 12 May 1217, William Marshal learned from his scouts that the French forces at Lincoln had been greatly reinforced and that the castle was in danger of falling, which would give Louis a huge boost in morale as well as a major stronghold in the region and the opportunity to thrust further north and west. Up until now the tactics of the Henrician camp (and of John before his death) had been a cat-and-mouse affair of strikes and withdrawals, but Marshal now realised that the fall or otherwise of Lincoln could mark a turning point from which there would be no recovery. He sent out a summons to every lord in his faction, as well as the notable waverers, to muster at Newark. He probably did not make the long and impassioned speech which the *History of William Marshal* attributes to him, in which he calls upon them to fight for the sake of their wives, children and loved ones, and to defend the honour of the Holy Church, and claims that it was God's will that they should be triumphant, but he was certainly persuasive enough to gather a large and powerful force. In Marshal's favour was the news, specifically included by the author of the *History* in his speech, that Louis was not there in person.

To Newark rode the Marshal, little Henry himself, the papal legate Guala, Peter des Roches the bishop of Winchester, Ranulf the earl of Chester and a veritable glut of Williams: Marshal junior, the earl of Salisbury, the earl of Derby, the earl of Aumale and Williams d'Albini and de Cantelupe senior and junior, among others. With them were Falkes de Bréauté and one John Marshal, an illegitimate nephew of the regent who had served his uncle and King John loyally since the Normandy campaign in the early 1200s and who had been among those sent to Rome by John in the immediate aftermath of the sealing of Magna Carta. The Church was also heavily represented: as well as Guala and Peter des Roches the host included the bishops of Bath, Salisbury, Lincoln, Exeter, Worcester and Hertford. Guala took the opportunity to remind everyone that they were engaged in a holy crusade; he re-excommunicated those besieging the castle, and this time also specifically included the citizens of Lincoln, a point to which we will return later. He made sure that the Henrician forces all wore white crosses on their clothes, and according to Roger of Wendover:

To those who had undertaken to assist in this war personally, he, by the power granted to him from the omnipotent God and the apostolic see, granted full pardon for their sins, of which they had made true confession, and as a reward to the just he promised the reward of eternal salvation.

The host remained at Newark for three days to allow time for everyone to reach them and to rest their men and horses, but during this time a spat arose between Marshal and the earl of Chester which threatened their enterprise. The regent had not been overly impressed by Chester's abrupt withdrawal from Mountsorrel without a fight (possibly conveniently forgetting that he had done much the same at Winchester), and he felt that Chester needed to redeem himself. Chester, as we have seen, was already smarting from the distribution of the regency arrangements, and he in turn was displeased that Marshal was being seen as their glorious leader and being begged by the other lords to have the honour of leading the attack and striking the first blow; there was also the question of Marshal's advanced age making him unsuitable as the physical spearhead. The *History of William Marshal* tells us: 'The earl of Chester ... was not one bit pleased, and, indeed, he told them plainly, without mincing words, that if he were not given the right to launch the first attack he would not join them in the army and they would not have his support.' As Chester's forces made up a good proportion of the host, the proposed attack to relieve the siege might well have been put in jeopardy if he were to withdraw in a sulk and take his men with him. The *History*, perhaps not liking to go into too much detail about an argument lost by its hero, notes a little tersely that 'the Marshal and those present did not like this dissension at all, so they granted his every wish'. The host now prepared in earnest: on 19 May 1217 Guala and Henry, as non-combatants, retired to Nottingham while the rest of the force started its march on Lincoln.

Inside the city, the joint forces of Gilbert de Gant, Saer de Quincy, Robert Fitzwalter and Thomas count of Perche were still bombarding the castle night and day, trying their utmost to take the fortification and get inside it themselves before the regent's host reached them. If they could do that, they stood a much better chance of holding out and keeping Louis's flag flying in the region. But how would they fare when the attack came? Military leadership by committee was seldom a great success, and they were about to face their biggest challenge yet without the presence of their most important weapon – Louis himself.

CHAPTER SEVEN

THE END OF THE ADVENTURE

WITHOUT LOUIS TO take personal charge, his representatives in Lincoln would have to prepare themselves for the forthcoming attack by the regent and his army, and deploy their resources to best effect.

The city was built on a hill, with the castle near the top (at the western edge of the northern half of the city) and the river at the bottom. The castle consisted of two fortified mounds with a large bailey encircled by walls, and was in a superb position: to the south the defenders could command the steep streets leading down towards the south city wall and the river, and to the west they could look out over a valley of open fields. The castle was surrounded by a deep ditch and had two principal gateways: one in the east wall leading into the city, and the other to the west, giving access to the open country. The fine position of the castle is one of the reasons it was able to hold out for so long; Nicola de la Haye was still energetically organising the defences, supported by experienced garrison commander Geoffrey de Serland and those knights and sergeants who had survived the dangers and illnesses of a three-month siege.

Louis's forces were spread throughout the city with the majority near to or surrounding the castle, which they had been bombarding from the south and east with siege machinery set up in spaces cleared by the razing of other buildings. In total they numbered some 600 knights and an unspecified but larger number of other men, including sergeants and the engineers who were working the siege machinery. But they themselves were inside the city walls, which were rectangular in design and included gates to north, south, east and west, so they ran the risk of being trapped between their two sets of opponents in steep and narrow streets, the only real open ground in the city being the siege area and the yard to the front of the cathedral. The best options available to Louis's men were therefore either to take the castle (without destroying so much of it that it became indefensible) so that they themselves could take shelter behind its walls, or to sortie outside the city and meet the regent's host on open ground, which would make fighting much easier for mounted knights than it would be in the confined and slippery streets. The leadership group – Thomas count of Perche, Saer de Quincy, Gilbert de Gant and Robert Fitzwalter – redoubled the assault on the castle, and waited to see from which direction the hostile force would arrive.

Marshal's forces did not take the most direct route from Newark, as this would have brought them to the south side of Lincoln where they would have had to cross the river and then access the city through or over the south wall before fighting their way up the steep slopes towards the castle. Instead they marched via Torksey, which brought them to open ground to the west of the city; the castle wall here formed the outside wall of the city so some communication might be possible with those trapped inside. The regent had a large force: 406 knights and 317 crossbowmen, according to the *History of William Marshal*, while Roger of Wendover says 400 knights and 250 crossbowmen. Although this appears fewer than the number of

Louis's men inside the city, the chroniclers do not include firm numbers for the foot sergeants and assorted others who would form part of the host; and of course Marshal could count on the assistance of those inside the castle, so the two armies were in fact fairly evenly matched.

At this point there is some confusion in the contemporary accounts over whether a representative from the regent's host was able to meet up with someone from inside the besieged castle. According to Roger of Wendover, a messenger was sent out to tell the newly arrived army of the situation inside and to offer them entry via the postern (a narrow door in the castle wall which would admit one or two men at a time). According to the *History of William Marshal*, the regent's nephew John Marshal met outside the castle with Geoffrey de Serland, who told them of a door they could use; John was then attacked by a party of French as he tried to return to the host. However, the *History* then goes on to say that Peter des Roches, the bishop of Winchester, managed to enter the castle and then the city, where, on a highly improbable walkabout while disguised as an ordinary citizen, he found a gate of great antiquity that was blocked but that could be cleared to allow the host entry. Whatever the exact details, it seems clear that some communication took place, which gave an advantage to the Henrician forces to the eventual detriment of Louis's men.

The events that followed are described in some detail (although also with some further conflicting points) in the *History of William Marshal* and by Roger of Wendover, and in shorter accounts by the Dunstable annalist, the Waverley annalist, William the Breton and the Minstrel of Reims. Therefore we can create a reasonable reconstruction of the momentous course of 20 May 1217.

* * *

Once his whole host had arrived and assembled, shortly after daybreak, the regent split his army into four divisions of knights and foot sergeants. The first was led by the earl of Chester, as per their earlier agreement; the others by Marshal himself with the support of his son, by William Longsword the earl of Salisbury, and by Peter des Roches. The crossbowmen were under the command of Falkes de Bréauté.

Meanwhile, having been informed of the direction from which the army was approaching, a reconnaissance party led by Robert Fitzwalter and Saer de Quincy left Lincoln and rode out to assess the force. Their initial conclusion was that they should sortie from the city and meet their opponents in a pitched battle, as Roger of Wendover describes:

> When they [de Quincy and Fitzwalter] had made a careful survey of the approaching enemy they returned to the city with their companions, telling them, 'The enemy are coming against us in good order, but we are much more numerous than they are; therefore, our advice is that we sally forth to the ascent of the hill to meet them, for, if we do, we shall catch them like larks.'

Battle was a hazardous tactic, as we have noted previously, but under these circumstances probably less so than risking being trapped in the streets between two hostile forces. And after several years of campaign, sieges, attacks, counter-attacks and withdrawals all over England the barons and their French allies were no doubt itching to spring into action in a mounted charge, to fight in hand-to-hand combat as they had trained to do all their lives.

Fitzwalter and de Quincy reported back to the count of Perche, who then rode out himself but managed to come to a different conclusion. In his inexperience he appears to have miscounted the number of troops, not realising that each knight had two banners (one with him and one in the baggage train) and so thought that the force was twice as big as it actually was. A pitched battle was one thing; a pitched battle against what he perceived as overwhelming odds was quite another. Amid several dissenting voices he overruled his compatriots and so Louis's men remained within the city; one part of their force was set to defending the city walls and gates, while the rest continued their attack on the castle. Had Louis been there in person, would he have acted differently? It is difficult to say, but on balance it is more likely that he would have elected for battle: nobody ever accused him of timidity in the face of an enemy, and by this stage he might have felt that all-out attack was the best form of defence, especially given the unpredictability of fighting in the city streets – a situation which had nearly cost him his life at Bailleul in 1213. This is a point to which we will return later. But certainly, leader-ship by one strong individual rather than by a group was preferable in a complex military situation such as this one, as events would demonstrate.

The French and barons prepared for the attack as they saw the regent's army split. The earl of Chester's division assailed the city's north gate and William Marshal's the west gate, each led by the earls in person; more troops had to be pushed into the confined spaces there to stop them, which meant less attention could be paid to the castle. But even if more men had been stationed around the south and east walls of the castle they could have done nothing about the tactic which was to swing the battle: Falkes de Bréauté and his crossbowmen entered the castle via the postern (which, as we have noted, opened outside the city and was defended by the outside wall of the castle, meaning that Louis's men had no control over it) and stationed themselves up on the castle walls, looking down on the besiegers and the streets.

The sheer press of men pushing at the north and east gates of the city meant that the French and baronial troops were forced to give ground as Chester's and the regent's men forced their way in. Fighting in the constricted streets was extremely difficult, with those on horseback too close together to mount a proper charge, so there were chaotic scenes as each man sought to defend himself as best he could, swords and daggers proving more effective than lances. The momentum was with the attackers, who were moving as they pushed their way in, while the French and barons were standing still or being forced backwards. The citizens, meanwhile, huddled in their homes and tried to stay out of the way of the furious combat.

As Louis's men gave ground from the north and the east many of them ended up in the open space around the castle, where the crossbowmen on the ramparts were able to rain their bolts down on men and horses, as Roger of Wendover tells us: 'By means of the crossbowmen, by whose skill the horses of the barons were mown down and killed like pigs, the party of the barons was greatly weakened.' The knights in their mail armour and padding were able to survive, although many of them lost their mounts; the more lightly armoured sergeants and the men operating the siege machinery were slaughtered. The dead men and horses clogged the ground still further; Falkes and his men took advantage of the chaos and made a sortie out of the castle to join the hand-to-hand fighting. The *History of William Marshal* provides a flavour of the combat:

> Had you been there, you would have seen great blows dealt, heard helmets clanging and resounding, seen lances fly in splinters in the air, saddles vacated by riders, knights taken prisoner. You would have heard, from place to place, great blows delivered by swords and maces on helmets and on arms, and seen knives and daggers drawn for the purpose of stabbing horses.

Slowly the French were forced east and south, down the hill. Their leaders were in different places, so there was no one focal point, but the count of Perche did the best he could by rallying his men in the flat open space in front of the cathedral where there was more room to fight; according to the *History of William Marshal* he 'performed many great feats of arms that day'. He must have been quite a sight: young (he was twenty-one or twenty-two) and tall, his surcoat and shield of a striking red and white chevron design, he would have been recognised by allies and foes alike as the ranking nobleman among the French as he fought furiously from horseback. This, of course, made him a target for every enemy knight who could potentially make a fortune out of capturing and ransoming him, so the press around him grew thicker and thicker as he battled on. He was called upon to surrender several times, not least by William Marshal, who had by now fought his way from the west gate to the cathedral. But Perche refused, bellowing that he would never surrender to those who were traitors to Louis, their lawful king and his. As he defended himself desperately against the multiple enemies closing in, a thrust from the sharp point of a sword or dagger entered the eye-slit of his helmet, stabbing through his eye and piercing his brain. Blinded and in agony, he managed three wild blows at Marshal before his body gave out and he crashed down from his horse, dead.

The loss of their leader and the focal point of their resistance in front of the cathedral was a crushing blow to morale for Louis's men, and they began to retreat in earnest southwards. There was another brief rally in a space at the top of what is now known as Steep Hill, but with the Henricians now having the significant advantage of fighting downhill, it did not last long. The earl of Chester's men, having finally fought their way through from the city's north gate, added to the Marshal's forces and the remaining French and barons were overwhelmed. Many tried to flee but Lincoln's south gate was very narrow, which caused a bottleneck of men who had no choice but to turn and make a last stand. Sergeants and footsoldiers were killed where they stood, while the knights and barons were captured for ransom. Saer de Quincy, Gilbert de Gant and Robert Fitzwalter were all among the prisoners, as well as Henry de Bohun, the earl of Hereford, and Richard de Clare, the earl of Hertford. Of the others, Roger of Wendover notes simply that there were so many that it would be 'tedious' to mention them; the Barnwell annalist says 380 knights were captured; while the Anonymous of Béthune's *History of the Dukes* says only 'a few' barons escaped.

In one day, Louis had lost half his army.

If the citizens of Lincoln were initially delighted that the regent's forces had defeated the army that had occupied their city for months, they were to be disappointed: on the pretext that they had been excommunicated by Guala and that they had collaborated with the enemy – or at least that they had not put up enough of a fight against the original attack in the spring – Marshal permitted not only the seizure of the belongings of the French and barons, but also the looting of civilian houses and shops. Indeed, as Guala had also excommunicated the entire clergy of Lincoln, even the cathedral was plundered.

Roger of Wendover, more sensitive than many other chroniclers to the plight of ordinary people, tells us:

Baggage, silver vessels and various kinds of furniture and utensils all fell into their possession without opposition. Having then plundered the whole city to the last farthing, they next pillaged the churches throughout the city, and broke open the chests and store-rooms with axes and hammers, seizing on the gold and silver in them, clothes of all colours, women's ornaments, gold rings, goblets and jewels.

Even the citizens themselves were not safe:

> Many of the women of the city were drowned in the river, for, to avoid insult [i.e. rape by the victorious soldiers], they took to small boats with their children, their female servants, and household property ... the boats were overloaded, and the women not knowing how to manage the boats, all perished.

According to the official accounts, the casualties of the battle were extremely low: only the count of Perche and a handful of other knights. However, we should remember that these narratives take no account of the losses among sergeants, other combatants and civilians, so the real number of those killed was certainly greater, to say nothing of those who were wounded or who lost their livelihoods. One of this latter group turned out to be Nicola de la Haye: in one of the most astonishing acts of ingratitude imaginable following her heroic defence, just four days after the battle she was removed by the regency council from her offices of sheriff of Lincoln and castellan of the castle, to be replaced by William Longsword, earl of Salisbury.

It would be too complex an operation to attempt to send the body of the count of Perche back to France, so he would have to be buried in the city where he fell. However, this caused some difficulty: like all Louis's adherents he was excommunicate and so officially could not be interred in consecrated ground either in the cathedral graveyard or in any of the churches in Lincoln. But given his status – he was, after all, both a cousin of William Marshal and a relative of Henry – a compromise was reached and he was buried in the grounds of the hospital in Lincoln. The bodies of the common soldiers and civilians were hastily dealt with to avoid the dangers of contagion and disease. The surviving citizens were left to clear up and put their lives back together as best they could.

William Marshal rode straight to Nottingham to tell Henry and Guala of the victory in person; the survivors from among Louis's forces who had managed to escape Lincoln fled southwards to apprise him of the news and to seek the security of his presence.

* * *

On Thursday 25 May 1217 the walls of Dover were still standing; the key to England stubbornly refused to turn. But Louis was only two weeks into what he knew would be a long and arduous siege, so he was not impatient; there was plenty of time to wait in his well-ordered camp while he broke down the defences and the will of the garrison. But as he directed the day's siege operations, a messenger arrived with the devastating news.

Louis's reaction was unsurprising: he was 'full of anger and rage once he heard how his men had been defeated so badly in Lincoln', says the *History of William Marshal*, while William the Breton tells us that 'chagrin, sadness and lamentation spread through the camp' when the news arrived. It seemed that only Louis's personal presence in a combat would guarantee victory and that his men could not manage without him; this was enough to make him furious and Roger of Wendover depicts him berating the survivors, telling them: 'That it was owing to their flight that their companions had been made prisoners, because if they had remained to fight, they would perhaps have saved themselves as well as their companions from capture and death.' The specific mention of death indicates that Louis was perhaps more upset by the loss of the young count of Perche than he would or could let on. He retired to think. He had lost his superior military position, so he needed to consider very carefully what he was going to do next. 'Surrender' does not appear to have been a word in his vocabulary, so he formulated plans to keep going and to make the best of the current position. The defeat at Lincoln had been a crushing blow but it was not a total disaster: he could still recover if he played his cards right. The key short-term decision was whether to stay at Dover, ever the thorn in his side, or whether to go back to London to ready it against the attack which would be the next logical move from the Henricians if they were bold enough.

But Louis was far-sighted enough to realise that Marshal and his party would be loath to mount an immediate attack on the capital; they needed time for their troops to recover, they needed to distribute and arrange for the imprisonment of their captives, and they needed to consolidate their position rather than overreaching themselves. So Louis elected to stay at Dover for another few days at least, in the anticipation of further reinforcements.

But once again he was to be disappointed in the support offered by others. The large force which Blanche was assembling was not yet ready, so what came across the Channel was a small fleet which was no match for the number of English ships still patrolling the Channel under Philip d'Albini; many were captured, and those that did manage to get through brought him a disappointing number of men: only eighteen knights and some sergeants and sailors. This was not enough. Louis wrote letters to his father and his wife asking them to send whatever they could muster as soon as they could manage it; he sent some of the ships back across to France with his messages and burned the rest so as not to let them fall into the hands of Hubert de Burgh, who would inevitably come out of his stronghold once Louis had gone to destroy or capture anything he could get his hands on. Then Louis set off for London.

Louis reached the capital in the first few days of June, where he was joined by some two hundred knights who had escaped the debacle at Lincoln. He took stock. The situation was, quite simply, that he did not have enough men to force a military solution at this stage. This was not helped by the fact that a large number of English barons and knights now deserted his cause (forswearing their oaths to him, as the Minstrel of Reims had depicted King Philip prophesying earlier) and went over to Henry, sensing a turn in Fortune's wheel. But Louis was not beaten yet: if success could not be found through military means he would have to seek a political solution, negotiating and holding off his opponents until such time as more reinforcements should arrive. He could not return to France again in person as this would be taken as a final abandonment of his cause. Instead he would need to stay put and await developments across the Channel.

* * *

Since his accession Pope Honorius had not been idle. We have already seen how he sent representatives to King Philip in France, and now a high-profile Church delegation arrived in England. It was led by Simon de Maugastel, the archbishop of Tyre (one of the crusader states in the east), who was in Europe to drum up support for the Fifth Crusade and to attempt to instil some cohesion into the English, French and imperial efforts towards it. The continuing war in England was having a detrimental effect on his recruitment drive, and it was no secret that Honorius wanted Louis to lead the crusade in person, which he could not do while he was over the Channel and excommunicate. The pope no doubt hoped that the exalted rank of the archbishop, who was accompanied by the influential abbots of Clairvaux, Cîteaux and Pontigny, would carry sufficient weight; it was agreed that the delegation would mediate between the two sides.

A meeting was arranged for 12 June 1217, to be held between Brentford and Hounslow. Neither Louis nor William Marshal was there in person, but they each sent four representatives accompanied by twenty supporting knights. This was not unexpected: even though his subordinates had not coped too well in battle without him, Louis could rely on his learned advisers and lawyers to argue for the best arrangement possible, while having the fall-back plan that they could not agree to anything definitive in his absence, so they would have to consult him in person – thus creating more time and space in which to make an informed decision.

After a discussion between the men from both sides and the prelates, a draft treaty was drawn up which included many points of detail: steps towards peace; the potential withdrawal of Louis and of Alexander of Scotland, still engaged in local conflicts in the north; the reissuing of Magna Carta to satisfy the barons; and matters such as prisoners, ransoms and the lifting of excommunications. However, there was a sticking point. The papal legate Guala insisted that four of Louis's advisers who were churchmen – Simon Langton, Elias of Dereham, Robert de St Germain and Gervase of Howbridge, the dean of St Paul's in London – should be specifically excluded from the treaty. He could not forgive the first three for ignoring and indeed preaching against Louis's sentence of excommunication, and the fourth for allowing their speeches to be given at his pulpit when Louis had first arrived in London. Their actions had been a challenge to his authority as the pope's representative, as the implication had been that he was not entitled to pronounce the sentence himself without further authorisation from Rome. He was offended at the slight and he wanted retribution.

But just as these four men had stood by Louis in his hour of need, so he now supported them in theirs: he refused absolutely to accept the treaty on such terms. The lessons he had learned long ago on the importance of a brotherhood of companions were still with him, and he would not let them be punished for their loyalty to him; better war than dishonour. The archbishop of Tyre wrote to the pope to say that it was clear that 'Louis would in no way make peace without them'. The talks collapsed and the Church delegation returned to France. The war for England would go on.

* * *

With the sides back on a war footing, Guala – possibly with little grasp of military logistics – was agitating for an all-out attack on London, but William Marshal and the other commanders were understandably less keen. The capital was fortified and was garrisoned by Louis's seasoned troops; the citizens were also on his side, which would make any potential assault dangerous. The Henrician forces could undo all their good work at Lincoln if they ended up dashing themselves fruitlessly against the high walls. Instead Marshal and his companions adopted a more softly-softly approach, offering induce-ments in the form of lands and castles to any English barons siding with Louis who decided that now was the time to defect. A number of them came over to Henry, but the decision of one of them to do so was to have unintended and serious consequences.

Reginald de Braose had no cause to love the Plantagenets: his father, William, had been persecuted and hounded to his death by John, and his mother and elder brother had met an excruciating end from starvation at John's order. But his father's ruin had meant the loss of some family lands, so Reginald was swayed by Marshal's offer of a pardon and the chance for pecuniary gain, and he decamped to swear allegiance to Henry. But Reginald was married to a lady named Gwladys Ddu; she was the daughter of Prince Llewelyn of Wales, a supporter of Louis (at least insofar as Louis's aims matched his own) who was not impressed with his son-in-law's actions. Llewelyn invaded Reginald's lands, capturing Swansea Castle, seizing control of the area and making inroads towards William Marshal's own territories in south Wales. Worried that the ground was being cut out from under his feet – an earl was an earl in name only and wielded no power if he had no lands – the regent left the London area and hurried to Wales; in his absence the question of a siege of the capital was dropped. Henry's council retired to Gloucester, reissued Magna Carta once more and summoned an assembly at Oxford for 15 July 1217, later postponed to 22 July.

All of this gave Louis some breathing space to do what he did best: seize back the military initiative. Now that the peace talks had ceased – Louis also refusing the advances of the pope's own confessor, who had been sent over to speak with him but who offered only the same terms which excluded the four churchmen – he was at liberty to restart his campaign. He had a strong base in London, in the Tower and surrounded by the city walls and citizens who supported him; he had the half of his army which had been with him at Dover, the escapees from Lincoln and the garrison he had left in London all along; and gradually he had those captured after Lincoln, as they were ransomed and found their way back to him.

Donning his armour once more, Louis and his men set out on a series of raids which would have the dual purpose of obtaining supplies and money for his cause and of reminding friend and foe alike of who was really in charge. Peter de Dreux made a foray which brought back much plunder, including 'great gains for the lesser men', according to the *History of the Dukes*; Adam the viscount of Melun (now recovered from his disgrace over the burned ship) evaded Henrician forces still stationed around London to launch a successful raid on Bury St Edmunds before taking captured booty back to London.

* * *

Meanwhile, in France, Blanche's efforts at recruitment had matured, and she was now ready to send over a large fleet, which she saw off personally from Calais on 20 August 1217. It was led by the high-ranking nobleman Robert de Courtenay, a descendant of King Louis VI and therefore a distant relative of Louis. But, alas, the fickle

Channel weather proved a problem once more, and the ships were close to Dover when they were blown almost all the way back to France by a storm. They turned again as soon as they could, but it was the night of 23/24 August by the time they approached English shores once more, and the delay gave the Henrician forces extra time in which to prepare.

Hearing of the preparations at Calais, William Marshal had travelled to Romney, where he summoned representatives from the Cinque Ports and promised them restoration of the rights they had lost under King John, and recompense by way of any plunder they could take from captured ships, if they would go out to fight the arriving French. They agreed and mustered a fleet at Sandwich, the extra three days giving them crucial time to prepare, as the *History of William Marshal* describes: 'They attended to the preparation of their ships, made ready their ropes, made seaworthy every one of their bowlines, guide-ropes and guys, their sturdy anchors and strong cables.' The men of the Cinque Ports joined forces with the ships of Philip d'Albini, who was still patrolling the Channel. Marshal himself would not go out to sea; on a practical level his age and the lack of opportunity to fight on horseback would count against him, but he was also Henry's personal representative, and as such he needed to stay on dry land to organise matters from there, and form an extra line of defence if the French were able to land in numbers. Thus, when the English fleet sailed out from Sandwich on the morning of 24 August, St Bartholomew's Day, it was under the command of Hubert de Burgh.

Hubert sailed on the best vessel available from the Cinque Ports, together with eighteen large ships which Matthew Paris tells us were 'well fitted out', some of them designed especially for fighting with iron prows for ramming enemy ships, and a number of smaller boats. He had with him a number of knights, including Richard Fitzroy, illegitimate son of King John and nephew to the earl Warenne;

Warenne himself was not of the seagoing party but the *History of the Dukes* tells us that he had furnished his nephew with a 'fine troop' and 'a ship with knights and men-at-arms where his banners were'. One of the English ships was a huge cog, a larger type of vessel of which several had been built during the reign of King John when he was keen to expand his navy. Lightly laden so it stood high out of the water, and with large 'castles' fore and aft, it would have the advantage of height. The cog was packed with sergeants, possibly those supplied by the regent.

Leading the French fleet was Eustace the Monk. His ship was at the front but, as the *History of William Marshal* tells us, it contained not only Robert de Courtenay and other leaders but also a trebuchet, treasure, coin and horses for Louis's use, and a contingent of fighting men. This meant that it was so overloaded that it 'could only sit so deep down in the waves that the water almost washed over it', and was therefore not easy to handle in the conditions. In addition to his own vessel, Eustace had nine other great ships, each packed with up to 125 knights and sergeants, and some sixty smaller boats carrying supplies. Their objective, on reaching the English coast, was to make for London, where Louis was waiting for them. Once he had reinforced his host there, in his well-defended main stronghold, he would be in prime position to move out in great strength to reconquer the land anew.

The English knew that London would be the target, so their own objective was simply to prevent the French reaching the capital. They sought to position their ships to windward, sailing in a column with Hubert de Burgh's at the front. Due to the formation, the French did not immediately see the whole fleet, and they thought they were being faced by only a few vessels, as William the Breton explains: 'While they were on the high sea they saw a few ships coming slowly from England, whereupon Robert de Courtenay caused the ship which he was in to be directed towards them, thinking it would be easier to capture them.' The result was disaster. Hubert's ship, sailing out in front, had already passed by – possibly as part of a feinting manoeuvre – but Eustace's ship struck the second in line, that commanded by Richard Fitzroy. Fierce fighting broke out; Eustace's men initially held their own, but then three more English ships from the column came up one by one and surrounded the vessel. The other French ships, possibly confused by the turn of events, or possibly finding it difficult to manoeuvre into an effective position to attack the English ships, hesitated. By this time the large English cog had also arrived, and with their height advantage the men on it were able to throw stones and shoot arrows down on the French. They also had a nastier form of missile, as all sources mention and as the *Romance of Eustace the Monk* describes: 'They began to throw finely ground lime in great pots upon the deck, so that a great cloud arose. Then the French could no longer defend themselves for their eyes were full of powder; and since they were before the wind it caused them torment.'

The wind blew the lime away from the English and into the faces of the French; the English were then able to take advantage of their blinded, choking opponents, jumping down onto the French flagship and cutting their way through the knights and men. 'Some had their arms broken,' says the *Romance of Eustace*, 'some their heads smashed, others a collarbone shattered.' Eustace, after an initial flurry in which he knocked down many opponents with an oar, fled below; he was eventually found and dragged out, and, despite offering a huge sum of money for ransom, was offered a stark choice: would he prefer to be beheaded on the trebuchet or on the rail of the ship? None of our chroniclers records his answer, but decapitated he certainly was.

The death of their admiral and capture of their flagship caused a loss of heart among the rest of the French fleet. They were rammed by the iron-prowed English ships; their rigging was cut so that their sails fell down on the crews; the unmanoeuvrable ships were then boarded and vicious close fighting took place with swords, daggers and axes. Philip d'Albini's archers and crossbowmen were particularly effective, raining their sharp arrows and bolts down on to the lower decks of the French ships. When the English boarded each ship 'they lost no time at all in killing those they found on board and throwing them into the sea as food for the fish', says the *History of William Marshal*; the water turned scarlet with blood.

The French loss was almost total: knights were captured, sergeants and sailors slaughtered where they stood; many chose to cast themselves into the sea, where they drowned. Robert de Courtenay and his three most senior magnates were among those taken prisoner; they were in danger of being killed by the now blood-crazed English common soldiers, who were stopped with some difficulty by their knightly superiors who saw the chance for monetary gain. And as a final insult Hubert de Burgh's ship, which had overshot the first phase of the conflict, had by now managed to turn around; he thus attacked from the rear of the French fleet, sailing serenely into the carnage and making himself a tidy profit by claiming capture of two ships. The haul of booty was enormous: the English shared out coins in bowlfuls while the French prisoners were taken back to land. Eustace the Monk's severed head was fixed on a lance and was subsequently taken to Canterbury and paraded in public there and in the country round about, amid the cheers of the coastal dwellers who had suffered from his raids for years. 'No one who is always intent on evil', concludes the *Romance of Eustace*, ominously, 'can live for a long time.'

The reinforcements were gone; the supplies were gone; the money, hard-won from Philip Augustus, was gone. None of it would reach Louis, and all Blanche's efforts had been for nothing.

* * *

Louis, in London, heard of the defeat on 26 August 1217; we may imagine him with his fists clenched as he took in the devastating news. 'He was enraged,' says the *History of the Dukes*, 'as he had a right to be.' Louis now found himself in the slightly odd position of not having been personally defeated in the field, but having been vanquished none-theless by the incompetence of his subordinates. Roger of Wendover tells us that he was more concerned about the defeat at Sandwich than he had been by the events of Lincoln, and he was right: with no hope now of further reinforcements, to fight on from his present position would be suicidal. Louis had no choice but to agree terms.

Robert de Dreux was sent under safe conduct from London to Rochester to meet William Marshal. Despite the customs governing embassies such as this, which promised ambassadors safety of their persons, Marshal took him hostage; as Louis's cousin, he was the second-ranked nobleman among the French and therefore a prize, and Marshal was well known for his acquisitive tendencies – he had already secured himself, for example, half of the late count of Perche's lands in England following the latter's death at Lincoln only three months previously. While keeping Robert de Dreux captive he sent Robert de Courtenay, lately captured in the battle at Sandwich, to Louis instead. We have no contemporary information on Louis's reaction upon hearing the news of Robert de Dreux's imprisonment, but he did agree to de Courtenay's mediation as he arranged talks between Louis, Marshal and Hubert de Burgh.

It would appear that those in the Henrician party were still a little afraid of Louis in person. Louis's own military reputation was still intact, and he would of course be king of France in due course, with all the power and the resources that entailed. The negotiations did not have the character of a victorious party dictating to a defeated one, but rather were couched in the language of truce and peace. On 5 September 1217, his thirtieth birthday, Louis met William Marshal in person – the first time they had come face to face – on an island in the Thames; they were accompanied by Robert de Courtenay and Hubert de Burgh respectively. The negotiation of terms began, and the talks lasted for several days before Louis retired to London, and the regent to Windsor, to consider their positions.

Louis's remaining French and baronial supporters in London pushed for a radical solution: they should make a vast and sudden sortie from the capital with all of their men in order to provoke a final battle. If Marshal, de Burgh, the earl of Chester or even little Henry himself could be killed or captured then the fortunes of the two sides would be markedly reversed. As the days passed and Louis received no word from the regent, the suggestion came to hold more merit, but it would be hugely risky. 'He did not know which way to turn,' says Ralph of Coggeshall, who describes the episode.

Would Louis have risked everything in one final, bloody chivalric endeavour? We will never know. On 9 September a letter arrived from William Marshal asking for a further truce and for the resumption of peace talks; Louis agreed.

On 11 or 12 September 1217 Louis and William Marshal met once more – this time also with Guala, who was not about to be left out of such a momentous occasion – to agree the Treaty of Lambeth, which ratified the peace agreement. Guala, in a spiteful gesture, tried to insist that Louis appear as a penitent, barefoot and shirtless; he was roundly ignored by both sides. William the Breton, Roger of Wendover, the *History of William Marshal* and the *History of the Dukes*, with varying degrees of detail, all agree on the salient points of the treaty. In short, Louis would be paid the sum of 10,000 marks of silver (amounting to about one-quarter of the English crown's annual income); in return he would agree to leave England and to make no further claim upon it, and would release from their oaths all those who had sworn fealty to him. King Alexander of Scotland and Prince

Llewelyn in Wales were to make peace on similar terms. The four clerics whose exclusion from previous conditions had caused Louis to refuse agreement were to leave the country in peace and travel to Rome to seek absolution from the pope in person. Both sides were to release all prisoners without further ransom (including Robert de Dreux, presumably to Marshal's chagrin), although ransoms already paid could be kept; those barons who had supported Louis were to be restored to the lands they had held before the war.

These terms were clearly not what Louis had set his heart on when he had sailed to England sixteen months previously; but neither were they the desperate terms of a defeated party seeking only to escape with his life. He had not succeeded in being crowned king, but he had not been personally defeated and could leave with his head held high and in possession of a heavy purse: 4,000 marks in cash and the promise of further payments by instalment. He was also granted absolution from the sentence of excommunication which had weighed heavily on him for so many months. The treaty was sealed on 18 September 1217, Louis's witnesses and guarantors including Hervé de Donzy, count of Nevers, Peter de Dreux, duke of Brittany, and Robert de Courtenay; Louis embarked from the coast ten days later.

Unsuccessful in his quest for the English crown but unbeaten and unbowed, Louis stepped on to his ship and sailed away. His adventure in England had lasted seventeen months; during that time he had succeeded in conquering about two-thirds of the realm and, as we will discuss later, could have gone further had he been in possession of greater resources. As it was, his feat remained unmatched for almost 270 years: the next successful invasion of England would be that of Henry Tudor in 1485.

Louis was never again to set foot in England, but his conflict with the English crown was far from over.

CHAPTER EIGHT

AFTERMATH

THIS WAS NOT the homecoming Louis had envisaged.

No cheering crowds thronged the quay, hoping for a glimpse of the English crown; no welcoming party knelt to a new king. Instead Louis and his companions simply disembarked, mounted their horses and began the journey of several days which would take them back to Paris. As Louis rode through the French countryside, a hive of activity at the end of the harvest season, he had plenty of time to consider his future. For almost a year and a half he had been in charge, had lived and governed on his own terms, but now he was back to playing the understudy, the heir, the king-in-waiting. It must have been galling, to say the least, but as pragmatic as he was he accepted that there was no choice. He would bend the knee to his father – which is exactly what he did when he arrived in Paris, although we have no way of knowing whether his teeth were gritted at the time – and over the next few years he would show a remarkable patience with his lot.

There were, of course, advantages arising from his campaign and his present circumstances. He may not have won the English crown, but he had done enough to ensure that England would be in no position to challenge or threaten France and the French monarchy for years to come. The last years of Philip's reign (for surely even he could not live forever) would not be marked by the incursions of an English king as his first years on the throne had been; and when the time came for his own accession, Louis would not need to fight off invaders on his own soil.

On a more personal level, Louis was also now reunited with his wife and sons, which must have given them all great joy. And it was through Blanche (or, more specifically, due to her ancestry) that another staggering offer arrived soon after his return: as Louis and Blanche were not to be king and queen of England, perhaps they would consider taking the throne of Castile?

Blanche's father, King Alfonso VIII, had died in 1214, to be succeeded by his youngest child and only surviving son, Henry, then aged nine; Henry's eldest sister Berengaria (formerly queen of León but now separated from her husband Alfonso IX and living back in Castile) acted as his regent. But the unfortunate boy was killed in an accident just three years after his accession when he was hit by a tile which fell from the roof of the royal palace. The crown then passed by hereditary right to Berengaria; she in turn immediately resigned it in favour of her sixteen-year-old son, who became Ferdinand III of Castile. However, this move was unpopular both with the pope (who considered Ferdinand illegitimate as Berengaria and her former husband had not sought the correct papal dispensation for a marriage which was consanguineous), and also with the Castilian nobles, who feared undue interference from León, Ferdinand being the heir to that throne as well. They unearthed a proviso whereby Alfonso VIII had decreed that should his son Henry die childless, the crown should pass to his daughter Blanche and her successors. Therefore, in the autumn of 1217 the Castilian crown was offered first to Blanche, and then to her and Louis for one of their sons if they would choose one and send him south.

A sense of déjà vu was in the air. Did Louis wish to become embroiled in another foreign campaign, after being offered a crown in right of his wife, who had a blood claim but was not the nearest heir? Did he wish to involve himself in the world of Castilian politics? He did not, and from the available evidence it would appear that Blanche did not press him on the point. Perhaps she now considered herself more Capetian than Castilian; she had, after all, spent rather more than half her life in France. She would be queen there and she was bringing up her sons in the French royal tradition. And so the offer of the crown was declined, firmly, by the whole family. Far from being bitter about the lost opportunity and regretting their decision in future years, Louis and Blanche had a very cordial relationship with Ferdinand, and indeed welcomed with all honour his betrothed, Beatrice of Swabia, as their guest in Paris in 1219. Ferdinand III went on to become one of the most successful Castilian kings, reigning for over thirty years, uniting the kingdoms of Castile and León, and leading great advances against the Moors in Spain, for which he was eventually canonised as St Ferdinand.

And so Louis and Blanche's lives proceeded for now unencumbered by a crown. They settled into something of a routine: their court was once again a literary hub; they accompanied the king on some of his peregrinations. It appears that they lived in a state of some domestic bliss: without exception every chronicle or account of Louis's life confirms that he never took a mistress – not even when he was away for over a year in England, despite suggestions from his companions – which was unusual for a man in his position at the time. His faith meant that he took his marriage vows seriously; he must also have been glad to be able to attend church services again now that his excommunication was lifted. Both Louis and Blanche were involved in teaching and guiding their sons: in subsequent years, as we shall see later, one of their children would be canonised as a saint and another would be beatified, and accounts of their lives credit their family background and upbringing as major factors in their saintliness.

But the bliss was not to continue for long. Tragedy struck in the summer of 1218 when Louis and Blanche's eldest son and heir Philip died shortly before his ninth birthday. He was just at the age when a noble boy would have moved away from the female-led care of his early life and started to undertake more masculine pursuits, but as his cause of death was not recorded (child mortality was, as we have seen, an occurrence so common that it was almost a part of everyday life) we have no way of knowing whether he met his end by illness or by accident. He was buried in the cathedral of Notre Dame in Paris, then still under construction. The loss of their son was a tragedy for the family and it also dealt a blow to France's future, the country having had great expectations of Philip: one unofficial record of his short existence appears in the margin of a document of the royal chancellery, where sometime between 1213 and 1218 a scribe jotted the words 'in the Year of Our Lord 1209, the ninth day of September, Blanche, once again a mother, gave birth to a son. This birth, so wished-for, gives a master to the French and the English.'

However heartbreaking Philip's death was for his family, it was not the disaster for the royal line of succession that it could have been. Louis and Blanche's next eldest surviving son Louis, aged four, became the heir; he had a two-year-old brother Robert as back-up; and now that Louis and Blanche were reunited and still relatively young (they were both thirty), they could have more children. The loss of young Philip did have a secondary consequence, however, which was that his betrothed, Agnes de Donzy – daughter of the loose cannon Hervé de Donzy, and heiress to the counties of Nevers, Auxerre and

Tonnere – was now back on the marriage market and available to provide a husband with a rich prize. It was therefore important that this husband was the right man. King Philip acted quickly, and (probably with encouragement from Louis) Agnes was married off to Guy de Châtillon, one of Louis's oldest and closest friends, a loyal servant of the crown, and the heir to the county of St Pol.

King Philip was still in robust health, and Louis could not expect to accede to the throne any time soon. But after a year back in France he was itching for more action, so he was no doubt pleased when an opportunity presented itself in the autumn of 1218.

* * *

The Albigensian crusade had been continuing unabated while Louis was in England. Despite the gains of Simon de Montfort which we recounted in an earlier chapter, the southerners never accepted that their cause was lost, and a fightback under Raymond (formerly Raymond VI, count of Toulouse, until his lands were officially bestowed on Simon) and his son Raymond the younger ensued. Raymond junior was turning out to be a very capable military leader and he made substantial gains, including the capture of the town and fortress of Beaucaire. Raymond the elder, who had been in Aragon for much of 1216 and 1217, was able to return to Languedoc in September 1217, just as Louis was arriving back in France, and to occupy the great southern city of Toulouse.

Simon de Montfort began the siege of Toulouse in October 1217. He encountered fierce and sometimes vicious resistance and doggedly remained there all through the winter of 1217 and the spring and early summer of 1218. On 25 June that year he was killed by a stone shot from a petrary mounted on the walls, which was being operated by women and girls from the city – every inhabitant was involved in the defence. The continuation part of the *Song of the Cathar Wars*, which gives a very detailed account of the siege, describes graphically the effects of being struck by such a missile: 'A stone arrived just where it was needed and struck Count Simon on his steel helmet, shattering his eyes, brains, back teeth, forehead and jaw. Bleeding and black, the count dropped dead on the ground.' The siege was lifted, the Toulousians celebrated, and leadership of the crusade against them fell into the hands of Simon's eldest son, Amaury de Montfort, who was then around twenty-three and who had already been part of the campaign for many years. But things were not to go smoothly. Simon had been an experienced and successful soldier and an inspirational leader to his troops; his death meant not just a military setback but also a huge loss of morale and the seeding of doubts among the crusaders – after all, was God not supposed to be on their side against the heretics? If so, why had He allowed this to happen? In the immediate aftermath of Simon's death the crusade lost ground.

On 12 August 1218 Pope Honorius wrote a letter to Philip Augustus to urge him to send help to Amaury de Montfort, in the form of an army led by Louis; on 13 August he wrote to Louis himself with the same request. Louis, predictably, was keen to undertake the campaign; Philip was less sure and sent no formal reply one way or the other. In September Honorius tried another approach and wrote again to Philip, saying that he would underwrite all the costs of the campaign, but Philip was still not convinced. His official truce with England (agreed with John in 1215; Louis's invasion was not considered to have broken the truce as it was not backed by Philip) was due to expire in 1220 and the minority of Henry III might provide some interesting opportunities for gain – but not if all Philip's resources were deployed elsewhere. This truce, incidentally, would be extended; both Louis ('his very dear and faithful eldest son') and Frederick II the Holy Roman Emperor ('if he wishes to be included') are named specifically in the terms, showing Philip's control or influence over both of them, but also recognition of Louis as a force in his own right.

However, Honorius was not finished yet and had another trick up his sleeve. Bypassing Philip, he offered leadership of the crusade directly to Theobald IV, count of Champagne (who, we might recall, was placed as a baby in the household of Louis and Blanche after being born after the death of his father, Theobald III; he was now in his late teens and approaching his majority). This goaded Philip into action: he might not be keen to commit himself to the crusade, but he certainly did not want to lose control of the campaign to a powerful vassal: the count of Champagne was one of the richest and most influential noblemen in France, and as well as a dash of French royal blood (his paternal grandmother had been Marie, daughter of Louis VII and his first wife Eleanor of Aquitaine) Theobald had other potential interests in the south due to a claim to the crown of Navarre via his mother. Philip accepted Honorius's offer on 19 November 1218 and Louis wasted no time in pledging himself, as Peter of Les-Vaux-de-Cernay tells us:

> On 20 November in the Year of Our Lord 1218 Louis, the illustrious eldest son of the King of France, took the cross, for the glory of God and the suppression of heresy in the Toulouse area, with the willing assent of his father. Inspired by his example many powerful French nobles also took the cross.

Louis began his preparations. The mustering of men and supplies naturally took some time and much of Louis's energy over the winter, and it was 15 May 1219 before his forces set off. As a designated crusade backed by papal authority, his army was packed with Church representatives: bishops, archbishops and abbots, including Guérin, bishop of Senlis, Philip Augustus's closest counsellor, and Bertrand, the papal legate to France. Louis was naturally also accompanied by his friends, among them Peter de Dreux of Brittany and Guy de Châtillon, as well as renowned fighters such as William des Roches of Anjou.

Instead of heading down the Rhône valley, as he had done in 1215, Louis and his host went through Poitou and Limousin. Their pace was slow: 'They brought carts, mules and pack-beasts, tents, pavilions, victuals and money, and travelled in short stages to let those at the rear keep up,' says the anonymous continuer of the *Song of the Cathar Wars*. They reached Marmande (a town some 50 miles or 80 km south-east of Bordeaux) in early June to meet up with Amaury de Montfort, who had been besieging it for several months.

As might be expected, the influx of a large and fresh force turned the tide; Louis had been there only a day or two when the ditches around the fortification were filled in and the barriers broken down. The leader of the defenders, Count Centule of Astarac, emerged to surrender and was taken to Louis's tent. There, says the *Song of the Cathar Wars*, 'the prelates of the Church attended upon the king [meaning Louis] and the barons of France took their seats before him. The king sat on a silken cushion and folded his right glove, rich with gold embroidery,' as he prepared to hear Centule's case. The atmosphere was tense, as 'everyone listened for the others to speak'.

What we should probably make clear at this point is that this particular war was being waged according to very different rules from the normal 'chivalric' encounters. Although the conflict was on French soil, it had been designated a holy crusade, so that the Cathars were considered sub-human heretics, on a par with the Saracens in the Holy Land. Therefore, they had not been accorded the mercy which might normally be expected by defeated opponents, even when they surrendered. Thousands of civilians had been massacred after the capture of the town of Béziers in 1209; after the fall of

Lavaur in 1211 some four hundred Cathars had been burned alive on a huge pyre, the castellan and eighty knights hanged, and the castellan's sister murdered by being thrown down a well-shaft and stoned to death. The southerners had retaliated in kind, and French soldiers captured during Simon de Montfort's siege of Toulouse had been paraded through the streets, their eyes gouged and tongues ripped out before they were hacked to pieces. So Count Centule was very much taking his life in his hands by approaching Louis's camp.

The opinion of the bishop of Saintes, readily stated, was that all those who had defended Marmande, including the count, should be put to death. According to the *Song of the Cathar Wars* Louis replied, 'since it is the Church who brought me here, her law shall not be challenged. The count is in dispute with the Church, so she may do what she likes.' But both Peter de Dreux and the count of St Pol leaped to their feet and protested that it was not right to execute a nobleman who had given himself up for mercy. The archbishop of Auch pointed out that the count, although he had been defending the town along with the heretics, was himself an orthodox Catholic, and that he could be exchanged for other prisoners who had been captured in earlier encounters. And so Centule was spared his life, along with four other nobles. But everyone else was not so lucky, and the population was massacred, as the *Song of the Cathar Wars* graphically describes:

> Clamour and shouting arose, men ran into the town with sharpened steel; terror and massacre began. Lords, ladies and their little children, women and men stripped naked, all these men slashed and cut to pieces with keen-edged swords. Flesh, blood and brains, trunks, limbs and faces hacked in two, lungs, livers and guts torn out and tossed aside ... not a man or woman was left alive, neither old nor young, no living creature ... Marmande was razed and set alight.

The author of this part of the text was a supporter of the southerners and on occasion in his work he exaggerates for effect. But in this case his account is backed up by William the Breton, supporter of the opposing side, who tells us that 'All the citizens were killed, along with their wives and their little children; every inhabitant, to the number of five thousand souls.'

Louis, it has to be said, does not come out of this episode with any great credit. From a modern perspective it is almost impossible to fathom how he could hear a discussion on how it would 'disgrace' him (in the words attributed to the count of St Pol) to execute an enemy combatant, and then stand by while a massacre of defenceless citizens – civilians, including women and children – took place. This was in marked contrast to the clemency he had often shown to defeated opponents in England. His silence is deafening: in neither account does he appear to command the massacre explicitly, but there is no doubt that he could have prevented it if he had chosen to. But it is dangerous to view historical actions though a modern lens, and here we have to remember two things. First, that thirteenth-century ideas of religion were very different – forgiveness came only after repentance, and even then was only for good Christians who followed the Church's doctrine, not for those who had departed so radically from the orthodox teachings. No less a personage than St Bernard of Clairvaux, the influential twelfth-century abbot and Doctor of the Church, had declared that the killing of heathens and heretics was not 'homicide' but 'malicide': the killing of evil. Therefore, not only was it permitted but it should be actively encouraged as an act of cleansing (this link with purification is one of the reasons why burning was a common method of execution for heretics). Secondly, we should also recall that although thirteenth-century noblemen saw other knights as 'one of them' even though they might be on the opposing side (they could be captured and offered for ransom rather than killed, and killing a knight once he had surrendered would be a 'disgrace'), they saw commoners differently. Thus, the massacre of the citizens of Marmande served multiple purposes: it rid the world of some five thousand heretics (or at least heretical supporters – the evidence suggests that Marmande was not, in fact, a hotbed of heretical activity), it deprived the enemy of resources and it acted as a warning to terrorise other towns in the region into submission. All this does not, from a modern viewpoint, excuse Louis's horrific actions, but it does go some way towards explaining them in context.

Leaving the bloody and smouldering ruins of Marmande behind him, Louis and his host set off for Toulouse, still in the hands of the southerners. The people there were naturally frightened, but the atrocities of the war had been such that they were almost inured to terror by now, and even the fate of Marmande did not persuade them to surrender. Instead it made them even more determined and they organised their defences, led by the younger Raymond who had taken charge of his family's campaign from his ageing father. He had a substantial garrison of knights and sergeants, as well as the civilians, and they prepared to withstand yet another siege.

The continuation of the *Song of the Cathar Wars* ends abruptly at this point, with a wish that the Blessed Virgin should defend and protect the inhabitants. But despite the huge and complex preparations on both sides, the siege was to prove an anti-climax. Louis arrived and began the assault on 16 June 1219; his troops surrounded the city and cut it off from reinforcement or resupply, and launched several vigorous assaults on the walls. But unfortunately for him, a specific aspect of feudal custom was about to throw a spanner in the works. The standard period of military service which was owed to an overlord was forty days per year: this meant that there was what might be termed a 'campaigning season' in the late spring and summer, when being on the road was more practical and the all-important harvest season was not interrupted. This limited period of service had not been the case for crusades to the Holy Land, for the obvious reason that the journey times were immense: those heading for Outremer, as the lands across the sea were known, simply accepted that they would be gone for months or even years, and they took a personal decision to travel. But the present campaign was somewhere in between the two: it was a crusade, yes (and those taking part in it were able to claim their indulgences for fighting in the army of God), but it was on home soil against rebellious vassals of the king. Therefore many of the lords and knights argued that forty days should be their default service here too, and in late July they simply packed up and went home.

With a dwindling number of men, insufficient to break down the mighty defences of Toulouse, Louis was forced to abandon the siege: it was lifted on 1 August and he headed back north. This rather sudden departure caused much celebration in Toulouse, and confused a number of chroniclers, who attributed it to anything from a secret agreement between Louis and Raymond to Louis coveting the southern lands for himself and therefore being unwilling to expend his energy on conquering them for Amaury's benefit. Roger of Wendover resurfaces at this point, describing 'a great famine among the French army ... dreadful mortality both of men and horses', and blaming this for Louis's decision to depart. But this is one of the instances in which Roger gets his facts mixed up, confusing this encounter with the earlier siege of 1218 in which Simon de Montfort was killed, so his account cannot be deemed reliable. It seems clear that it was simply the lack of men that forced Louis's hand: he was enough of a military leader to know when a victory was possible and when he was facing a lost cause. To put it bluntly, while he was restlessly driven, lived for campaign and did not have much else to occupy his time, other lords were not so keen and did not want to be away from their lands for long periods.

The net result of Louis's withdrawal was the one which could be expected: Amaury de Montfort lost the gains he had made. The crusade was not over yet; the carnage in the south would remain a festering sore on the map of France and Louis would be back.

* * *

All around him, Louis's friends and boyhood companions were succeeding to their inheritances. Theobald had, of course, been count of Champagne since his birth; he reached his majority in 1221. Peter de Dreux had been duke of Brittany since his marriage to the heiress some years before; his elder brother Robert succeeded their father as count of Dreux in 1218. Guy de Châtillon's father, the count of St Pol, died in 1219, and in 1222 his mother (who was countess in her own right) ceded the title to him. But Louis was still in his father's shadow. How was he to occupy himself?

From what we can gather from the available evidence, Louis was not exactly kicking his heels, but he was not overtly associated with royal power either. He had still not been crowned as 'junior king', and neither had he been named count of Artois – all his acts from this period, including those relating to Artois, list him as 'Louis, eldest son of the lord king of France' (the same style he had used in England) rather than as count. He did play some administrative role in Artois, which was useful practice for eventual government: we find him engaging in day-to-day tasks such as confirming a grant of land, or the assignment of a dower, or a peace treaty between two vassals. However, he did this without having Artois as his principal residence; we can tell from the various charters and acts which contain names, dates and places that he was more often in royal residences elsewhere, such as Paris, St Germain, Compiègne and Fontainebleau. Louis also kept himself busy administering the county of Boulogne while his half-brother Philip Hurepel was a minor (we will remember that

Philip Hurepel was married to Matilda, daughter of Renaud de Dammartin, who was still in prison following his defeat at Bouvines, and that Renaud had been forced to resign his county to her). And Louis and Blanche did their duty to guarantee the royal line: three more sons, of whom we shall hear more in the next chapter, were born in quick succession in 1219, 1220 and 1222.

In March 1222 there came a renewed appeal from the pope to King Philip regarding the Albigensian crusade. Amaury de Montfort, perhaps tired of fighting a bloody and endless war which had taken up most of his life since he was in his early teens, and which had cost him his father and younger brother, had been offering his lands and claims to Philip since the beginning of the year. Meanwhile, Raymond VI of Toulouse had died and his son Raymond VII had declared himself the loyal subject of Philip and asked to be reinstated as count of Toulouse, to the lands which had been taken from his father and awarded to Simon de Montfort some years before. Raymond was another young man – around twenty-five at this point – whose entire existence to date had been dominated by the conflict and who might justifiably be dreaming of a different and more peaceful kind of life. A decision would have to be made. Over the summer the cardinal legate, Bertrand, travelled to Languedoc to mediate, and he arranged for an assembly to be held once all parties were in a position to travel to Paris.

However, in September 1222 King Philip, now fifty-seven, began to suffer from bouts of a violent fever. This may or may not have been linked to the serious illness of his youthful crusade to the Holy Land, which had affected his life ever since, but it was debilitating enough for him to stop what he was doing and to draw up his testament. In this he salved his conscience by apportioning vast sums for the recompense of lands unjustly confiscated, for the Christian cause in the Holy Land, for widows, for orphans, for lepers – and no less than £10,000 for his long-suffering wife Ingeborg (who would go on to outlive him by thirteen years). The fever was described as quartan, meaning that the worst attacks happened every fourth day. In between these times Philip managed to continue with his duties as best he could. His doctors advised him to go on a diet and to abstain from wine, but – ever the *bon viveur* – he refused. After all, everyone had to die of something, and making his life miserable would not ease his last months or years. But this still provided no opening for Louis to take over any kingly duties: Philip would hold the reins of power fast in his own hands until his dying breath. Both William the Breton and Roger of Wendover note that the onset of Philip's illness was accompanied by the ill omen of a 'fiery-tailed comet' – the tendency in medieval chronicles to link important events with phenomena which must at the time have seemed supernatural is often taken as metaphorical, but in this particular case it is possible that Roger and William were depicting astronomical fact: one of the appearances of Halley's comet is calculated to have taken place in September 1222.

In July 1223 an assembly of bishops was in Paris discussing the Albigensian question. Philip, who was at Pacy-sur-Eure in Normandy, decided to try to travel to Paris to join them. However, he had made it only as far as Mantes (some 35 miles or 55 km away from the capital) when he was struck by another severe bout of fever and had to stop. This time he knew it was serious: both Louis and his son young Louis were summoned to his side. The deathbed scene would remain etched in the mind of the little boy in later life, and Louis, too, was emotional. A chronicler named Conon de Lausanne was in Paris at this time (he was later present at Philip's funeral), and he describes the scene eloquently. Louis's final reward from his father was in the form of simple words: 'My son,' said Philip, 'you have never caused me any trouble or pain.'

Philip Augustus died on 14 July 1223; he was just short of his fifty-eighth birthday and had ruled France for forty-three years, during which time it had grown from a small kingdom precariously sandwiched between the Plantagenet domains and the Holy Roman Empire to become the dominant force in western Europe. Philip's body was taken in state to Paris, to be buried in full regalia at the abbey of St Denis in the presence of all the assembled bishops and archbishops and, among others, his sons Louis and Philip Hurepel, and John the king of Jerusalem.

The Minstrel of Reims records Philip's passing quite simply: 'Death, which spares nobody, neither great nor small, came for him ... he confessed and repented of his sins.' The *Chronicle of Tours* offers a factual yet nonetheless informative assessment of the king and his life:

[He had] an agreeable appearance, well-formed body, cheerful face, a bald pate, ruddy complexion. [He was] given to drink and food, prone to sexual desire, generous to his friends, miserly to his foes, skilled in stratagems, orthodox in belief, solicitous of counsel, holding to his word, a scrupulous and expeditious judge, fortunate in victory, fearful of this life, easily moved, easily assuaged, putting down the wicked of the realm by sowing discord among them, killing no-one in prison, availing himself of counsel of lesser men, bearing grudges only momentarily, subduing the proud, defending the Church, and providing for the poor.

William the Breton, perhaps understandably, gets a bit teary-eyed:

He was a man prudent in his address, strong in courage, great in his actions, of illustrious renown, victorious in combat, distinguished by many and great victories, who augmented marvellously the rights and the power of the kingdom of the French and enriched it considerably ... Defender and zealous protector of the Church ... most generous distributor of alms to the poor ...

He continues in this vein for some while, and then draws his chronicle of the *Deeds of Philip Augustus* to a close, dedicating it to Louis.

For there was a new king in France, a new power in western Europe. As he rose from Philip's deathbed, as he accompanied his father's body back to Paris, and as he saw the coffin lowered into the ground, he kept his own counsel. But once he walked out of the abbey of St Denis on that July day, Louis began to make his plans for the future.

CHAPTER NINE

KING OF FRANCE

[In the year 1223] died Philip, the wise king of the French, and was buried at St Denis . . . he was succeeded by his son Louis, but how dissimilar were the father and the son! (Matthew Paris)

L OUIS WAS THE king. Despite being in the unusual position, for a Capetian, of not having been crowned during the lifetime of his father, there was no question over his accession; no better-qualified rival claimant could possibly appear, so the throne passed smoothly from father to son once more. There was a great deal which required the new king's attention: the appointment of royal officers, the handover of government and administration, and the preparation of official communications, to name but a few, but the most important immediate task was to organise a coronation ceremony. This was arranged speedily for 6 August 1223, the feast of the Transfiguration, and Louis and Blanche set off from Paris a week beforehand so that they could ride in state, at a leisurely pace, through the countryside to the great cathedral at Reims where all French kings were crowned. The nobility and clergy of France had been summoned and all who were able made their way to Reims too, gathering ready on the morning of the big day.

Despite the time of year the summer's heat would not have penetrated the thick stone walls of the cathedral, which had been reconstructed during the preceding decade after being damaged by fire in 1210. The assembled throng included well-dressed and bejewelled nobles, clerics in their finest robes, and notable guests including John de Brienne, king of Jerusalem; they gathered in the cool and airy space as they waited for the king and queen to arrive. Louis and Blanche made a ceremonial entrance and walked up the towering nave, through the crowds, towards the altar. The coronation was to be performed by William de Joinville, the archbishop of Reims, as was his right. Various nobles were tasked with bearing items of regalia during the ceremony. The privilege of carrying the new king's sword had briefly threatened to become the subject of conflict among his companions, but the honour eventually went to Philip Hurepel, Louis's half-brother, who had now reached his majority and assumed his inheritance, in right of his wife, as count of Boulogne.

The first part of the coronation was spiritual: a solemn Mass was sung, and then the archbishop anointed Louis with sacred oil from the holy ampoule, a vial of Roman glass which was reputed to have been associated with the baptism of Clovis, the first Frankish king to convert to Christianity, in the year 492. The sceptre was put in Louis's right hand, and a rod known as the 'Hand of Justice' in his left. And then, finally, after all his years of waiting and the missed opportunities, a golden crown was placed on Louis's head. How he felt when the cold weight, and its attendant responsibilities, pressed down on his brow we can only imagine.

The second part of the ceremony was military: Louis was the first knight of the kingdom and the leader of the armies of France, and this was reflected in the giving of martial symbols. He was presented with his sword, shield, spurs and standard. Then, amid wild applause, he moved to sit on his throne while the shorter coronation of the queen – who was crowned and presented with a small sceptre – followed.

And then the celebrations could begin. A huge banquet costing some £4,000 (approximately one-fiftieth of the total annual royal income) had been arranged: 'the feast was the most beautiful and the richest which had ever been seen at a king's coronation,' says the Minstrel of Reims, alas without giving us any information about the menu, which remains a mystery to this day. The following day Louis and Blanche started to make their way back to Paris to make a formal entrance into their capital. Nicholas de Bray, chronicler of Louis's reign, is in fine form as he describes the scene:

> The light is outshone by a new light; the sun thinks that another sun has come to illuminate the earth, as its accustomed splendour is eclipsed. In the squares, at the crossroads and in the streets there is nothing to be seen but garments resplendent with gold; fabrics of silk shine from all sides ... the churches are decorated with garlands, the altars surrounded with gems, the perfume of incense lifts into the air ... joyous young people dance and sing in the streets.

Nicholas is probably (not for the first or the last time) exaggerating here, but there was certainly reason for the citizens to celebrate. As there had not been a coronation for forty-three years, this was a new experience for many if not most of them, and they were determined to enjoy it. They had further cause to rejoice in the peace with which the crown had passed on: there was a new king but he was a familiar and trusted figure in Paris, and there would be no upheaval in their daily lives.

Louis and his nobles reached the royal palace on the Île de la Cité and prepared to receive the citizens and the gifts they offered. The king was able to relax at last, safe in his position and looking forward to the future. Nicholas de Bray, as we noted in the Introduction, is very fond of both hyperbole and obscure references to ancient or mythical figures, but just occasionally in his writing there is a touch of the eyewitness's realism and an unexpected gem to be found. Here we find one such passage, and in the hot and crowded palace we can peer through the throng and get that rarest of things, a brief glimpse of Louis in person: 'Seeing so many of his illustrious friends gathered together in front of him, the king cannot contain in his heart the joy which he feels. It shows on his face: his cheeks colour and his features become animated with a vivid expression of energy.'

* * *

Once the emotion of the coronation was over, it was time for work. Louis was now thirty-five, not the hot-headed youth he might once have been, but a mature man. But how to step into his father's shoes? As Matthew Paris points out in the quote at the beginning of this chapter, Louis was indeed different to Philip, but they shared many of the same goals; Louis would carry on his father's dynasty-building work, consolidating his gains and extending the Capetian domains and influence still further.

There has long been a view among some historians that Louis and Philip were in conflict for much of Louis's life, but as we discussed earlier there is little hard evidence for this supposed antipathy. If the father–son rivalry had been intense we might have expected that one of Louis's first acts on his accession to the throne would have been a wholesale clear-out of Philip's counsellors, the men who represented the old regime. In fact, Louis did nothing of the sort. He kept on both of his father's closest advisers, Bartholomew de Roye and

Guérin, bishop of Senlis; indeed, he officially named the latter as chancellor, a role he had long been performing without the title, which Philip, with characteristic unwillingness to let anyone have too much power, had not bestowed upon him. Louis also retained Philip's marshal: although the office was not strictly hereditary, this was John Clément, who had held the office since the death of his father, Henry, on Louis's campaign at La-Roche-aux-Moines in 1214. Ours de la Chapelle, who had accompanied Louis on his English expedition, retained his position as chamberlain. Louis did add to his circle of advisers by taking on some men of his own: among those welcomed into the new king's household was Simon Langton, now forgiven by the pope for his part in Louis's English campaign and his excommunication lifted.

So the early months of Louis's reign were characterised by both stability and renewal. As part of the process of consolidation, Louis decided to visit straight away the kingdom's most recently annexed domains, where loyalties were the newest and therefore potentially the shakiest. In September 1223 he and Blanche rode through Touraine, Anjou and Normandy; they made a second journey in November, this time heading north to Arras and Flanders. On both journeys Louis received homage and oaths of fidelity from his nobles, and was welcomed by the people, who were no doubt glad to have a strong and proven man as the new king, which would mean peace. 'No rebel dares to raise unjust arms against the power of royal majesty,' says Nicholas de Bray; 'Normandy does not lift its head, and Flanders does not refuse to wear the yoke of this powerful prince.'

But Louis was not content simply to coast on the back of his father's achievements; he wanted to add more of his own. And one way in which he could do this was to restart his war with the English crown. The truce which Philip had extended in 1220 was due to expire at Easter 1224, so once Louis returned from his peregrinations he turned his mind to the question of how best to ensure the ascendancy of the French crown over the English one. Invading England again was not a realistic scenario at this point, but he could certainly aim to drive the English out of France.

All had not been peace and prosperity in England during the previous six years. The regent William Marshal had died in 1219, his proto-dynasty as earl of Pembroke and Striguil later to come crashing down as all five of his sons died childless one after the other. The other high-ranking noble who had supported Henry's cause during the war, the earl of Chester, had left England in 1218 to go on the Fifth Crusade. The regency was therefore for some time held by the trio of Hubert de Burgh, the justiciar, Peter des Roches, the bishop of Winchester, and the papal legate Pandulf, who had replaced his compatriot Guala in 1218 when the latter returned to his native Italy. The major achievement of the triumvirate had been to ensure the re-coronation of Henry in May 1220, this time at Westminster Abbey and with the ceremony conducted by the archbishop of Canterbury so that no doubts could surface over the validity of Henry's kingship. But they were not a comfortable group, falling out with each other and finding that rule by committee was time-consuming and tiresome. Pandulf resigned as a legate in 1221 and Peter des Roches left his position as Henry's guardian shortly afterwards, leaving Hubert in sole charge with a council to consult over major decisions. However, Hubert was not from one of England's foremost noble families and some of the lords resented his power. There had been a number of revolts against him, including one by William de Forz, the earl of Aumale, who as we might remember was one of the notable waverers during the war. In the spring of 1224, as the truce with France was about to expire, Henry was sixteen years old (and still some way off taking the reins of government into his own hands) and Hubert was embroiled in fighting off a rebellion led by Falkes de Bréauté, erstwhile favourite of King John. The time was ripe for Louis to strike.

Some indication of the confidence, indeed bullishness, of the atmosphere of Louis's early kingship can be found in the writings of William the Breton. His *Deeds of Philip Augustus*, as we have seen, terminates with the old king's death, but in 1224 William penned an addendum to his *Philippide*, known as the *Conclusion and Exhortation to the New King Louis*, in which he anticipates some rather ambitious aims:

[Poets] will sing of the brilliant start to your reign, and will tell of the transports of joy and the applause with which France welcomed her new king . . . you will be a subject worthy of their songs . . . you will suffer no longer to reign in peace this new king who dares to bear the English sceptre which, taken from his father by just sentence, belongs only to you, is reserved only for you through the rights of your wife, and which was conferred on you by the unanimous election of the clergy, the people and the nobles of England. This enterprise calls you, and you will prepare for it after Easter following the expiration of the truce which John begged from your father. Therefore, joyfully taking up arms under favourable omens . . . start to re-establish the rights of your kingdom, and add a kingdom to a kingdom, giving the signal for combat . . . take no rest until the child of England, vanquished by your armies, has resigned into your hands the sceptre to which he has no right, so that you may at last reign over both realms.

Louis did not renew the truce, a decision which was formally announced on 5 May 1224. Then he rolled up his sleeves and got started on his long-term plan, turning his attention to Poitou, a region of Aquitaine. Aquitaine had once been subject to the overlordship of the king of France, but it had passed into the control of Henry II of England when he married Eleanor of Aquitaine, who was duchess in her own right. By 1224 'duke of Aquitaine' was one of the titles of Henry III. During May Louis scored a masterstroke in advance of the campaign when he agreed terms with Hugh X de Lusignan. Hugh wielded great influence in the region as he was both count of La Marche (having succeeded his father, Hugh IX, in 1219) and count of Angoulême via his marriage to Isabelle, widow of King John and heiress to that county as her father's only child. The fact that his wife was the king of England's mother did not seem to bother Hugh as he responded readily to Louis's overtures. Hugh had long coveted the Isle of Oleron, off the French Atlantic coast just south of the major port of La Rochelle; it would have been part of the dowry of Joan, Henry III's sister, when she was betrothed to Hugh, but had not formed part of his marriage settlement with Isabelle. Louis agreed that if he could use Hugh's lands in Poitou as a base for his attack against the remaining English territory in the region, then control of Oleron would pass to Hugh as soon as they captured it. Hugh agreed, so Louis was able to move forward with his plans.

Now that he was king, Louis had the resources of the French crown at his disposal, and so was much better equipped for this campaign than he had been for his invasion of England. Not only could he summon all royal vassals to join him, but he also benefited from the frugality which Philip Augustus had exhibited with his annual income: during his reign Philip had doubled his revenues, quadrupled the size of the royal domain, and in his later years spent only around two-thirds of his income each year, so he had built up a significant store of treasure which Louis could call on.

Louis mustered his army at Tours on 24 June 1224: the *Life of Louis VIII* says that 'he assembled a great company of bishops and prelates, and a large host of barons, knights and sergeants'. Nicholas de Bray adds the detail that the host included combatants from Brittany, Normandy, Flanders and Champagne – local differences put aside, almost the whole realm was represented. Nicholas attributes a very flowery speech to Peter de Dreux, duke of Brittany, saying that he and his companions would be loyal to Louis forever, and that they would follow him whatever the dangers; although it is possible that the real Peter did not make *quite* so many classical allusions to Scylla, Charybdis, Cerberus and so on, the enthusiasm strikes a plausible note. These men had been with Louis since their boyhoods; they were his companions in arms, they were now the great peers of France, and he was the king. Adventure and glory awaited.

Among those in the host were Guérin, the chancellor; Philip Hurepel, Louis's younger half-brother; Robert, count of Dreux; Guy, count of St Pol; and Theobald, count of Champagne. Also included was John de Brienne, the king of Jerusalem, who had attended the coronation the previous year. A French nobleman by birth (the second son of the count of Brienne, a fiefdom in Champagne), he had gained the throne by marriage to Maria de Montferrat, the heiress of Jerusalem. At the conclusion of the unsuccessful Fifth Crusade he had arrived in western Europe and was now on a tour there trying to find more help for his kingdom. Possibly he thought that fighting for Louis at this point would do his cause good, but he was to wander through France, England, Italy and the Holy Roman Empire before finally finding practical support in León in the shape of an alliance with Alfonso IX and a marriage to Alfonso's daughter Berengaria, who was Queen Blanche's niece. But that was still in the future: for now John was an experienced knight with forty years of tournaments and fights behind him who would be a useful addition to the host.

Notable by his absence on the march was Peter, duke of Brittany, but this was because he had been assigned a different role to play: perhaps suspicious of Hugh de Lusignan's new-found loyalty (his family did, after all, have a conspicuous history as vacillators), Louis had inserted a clause in his agreement with Hugh that he would turn his castle of Lusignan – some 15 miles (24 km) south-west of Poitiers – over to the duke of Brittany for the duration of the campaign. Thus Peter was ensuring peace and stability behind the main advance. Possibly he chafed at the relative inaction, but he obeyed his orders nonetheless.

This gave Louis a safe space to the rear of his army as he advanced. First he marched on Montreuil-Bellay and secured a truce with the viscount of Thouars; then he turned south-west through Poitou with the eventual aim of reaching La Rochelle. The town of Niort, with a garrison commanded by the English seneschal of Poitou, Savari de Mauléon, surrendered after a short siege from 3 to 5 July; Savari and his men were permitted to retreat to La Rochelle with their lives and weapons. Next in Louis's path was St Jean d'Angély, but the inhabitants there surrendered without a fight: the *Life of Louis VIII* tells us that 'when those in the town heard of the approach of the king they doubted themselves and took counsel ... they gave themselves up and received the king and his people honourably in the town'. Louis was treated to a reception as lavish as St Jean d'Angély could provide, and he could plan his next and biggest move: the assault on La Rochelle.

La Rochelle was of pivotal importance. It was the major port on that part of the Atlantic coast; the nearest alternatives of similar size were Bordeaux, 120 miles (190 km) south, or the inland port of Nantes some 85 miles (135 km) north. La Rochelle was the place where English kings landed when they came to visit their territories in France, as it was big enough both to disembark troops and to take refuge in if defeat threatened. The town's wealth was built on trade, principally the wine trade with England, upon which it depended for much of its prosperity. The sympathies of its people could therefore be expected to lie with England; moreover, it was defended by an English garrison. Matthew Paris, recognising its importance, notes that 'if [the king of France] can in any way subdue the town of La Rochelle, thenceforth he will easily possess the rest of the land of Poitou'.

As Louis rode with his army, he encountered some familiar issues with his nobles and the terms of their feudal service. The campaign had so far lasted for some twenty days, so some of the lords, Theobald of Champagne the most vocal among them, thought that starting the siege of a well-fortified city would take them beyond their statutory forty days' service and should therefore not be attempted. Louis, predictably, was not in agreement, and he was supported by the churchmen present, including the chancellor Guérin, who thought that the campaign must be pushed to its end now they had got this far. The nobles were persuaded and the host moved on to La Rochelle.

Louis began the siege on 15 July 1224. The siege engines, the pieces of which had been rumbling along behind the host on carts, were unloaded, and the army began making ominous preparations, as Nicholas de Bray describes:

Here a knight polishes his helmet to remove traces of rust. Shields are made ready; swords are sharpened so that their steel points can inundate the earth with blood and turn the green grass red ... footsoldiers make ready their catapults, and a mass of lead is converted into balls; machines are constructed which are destined to break down the walls and to cast blocks of stone to destroy towers and houses, to kill enemies ... hands are full of darts and javelins, quivers are filled with arrows ... they are not short of bows, heavy blades, cruel axes or falchions; each also arms himself with a sharp steel sword.

The bombardment began.

At first the garrison (augmented by Savari de Mauléon and his men from Niort) were in buoyant mood, having been warned of the royal army's approach and having stocked up on barrels of grain, meat, fish and wine; they erected engines of their own and returned missile for missile for the first week and a half. However, if La Rochelle was to survive then it needed reinforcements and supplies sent across the Channel, and (in a neat reversal of Louis's experiences in England) these were not forthcoming. Ralph of Coggeshall, documenting the situation from his point of view in England, tells us that the citizens 'despaired of help from King Henry, who was meanwhile besieging the castle of Bedford'; Hubert de Burgh, the royal forces and a huge amount of resource were embroiled in a struggle there as they sought to wrest control of the castle from William de Bréauté, who was holding it in the name of his brother Falkes and keeping captive Henry de Braybrooke (whom we last saw defending Mountsorrel Castle in 1217), a royal judge who was hearing cases against Falkes which could lead to his downfall. After an eight-week siege Bedford would eventually fall, resulting in the hanging of the eighty-man garrison as well as William de Bréauté, but by then it was too late for La Rochelle.

By the beginning of August the garrison and the citizens there were not yet at their last extremity, but, knowing that no help would be forthcoming, they saw that there was no point in fighting on: the outcome was inevitable. They did not have enough troops to mount a sortie to try and break the siege; all they could do was sit tight and endure the bombardment until the walls gave way and the royal army came pouring in. It would be better for the inhabitants to accept the inescapable, in the hope of securing a settlement. La Rochelle surrendered to Louis on 3 August, and after a triumphal and peaceful entry into the town, the king allowed the garrison to leave with their lives and their arms; the burgesses swore fealty ten days later. The *Life of Louis VIII* is in jubilant mood as the English sail away: 'they gave up the town, saving their lives, and fled to England. And in this way the

English, who had long been lurking in this part of Aquitaine, left either voluntarily or under duress the kingdom of France.' The icing on the cake came when the Isle of Oleron submitted to Louis without a fight; he kept his word and handed it over to Hugh de Lusignan. On French soil Henry III now had control only of Gascony, and could land only by sailing as far south as Bordeaux.

The king was victorious, and he was in a confident mood. When Hubert de Burgh knew that Louis was advancing on La Rochelle and that he would not be able to provide any military support, he had written to the pope, sending envoys to Rome with his message. This resulted in a letter from Pope Honorius to Louis dated 3 August 1224 (the very day on which La Rochelle had fallen), expressing his regret at the non-renewal of the truce with England and his shock that Louis should have resorted to war at a time when he could have been instead supporting the needs of the Holy Land. Louis was 'asked *and begged*' (note the wording) to stop attacking the lands of the king of England. By the time Louis received this letter the campaign was done and dusted, so he replied in vigorous fashion that King John had been justly sentenced to forfeiture, that England was a papal fief and that yet its resources were being used to oppose him in Poitou. Was this happening with the pope's knowledge and consent? If so, he was 'asked *and required*' to ensure this was stopped. Louis's envoys reached Rome with this letter in December 1224 and wasted no time in circulating rumours that Louis might just mount a second invasion of England if the pope did anything against his interests, and that the English barons might just be prepared to hand the crown over to him.

While various envoys were en route, Louis stationed garrisons in the towns of Poitou and successfully convinced the inhabitants that they would be safer and more prosperous under his rule than Henry's. He then withdrew to Poitiers and thence to Paris.

Once in his capital he laid down his sword for a while and set about consolidating his conquests on parchment by making deals with nobles and by issuing charters to towns in Poitou which confirmed their privileges. It was in their best interests to stay loyal to him rather than rebelling on behalf of the absent (and unlikely to return in the near future) 'duke of Aquitaine', and the charters were accepted without challenge or complaint. Meanwhile, Savari de Mauléon had travelled back to England to explain what was under the circumstances an entirely justifiable surrender, but he was badly received, his explanations ignored and his motives suspected. Threatened with a charge of treason, he sailed back to France and threw in his lot with Louis, offering the king his sword in mid-December 1224. On submitting his castles as security, he was entrusted with the command of the new garrison of La Rochelle and the guard of the coast.

The next year or so would see a series of complex negotiations between Louis and Hubert de Burgh about peace and over merchant and shipping rights. For once out of his armour and his saddle and away from military camps, Louis was able to carry out this task from the comfort of Paris and the various royal residences, giving him at last some time in which to enjoy family life.

* * *

In May 1225 Louis and Blanche had been married for twenty-five years – two-thirds of their lives. During that time Louis had remained utterly faithful to her: unusually for a medieval king he fathered no illegitimate children, and no chroniclers, not even the hostile ones, mention any kind of mistress or even a passing liaison. Indeed, they show the opposite: the worst anyone could say on the subject was Matthew Paris's comment that Louis was so devoted to his wife that he was too much under her influence. But then, she was an exceptional woman.

Blanche was as devoted to Louis as he was to her; she supported him in all endeavours to the point of facing down his all-powerful father, as we have seen, and riding around to harangue the nobles of France into raising troops for him. Blanche makes very few appearances in official documents. Of the 460 acts of Louis's reign she appears in just three, all to do with family matters: the confirmation of her dower lands, the appointment of a chaplain to sing Masses in memory of their late son Philip, and Louis's testament providing for his children, which we will explore later in this chapter. But it would be a mistake to assume that she played no part in Louis's government – it is likely that they discussed matters in private and that he benefited from her advice. The intermediary role of queens during this period was well established, and indeed Pope Honorius wrote to his 'dear daughter in Christ, the illustrious queen of France' in May 1224 to ask her to intercede with her husband on the subject of aid for the emperor of Latin Constantinople.

Blanche was loyal not just to Louis but to France; by now she saw herself as a Frenchwoman, having left her home country when she was twelve and never returning. She had few remaining ties to Castile: her parents had died within three weeks of each other in October and November 1214, and she had never met her younger brother Henry, who inherited the crown of Castile, as he had been born four years after Blanche's departure.

One of the principal duties of a medieval queen was to bear children, and in this regard Blanche was very successful; allowing for Louis's frequent absences on various campaigns, she became pregnant at almost every opportunity. The agonising waits for a male heir, with the Capetian dynasty hanging on a single thread, which had characterised the previous two generations, became a thing of the past as son after son was born to the couple: after their short-lived daughter in 1205 Blanche gave birth to Philip in 1209; twin boys, possibly called John and Alfonso, in 1213; Louis in 1214; Robert in 1216; John in 1219; Alfonso in 1220; and Philip-Dagobert (the second half of the name being a reference to his Carolingian ancestors) in 1222. But a king needed daughters as well as sons, in order to form advantageous matrimonial alliances, so it was probably with more celebration than was usual at the birth of a girl that Isabelle, named for Louis's barely remembered mother, joined the family in 1224. And two more sons were to follow: Stephen in 1225 and Charles in 1227.

We have already noted that child mortality was endemic in the thirteenth century, and unfortunately for Louis and Blanche, their royal rank did not exempt them from tragedy. Of their twelve children only five would reach adulthood; four (their first-born daughter, the twins and Stephen) would die in infancy, while Philip, John and Philip-Dagobert would all perish between the ages of eight and ten.

Royal children needed providing for. Louis might have many offspring, but he also had significant lands in his gift thanks to his own conquests and those of his father. In June 1225 he drew up a testament to distribute lands and to provide for his children. His eldest son, Louis, then eleven, was of course to be the next king of France, inheriting the crown and the royal domains, but what of the others? There were to be titles for almost all his sons: Robert, aged nine, was to be count of Artois, lord of Louis's inheritance from his mother; John, six, would be count of Anjou and Maine; Alfonso, five, would be count of Poitiers and Auvergne. Three-year-old Philip-Dagobert would enter the Church, as would any further sons born to the king and queen. This giving of children to a religious life was common at this time, particularly in large families where there were too many sons to provide for comfortably. The boys in question would not end up as simple priests but rather as high-ranking clerics – bishops and archbishops who were socially and politically on a par with the great noblemen of the land. Unfortunately they tended to be chosen based on their order of birth within the family rather than on any particular aptitude or piety, so the end results varied considerably from great and ascetic scholars, to canny politicians such as Peter des Roches, to bullish warriors such as Philip Augustus's cousin the bishop of Beauvais, who had battered the earl of Salisbury into submission at Bouvines and fought in the Third Crusade, his clerical status notwithstanding. Surplus girls could also be handed over to the Church – again, generally to become abbesses rather than simple nuns – but Louis had only one daughter, so it was envisaged that baby Isabelle would make a great marriage; she would have the enormous sum of £20,000 as her dowry.

As it transpired, Louis and Blanche's son Philip-Dagobert died at the age of ten and so never started on his ecclesiastical career; John had passed away four years earlier, at nine, and his inheritance of Anjou and Maine eventually went to the youngest son, Charles, who had not yet been born when Louis drew up his testament. Great futures awaited all Louis's surviving children. Charles would inherit his counties and would later be crowned king of both Sicily and Naples. Alfonso became, as envisaged, count of Poitiers, and also subsequently count of Toulouse via his marriage to Joan, only child of count Raymond VII. When Alfonso and Joan both died in 1271, without heirs, the county of Toulouse reverted to the French crown, adding considerably to the royal domain. Robert, count of Artois, was a steadfast and loyal retainer of his elder brother, accompanying Louis on crusade, where he was killed at the battle of Mansourah in 1250. And Louis went on to become one of France's greatest kings, a crusader and a reformer of justice who reigned for forty-four years, renowned throughout Europe for his piety and known to posterity not as King Louis, but as Saint Louis. Isabelle would never marry, despite being pressed by Pope Innocent IV to marry Conrad, the son of Holy Roman Emperor Frederick II who had been Philip Augustus's ally; she chose instead a religious life, and supported by her brother she founded a convent of poor Clares in honour of St Clare of Assisi, one of the first followers of St Francis. Isabelle never took holy orders, preferring to avoid the inevitable rise to the rank of abbess which would follow; instead she lived quietly in the community she had founded until her death in 1270. She was later beatified; she is revered as a saint in the Franciscan order, so Louis and Blanche, although they did not know it in their own lifetimes, would be in the unusual and distinguished position of being the parents of two saints.

* * *

Louis would no doubt have been delighted if, in the summer of 1225, he could have looked into the future to see the destinies of his children, particularly the religious lives of Louis and Isabelle. But in thirteenth-century France religion meant conflict as well as comfort, and the king now found himself faced once more with the Albigensian question.

The war in Languedoc had been continuing on its bloody and destructive course. Raymond VI of Toulouse had died in 1222 but his son Raymond VII proved a more effective military leader; aided by the teenage Raymond-Roger de Trencavel, son of the old count of Carcassonne – and now titular holder of that honour although all his lands were in the hands of the de Montforts – he oversaw victory after victory. Conversely, Amaury de Montfort had proved less able than his late father, and he suffered loss after loss: Lavaur, Puylaurens, Montauban, Castelnaudri, Agen and Moissac were taken from him one by one by the resurgent southerners. The Cathars and the Perfecti who had been in hiding during the ascendancy of the crusaders emerged in public once more, and Catharism regained much ground at the expense of orthodox Catholicism. Amaury's position became so perilous that he fled Languedoc altogether in January 1224. The cause was in danger of being lost beyond repair, and the pope appealed to Louis. Only a large-scale intervention from the king of France himself could swing the balance.

Before Louis mounted any military action he needed legal and ecclesiastical justification. The pleas of the pope were weighty, but what of the French clergy? A council was held at Bourges on 30 November 1225 at which the cases of the two claimants to the title of count of Toulouse were put to a council of forty archbishops, 113 bishops and 150 abbots, presided over by the new cardinal legate to France, Romanus of St Angelo. The result was something of a foregone conclusion: on the one hand there was Amaury de Montfort, son of the great crusader and champion of the Church; on the other was Raymond VII, excommunicate and suspected of being a sympathiser of the heretics. Amaury's claim was upheld. The sentence of excommunication against Raymond was reaffirmed on 28 January 1226 at a general assembly of the nobles and clergy of France, at which point Amaury ceded his territorial rights to Louis, who became, officially, the overlord of Languedoc.

Having the title in theory was one thing; claiming it in practice was another. Louis needed to ride at the head of an army and take his new lands by force. Fortunately for him, this is something he was more than willing to do: not only would he be in the situation of being able to enlarge the royal domain, to his lasting fame and the credit of his dynasty, but he would also be fighting for his beloved Church in a legitimate cause. The campaign would be given the status of a crusade, meaning that Louis and his men would be granted the same privileges extended to crusaders in the Holy Land: they, their families and their lands would be placed under specific papal protection, and if they died on campaign they would go straight to heaven.

But there was more for Louis to take into account than there had been previously in 1219 and 1222. The last time Louis had mounted an expedition to Languedoc he had been a prince; now he was a king with the welfare of the rest of his realm to consider. The support of the laity, as well as that of the Church, must be gained: twenty-nine of the principal nobles of France put their names to an act confirming that they had advised him to undertake the crusade and that they would support him in it. Finances must be considered, so that the national coffers would not be emptied: taxes were levied, including a tithe of 10 per cent of the income of all clergy. And Louis must be able to prioritise the needs of France over the needs of the Church if necessary: he agreed with the pope that he would stay in Languedoc 'only as long as he pleased'; that his vow to complete the crusade was not binding on his heirs if anything should happen to him; and that if Henry III of England should attack any French lands while Louis was away, he would fall under sentence of excommunication.

A huge army was mustered. The figures of tens or even hundreds of thousands of men given by the chroniclers are exaggerated, but it is safe to say that it was a larger army than was normally seen in western Europe at the time. It set out on the road in June 1226, travelling south via the Rhône valley and using the river to transport some of the baggage and supplies. There was a great deal to be moved: as he was making his way through friendly parts of his own realm Louis brought food, cattle and fodder with him so that his army was self-sufficient and had no need to ravage, requisition goods or live off the land. News that the king was on his way in person sped ahead of the host. Louis's reputation both for victory and, when called for, for ferocity preceded him and many of the minor southern nobles fell over themselves to submit to him. 'We are zealous to place ourselves beneath the shadow of your wings, and under your wise dominion,' wrote one Bernard-Otho de Laurac. How much of this zeal was motivated by fear it is impossible to guess. Cities followed suit: Béziers, Nîmes, Puylaurens and Castres had all submitted before Louis got anywhere near them.

But Raymond of Toulouse was not going to give up so easily. He summoned those vassals still loyal to him, and appealed for help to his cousin Henry III of England (Raymond's mother had been Joanna, sister to King John) and to Hugh de Lusignan, count of La Marche and Angoulême. He was unsuccessful: Henry was a pious son of the Church and did not wish either to associate himself with the forces allied with heresy or to put himself at risk of excommunication due to Louis's agreement with the pope. More pragmatically, Hubert de Burgh would have seen the benefits of Louis being occupied in Languedoc, slugging it out with Raymond while England stood on the sidelines. Hugh de Lusignan, meanwhile, was – for now – comfortable in his alliance with Louis, which, as we have seen, had brought him great benefits, so he declined to join Raymond.

As the royal army advanced further south into Languedoc, one of the obstacles in its path was the great and supposedly impregnable city of Avignon, with its large bridge across the Rhône. Avignon was in the county of Provence rather than the county of Toulouse, so it had no reason to hold out against Louis, and he had no quarrel with it. Initially it appeared that the king and his host would have free passage through or around Avignon to cross the river and continue their journey, but this turned out not to be the case. Accounts differ as to how and why this happened.

A story which appears in Nicholas de Bray's work and in another chronicle by a cleric from Ghent named Philip Mousket, but not in any of the official acts and documents of the campaign, is that Louis sent an embassy into Avignon led by Guy the count of St Pol, but the citizens, mistaking the count for the king himself (they were of similar age, and we may imagine that the embassy carried some kind of French royal banner), shut the gates behind them and celebrated their capture of the king, at which point Louis recognised their treachery. Other sources, including the generally reliable *Chronicle of Tours* and some letters of various barons, as well as Nicholas de Bray (who, rather confusingly, includes both tales), say that some of Louis's army were already on or over the bridge when the citizens suddenly took fright at the sight of so many approaching armed men, refused entry to the king and the legate, shut the gates and sent out a party to destroy the bridge.

Whatever the precise reason for the decision, what is clear is that Avignon refused passage to the army, and that it now presented both an obstacle to the crusaders and a direct challenge to the king's authority. This was not to be borne, so the following day, 10 June 1226, Louis ordered his siege engines to be set up around the city. A temporary bridge made of boats was built to enable those who had already crossed the river to return and rejoin the main host.

Avignon was garrisoned not only by local citizens but also by a large troop of mercenaries who were willing to defend the city. A description from inside the city appears in the chronicle of Roger of Wendover: Roger, of course, was far away in England (unlike Nicholas de Bray, who was actually present at Avignon) and is occasionally confused in his accounts of events overseas, but sometimes his descriptions are so vivid and detailed that he appears to have based them on eyewitness accounts. This is plausible as he was based in the influential and well-situated abbey at St Albans, meaning he was able to talk to guests who had travelled all over Europe and so glean many valuable details for this writing. Of Avignon he says:

The city, until that time unattempted by hostile troops, was well defended by trenches, walls, turrets and ramparts outside, while within it was well garrisoned with knights and thousands of soldiers, and well supplied with horses, arms, collections of stones for missiles, engines and barriers, and was well stored with provisions, and did not therefore fear the assaults of the besiegers; for the defenders of the city bravely hurled on them stone for stone, weapon for weapon, spear for spear, and dart for dart, inflicting deadly wounds on the besieging French.

One of the casualties of the early stages of the siege was one of the rarely named common men in the host: Amaury Copeau, chief of the engineers and miners without whom no siege could succeed. He was replaced by another man promoted to chief, and the siege went on. The walls were high, and the French army was separated from the city by the river, but the king was determined in his course of action and so the siege continued all through the summer. The besiegers suffered all kinds of ills. Not only were they subject to missiles from inside the city, but the outlying parts of the host were attacked in raids by Raymond of Toulouse and his men, who also destroyed all nearby fields and crops so that the host had to travel further and further afield to find ever-dwindling supplies of food. As they remained there, exposed to the burning Provençal sun of June, July and August, many of the troops fell sick and died, and the difficulty of disposing safely of the corpses of men lost through illness or assault only added to their problems. Roger of Wendover is again descriptive as he notes:

At this siege the French were exposed to death in many ways, from the mortality which was raging dreadfully among their men and horses, from the deadly weapons and destructive stones of the besieged who bravely defended the city, and from the general famine which raged principally among the poorer classes, who had neither food nor money. In addition to the other miseries,

217

which assailed the army without intermission, there arose from the corpses of the men and horses, which were dying in all directions, a number of large black flies, which made their way inside the tents, pavilions and awnings, and affected the provisions and liquor; and being unable to drive them away from their cups and plates, they caused sudden death among them.

By early August discussions were taking place about the best way forwards. It would not do to be stuck outside the walls of Avignon for too many more months; but on the other hand if the siege were abandoned then a hostile city would be left behind the host – always dangerous – and Louis's army would have to find another place to cross the Rhône. The knights and nobles, as ever, had been chafing at the lack of direct engagement with the enemy, and now Guy the count of St Pol (presumably escaped from his captivity, if indeed he was ever taken prisoner) became animated and urged an all-out assault, as Nicholas de Bray tells us:

> The illustrious count of St Pol responded in these words: 'What madness to waste our time with words! While we have been talking, we could have been knocking down the walls and attacking a thousand breaches. The sun is already setting in the west, and we cannot call back the hours we have lost. Whatever may be the determination of others, I will be the first to make an attack with my forces against the enemy!'

The other nobles agreed, and Louis – possibly against his better judgement, given what we know of his tactical acumen – allowed the assault to go ahead. It proved a total disaster. In order to get close to the city walls the army had to cross the river; they attempted to surge over a secondary bridge which was not sturdy enough for their weight, while being bombarded from inside the city. Nicholas de Bray's eyewitness account has him dodging the missiles himself, while describing what he sees around him:

> Arrows are falling more heavily than rain, causing injury and death on all sides. Thousands of stones flying through the air cause similar carnage. One perishes under the stones, another falls, pierced through the side by an arrow; a third receives a leg wound. This man here has his brains scattered after his helmet has been broken; that man there, exhausted by the weight of his shield, can carry it no longer; another succumbs, burned by a substance made of fire and sulphur.

The bridge collapsed and hundreds of men were thrown into the river, where they drowned, screaming as they were dragged under the water by the weight of their armour and equipment. The missiles did their work, too, and Guy, the brave and impetuous count of St Pol, was killed when a stone hit him directly on the head, an incident mentioned by all chroniclers of the event. 'His brains were completely knocked out,' says the Minstrel of Reims, bluntly; and this was 'a great shame', says the *Life of Louis VIII*, as 'he was a valiant man, courageous in arms and fervent in faith'. Louis was devastated by the loss of his lifelong friend, his companion since boyhood, but his sorrow soon turned to anger. 'He does not weep,' says Nicholas de Bray, 'because the bitterness of his feelings has dried his tears'; the Minstrel confirms that 'when the king saw his friend dead, he was so enraged that he was almost out of his mind'. Louis 'swore that he would not leave the siege until the city had been conquered,' says the *Life of Louis VIII*, but now he would try a different approach. He forbade any more frontal assaults and settled in for the long haul: Avignon would surrender or starve.

The body of Guy de Châtillon, count of St Pol, was embalmed and transported in a coffin to a convent which had been founded by his family, where he was given an honourable burial. He was a widower, his wife Agnes de Donzy having died the previous year when barely out of her teens; their two children, a son of three and a younger daughter, were taken into the care of their maternal grandmother, Matilda de Courtenay, dowager countess of Nevers and one of the great matriarchal figures of the thirteenth century. The power bloc which Guy's loyalty to the crown had produced (following the death three years previously of Hervé de Donzy, Guy was count not only of St Pol but also of Nevers, Tonnere and Auxerre, in right of his wife) was split, his son receiving the maternal inheritance and the county of St Pol going to Guy's younger brother Hugh. By strange coincidence, Hugh would also be killed at Avignon by a stone from a catapult, in the service of Louis IX in 1248.

Louis grieved and his army sat tight around Avignon, allowing no supplies in and no people out. His overall situation was improved by the submissions of other towns which came to him while he remained *in situ* – Carcassonne, Albi, Marseille, Beaucaire and Narbonne, among others. If only Avignon could be taken, the rest of Languedoc lay open.

Eventually the citizens bowed to the inevitable. Help would not be forthcoming: no doubt the news of other submissions was shouted to them over the walls in order to sap their morale, and Raymond, still at large in the surrounding countryside, did not have sufficient troops to attempt the full-scale attack which would be needed to break the siege. Sometime in late August or early September (we do not have the exact date) Avignon capitulated. After the surrender of hostages for good faith the inhabitants opened their gates to the king. There were immediate repercussions which were both religious – the legate entered the city, performed absolutions, purified the churches, established new priests in post and appointed a new bishop – and military in nature: the ramparts, along with any houses considered to be fortified, were razed and ditches filled in. The citizens handed over all their weapons, siege engines and 6,000 marks to Louis. There were to be no executions, no massacre of the population; however, as Louis had to leave again almost immediately, he needed to leave the city in the charge of someone who would rule strictly in his name. His choice fell on William, the young count of Orange, whose father had been captured and burned alive, the remains of his body cut to pieces, during the crusade of 1218. William could be relied upon not to develop any sympathy for the defeated southerners.

Avignon had been reputed to be invincible, and Louis had taken it in three months. The French army now headed for Toulouse with no other towns standing in their way.

However, it was a reduced army. Once more Theobald of Champagne had been more concerned about his statutory forty days of service than about the overall success of the campaign. He had arrived belatedly, only once the siege of Avignon was under way, and had sought an audience with Louis as soon as his forty days were up. It is possible that he was jealous of the success of the king's campaign, which brought glory to Louis and no particular gain to Theobald, all the more aggravating because things could have been so different. After all, if Philip Augustus had not acted as he did in 1218, Theobald could have been at the head of a crusade himself, his wealth and his prospects in the south being considerably enhanced thereby. He had not put his name to the act of January 1226 in which the nobles of France affirmed their support for Louis and his crusade, and he was not prepared to continue there any longer. We do not know exactly what was said, but there seems to be agreement among the chroniclers that there was a blazing row, and Theobald certainly left the army to return north. The author of the *Chronicle of Tours*, normally dispassionate in his writing and therefore considered a reliable source, is on this occasion scathing:

> The count of Champagne, relative of the king, brought up in the palace of Philip Augustus, whom Louis defended with all his might . . . forgetting all honour and all affection, abandoned his lord and king in the middle of his enemies, in pressing peril, returned to France to the dishonour and ignominy of his name.

And so Louis marched on without one of his greatest vassals. The summer was over; by the time the army arrived at Toulouse it was mid-October. A siege of Toulouse would take many months, and winter, as we have already noted, was not a good time for campaigning. Louis was an eager knight and soldier, but he was also a leader, a strategist and a pragmatist. His army was tired. Many of the knights and men were sick. They were still being harried by Raymond's forces and were sustaining losses. The only realistic decision was not to launch a siege of Toulouse at this point; instead Louis would lay the groundwork for another expedition the following spring to finish the crusade once and for all. He appointed seneschals and placed loyal garrisons in the towns which had submitted. Orthodox churchmen were placed in positions of clerical authority. While this was taking place he suffered more losses from illness, the great men being no less susceptible than the commoners: among the dead were William de Joinville, the archbishop of Reims who had crowned Louis, and Philip, count of Namur. Dysentery ravaged the army and they set off for home in late October.

* * *

It was not long after they turned back that Louis was first struck by severe stomach pains. As an experienced campaigner he can have been under no illusions as to the cause, and the danger it presented.

Various rumours flew around – mentioned in passing by some chron-iclers and even aired in public some years later by Philip Hurepel – that the king had been poisoned by Theobald, but as the count had been gone over a month and Louis had spent that time sharing a camp with an army packed with diseased men living in cramped and unsanitary conditions, there can be little doubt that he was suffering from dysentery. He tried to hide it as long as he could, riding on in grim determination so as not to affect the morale of the host, but by the time they arrived at the castle of Montpensier on 3 November 1226 he was suffering greatly and was taken to a bed to rest. Doctors were summoned, but everyone knew there was little they could do.

As the days went by it became clear that Louis was unlikely to recover. There were urgent matters to attend to: the king needed to make a last testament in front of as many high-ranking witnesses as possible. The archbishop of Reims was dead and Guérin, the elderly chancellor, had already returned to Paris ahead of Louis. It was too late to summon anyone else, so decisions would have to be made by those who were on the spot: Philip Hurepel, Amaury de Montfort, the chamberlain Ours de la Chapelle, the marshal John Clément and the archbishop of Sens were among those who swore that they would crown as soon as possible Louis's eldest son Louis, or if he had died – for who knew what had happened in Paris since the last communi-cation from the capital? – then his second son Robert. They affirmed that they had sworn this oath in Louis's presence. Young Louis was only twelve, so a regent would need to be named: by custom this would have been the nearest male relative to the child king – in this case Philip Hurepel – but Louis, 'in agony but still of sound mind', according to the testimony of three bishops, named Blanche.

The testament was complete. Louis would never see his beloved family again and he could do nothing more for them except to pray that they would survive his loss.

223

The doctors apparently had one last ploy. In a possibly apocryphal tale told by William of Puylaurens, they decided that such an excess of chastity as the king had demonstrated while he was on campaign was hindering his recovery. The solution was for him to deflower a virgin, so they found a suitable young woman and placed her in his bed while he was asleep. When Louis awoke he demanded to know what she was doing there; upon hearing the explanation he thanked her but declined, as he would rather die than commit a mortal sin and live as an adulterer who dishonoured his wife in such a way. Faithful to Blanche until the end, his mind remained clear enough for him to make a confession and receive absolution before he breathed his last on 8 November 1226.

At the age of thirty-nine, Louis was dead.

CHAPTER TEN

LEGACY

THERE WAS SILENCE.

Louis had reigned over France for just three years and three months, dying in his prime too young, too soon, too suddenly, and the consequences for the realm could be serious.

The first considerations for those of the king's advisers who were present were practical: the body must be dealt with before putrefaction set in. Louis's entrails and heart were removed and buried in the abbey church at Montpensier (since destroyed); this may sound somewhat macabre but it was not unusual for the bodies of medieval kings to be divided in this way and the honour of their burial distributed among different places. His body was then embalmed to preserve it temporarily, wrapped in cloth, sewn into a leather covering, and placed in a coffin ready for the slow and sorrowful journey back to Paris.

Decisions needed to be made, decisions which would normally be left to those of higher rank. However, as neither the chancellor nor any of the great peers of the realm was present, those who had attended the dying king were forced to take action themselves. They had sworn to crown young Louis, and under the circumstances speed was of the essence: there was no time to send word to Paris to consult on the best date for the coronation as this would cause unwanted delay. Instead the bishops and nobles set the date for 29 November 1226 – just three weeks after Louis's death, almost the minimum which could be managed given the travel times involved in contacting the lords and then their journeys to Reims – and sent out invitations there and then.

News of the king's death travelled to Paris faster than his body, and the funeral was planned and ready to take place almost as soon as the cortège arrived. Louis was laid to rest on 15 November 1226, his body interred next to that of Philip Augustus at St Denis, the traditional burial place for French monarchs. Nobody could have predicted that the funeral of the son would follow so quickly after that of the father, and the grief of the mourners was intense.

And there, as Louis went to his eternal rest amid the tears of his family and friends, his story should have ended. But there was to be a sad addendum; he was not to be left in peace. In 1793 the French Revolutionary government, having executed their present king, turned their attention to the monarchs of the past and all the royal tombs at St Denis were broken into. The bodies were exhumed, thrown with deliberate carelessness into a ditch dug on the north side of the church, and covered in lime. Louis's grave did not escape the desecration, but before it was disposed of his body became the subject of a study by Alexandre Lenoir, an archaeologist and historian who made notes on what he discovered. Once the coffin was opened he found the corpse wrapped in cloth of gold; underneath it was still in the leather covering which had been sewn around the body shortly after death. Inside this the skeleton was well preserved, and Lenoir was able to confirm that Louis had indeed been small and slender as per contemporary descriptions. On the king's head was a simple diadem, and in his hand the remnants of a wooden sceptre, no doubt all that could be found of royal dignity in the rush to deal with his body far away from home. Lenoir was allowed to make a drawing of the corpse – a drawing which still exists and is now in the Louvre museum – but once this was complete Louis was taken away and tossed into the ditch along with his father, forty other kings, thirty-two queens and various other royal family members from throughout the ages. The only royal remains at St Denis to escape the desecration were those of Louis's son St Louis IX, whose bones had been carefully exhumed and transferred to a reliquary elsewhere upon his canonisation in 1297.

When the monarchy was eventually restored in France after the Revolution the 'Capetian ditch' was dug up once more, but the bodies and the bones it contained were so deteriorated and mixed together that it was impossible to tell who was who. They were all tumbled into four great coffins, black and embossed with fleurs-de-lys, which were placed in the crypt at St Denis. Plaques were erected around the crypt listing those reinterred; one of the names carved there is Louis VIII, the only indicator of his physical resting place.

* * *

Louis was a man of both extraordinary energy and extraordinary patience. He loved his wife and his family and respected his father, but he was not content to stay at home, sit still and let events take their course around him; he needed to be at the centre of the action, and if that action was martial then so much the better. He was never happier than when he was on campaign, but he was able to temper his knightly fervour with good sense and leadership. None of this is contested, but over the years these basic facts have become embroidered, particularly by two persistent misconceptions about Louis: first, that he was at loggerheads with his father for much of the time;

and, second, that he was sickly and suffered from ill-health throughout his life. Neither is true, or at least not to the extent previously thought.

In terms of any conflict with Philip Augustus, there was certainly no hint of this in public at the time, which naturally leads us to question whether Louis was genuinely content with his lot or whether he was putting on a very convincing mask. If the latter then he was an excellent actor indeed; it would be very difficult to keep a seething resentment hidden for so long – almost two decades from Louis reaching adulthood until the death of his father – and given how closely their lives were chronicled, we might expect to see some hint of discontent in at least one of the contemporary sources. But what we find, as we have seen, is the two men operating in tandem, Louis as Philip's 'very dear and faithful eldest son', Philip confirming the agreements Louis makes, Louis working on behalf of his father, and Louis retaining his father's advisers once he became king. They were dissimilar in character but they shared many of the same goals, even if they preferred to work towards them in different ways. Later writers have inferred that the often difficult positions in which Louis was placed by his father cannot possibly have been palatable to him, and that he therefore must have harboured a deep resentment, but it seems probable that Louis – devout and dutiful as well as skilled in combat – did not have the wild personal ambition of Henry the Young King or Richard the Lionheart which led them to rebel against their father, Henry II. Rather, he was content in his role as heir to the throne as it meant that he was able to undertake his favoured military activities with greater freedom, leaving the politics and the talking – at which he was less adept – to Philip.

With regard to stories of lifelong illness, we should note that if a myth is repeated often enough it appears to become a fact, and this is what has happened here: later commentators only mention it because earlier ones did, without explaining why. When we look at the actual evidence put forward for Louis's supposed ill-health, we find it distils itself into four elements: he was ill with a stomach complaint, possibly dysentery, when he was four years old; he was kept well guarded in the royal household when he was a child; he was small and thin; and he died of dysentery. All of these need to be examined more closely before any general pronouncement on his health is made.

In the late twelfth and early thirteenth centuries, childhood ailments were overwhelmingly common, and Louis's falling sick at one point does not necessarily imply a propensity for illness. Indeed, the opposite could be argued: at a time when large numbers of children died from such ailments, Louis survived, which implies he was robust enough to fight it off. There are no other mentions of sickness in his youth; his education and chivalric training do not appear to have been disrupted. And after the travails which had attended the wait for a male heir for the dynasty (both for Philip and for Louis VII before him) was it not natural that Louis should be well guarded as he was the only son, indeed the only child for most of his childhood? Louis was eleven by the time his half-sister Marie was born, and Philip Hurepel did not appear until Louis was thirteen, at which point his household of other youths was formed and his training became more serious.

The evidence that Louis was small and thin is irrefutable; however, this does not in and of itself point to ill-health – it is perfectly possible to be of slight stature while remaining healthy. His military exploits show that his size did not prevent him from participating fully in knightly life. It was of course those same military exploits that led to his death, but anyone could be struck down by illness in the unsanitary conditions of a medieval siege camp, and dysentery was a frequent cause of mortality. The death some years later from the same disease of Edward the Black Prince – also among the greatest warriors of his own age and the military son and long-time heir of a strategist father – is not generally used to demonstrate that he was weak or illness-prone. Nearer Louis's own time, Richard the Lionheart was ill to the point of death at Acre in 1191, and he eventually died of blood poisoning in a siege camp: historians do not tend to put this forward as evidence that he was sickly throughout his life.

And once again, there is no *contemporary* evidence of Louis being in continual ill-health. If he was then we might expect to find mention of it in the chronicles and other official records; perhaps the odd reference to a journey being delayed a day or two because Louis was not well enough to travel, or his absence from a meeting as he was not able to leave his bed, or a description of him struggling with the weight of his armour. But we do not. Instead we can use contemporary evidence to reconstruct an active life, that of a man full of energy who loved the knightly life of riding and fighting. We might even characterise Louis as restlessly driven: ever ready – too ready in some cases – to leap into his saddle and lead his men from the front. He had two great quests in his life, which were, firstly, the reduction of Plantagenet power and the corresponding increase in Capetian fortunes; and, secondly, the conquering of the heretical region of southern France. To these ends he exhibited a single-minded determination and a willingness not to be put off by setbacks, political, personal, military or otherwise.

Although perhaps not quite as intellectually gifted as his father, Louis demonstrated an interest in academic learning, particularly that of a religious nature, and he took the tenets of the contemporary Church to heart. He was, as we have seen, faithful to his wife; he was not given to drunkenness or gluttony; and although he dressed as a man of his rank, he was not ostentatious or flamboyant. He did not waste his time on display, hosting no grand feasts (other than the one following his coronation, which was to be expected) or tournaments.

Equally, he was not an ascetic and did not allow his faith to remove him from day-to-day life – he was all business, all of the time. Many of his motives for action stemmed from his religious faith but he was, unlike his son, never going to be considered a saint: he was too human in his tempers and too concerned with military matters. When in the summer of 1216 he was faced with the choice of submitting to and reconciling with the Church or continuing his quest for the English crown, the latter took priority.

In an age when the rages of other kings were well documented, Louis remained in control of himself – most of the time. It took some provocation for him to lose his temper: if we look at the occasions we have highlighted in these pages, we see that the common factor seems to be frustration, and particularly frustration that his opportunities for military advancement were being curtailed. He certainly lost his temper with the papal legate Guala at the Assembly of Melun in April 1216, when Guala did his best to prevent Louis from invading England; he became enraged outside Dover later that year when the siege was going nowhere and the situation was holding him up from making gains elsewhere. The viscount of Melun was the target of his ire in 1217 for not posting adequate guard when the fortified ship was destroyed, thus weakening Louis's position ahead of the ensuing combat; and Theobald of Champagne was on the receiving end of a tirade when he wanted to leave the siege of Avignon in 1226.

What is noticeable about these occasions is that none of them resulted in an atrocity: perhaps Louis could see that any rash action due to his anger could have long-lasting consequences and he was able to rein himself in accordingly. Conversely, those occasions when barbarity was committed by him or in his name appear to have been the result of a more cool-headed decision to punish or to make an example, rather than of a wild bout of temper. The towns of Flanders were burned in 1213 to send a message to the count who had betrayed his king; Sandwich was razed in 1217 both as a punishment for changing sides in the war and as a tactical manoeuvre so it could not aid the enemy; and the horrific, unjustifiable massacre at Marmande in 1219 was intended to spread terror in the region so that others might surrender without the need for battle. In committing these acts (or in allowing them to be committed in his name) Louis does not appear to best advantage, but he was behaving in a manner which would have been understood at the time.

It is difficult to offer a proper assessment of Louis's reign in France as a whole as it was so short. Given that he had more or less achieved one of his lifetime aims – the curtailment of Plantagenet influence – that he was making progress towards the other, the subduing of southern France, and that he left an enlarged and stable realm which survived inheritance by a minor, we can safely characterise his reign as good, if not yet great. Whether he might have gone on to achieve greatness had he lived longer, we will never know.

Louis was known in his own time as a fearless and just man; even those chroniclers who are hostile to him cannot find many grounds on which to criticise him on a personal level. And among those who are more sympathetic towards him the opinions are remarkably similar across the years. The only surviving manuscript of the work of Nicholas de Bray is, unfortunately, incomplete and so we do not know what he wrote about Louis after his death, but other epitaphs bear a resemblance to each other: the Minstrel of Reims says that 'this Louis was brave and hardy and combative and had the heart of a lion', while the *Life of Louis VIII* concludes that: 'During his lifetime King Louis was as brave as a lion towards his enemies, and marvellously peaceable towards the good.'

* * *

But, as the Minstrel of Reims continues in his narration of the aftermath of Louis's demise, let us now leave the dead in peace and speak of the living.

Blanche, in Paris in the autumn of 1226, had heard that Louis was on his way back from Languedoc, the southern campaign terminated for now; she was no doubt preparing to welcome him home when the dreadful news arrived. Her grief was extreme, worsened by the fact that she now found herself in a very difficult position both personally and politically. On a personal level the situation was catastrophic: she had lost her beloved husband, the man to whom she had been happily married for more than two-thirds of her life since she was twelve years old; she had seven young children (one of whom, baby Stephen, would die within months, compounding her grief) and was pregnant with an eighth who would never know his father. But more than this, her eldest son, the new king, was a minor, and this was a dangerous political situation in the thirteenth century. Once more the Minstrel of Reims is sympathetic to her plight: 'her children were small and she was a lone woman in a foreign country. She had to outwit a number of the great lords.' For the nobles of France were not all in agreement with Louis's deathbed decision that the queen mother was the best choice for regent, and trouble lay ahead. Blanche would need to have her wits and her courage about her in the weeks, months and years to come – she had no time to mourn her loss and could not allow her grief to overwhelm her.

At first glance it might seem a little odd that the regency was left to a woman when there were male relatives available. But there were good reasons for this and there was plenty of precedent: for example, we will recall that when Philip Augustus departed on his crusade in 1190 he left his mother, Queen Adela, in charge; Richard the Lionheart of England had also confided the rule of his kingdom to Eleanor of Aquitaine during his numerous absences from England.

The rule of a mother during a minority was also a well-established custom among the nobility of France: Blanche of Champagne had been in control of that county until her son Theobald came of age, and the current duke of Burgundy was the child Hugh IV, again under the tutelage and rule of his mother. On a more personal level, it was for obvious reasons not entirely safe to entrust the care of a boy king to a paternal male relative who might himself have a claim to the throne; a mother, on the other hand, could be relied upon to do her utmost in the cause of a son. Nobody could doubt that Blanche would devote herself wholeheartedly to the care and guidance of young Louis, and all was not black politically: 'foreign' she might have been, but as a member of the Castilian royal family she was above internal French rivalries; she was not allied to any of the great French houses and would therefore not be suspected of trying to favour one at the expense of the others.

Young Louis had not been crowned in the lifetime of his father, although this is not surprising given that he was only twelve: Louis VIII had evidently expected to live much longer, and (despite or perhaps because of his own experience) may have been intending to return to the tradition of crowning the junior king once his son was a little older. But the lack of prior coronation meant that it was all the more imperative that the crown should now be set firmly upon Louis IX's head, and that he should be anointed with the holy oil as the one true king of France. And so mother and son found themselves riding towards Reims very shortly after the funeral. On the way, young Louis was knighted at Soissons; if he was to be the first knight of the armies of France, as symbolised in part of the coronation ritual, he needed to have received the accolade himself, regardless of his youth.

The coronation took place as anticipated on 29 November 1226. There was no archbishop of Reims, as William de Joinville had died only a few weeks beforehand and the see was still vacant, so the ceremony was performed by the bishop of Soissons, assisted by Guérin, chancellor and bishop of Senlis. We may imagine Blanche's mixed feelings as she sat in the same throne in the same cathedral as she had done at the great moment of triumph only three years previously, but this time at the side of her son rather than her husband. Once Louis had been crowned, the nobles swore oaths of allegiance not only to him but also to Blanche as regent, thus publicly recognising her position.

Notable by their absence from the coronation were three great lords who were to stir up much strife during the next few years. The names of two of them could have been predicted; the other came as something of a shock.

Theobald, count of Champagne, was the first. It is probable that he was banned from attending the ceremony on Blanche's orders, either because of rumours still circulating about his suspected poisoning of Louis, or (more likely) due to his undoubted desertion of the army while the king was still in the field at Avignon, which the widowed queen could not forgive. The second was Hugh de Lusignan, count of La Marche and Angoulême, who, perhaps sensing a chance for gain, had lived up to his reputation as a man of loose loyalties and had thrown in his lot with Theobald. But it was the third absentee who was the surprise, the major blow to the grieving queen: Peter de Dreux, the duke of Brittany.

Peter had been one of Louis's closest companions since their boyhood; he had ridden with him on numerous campaigns, including to England, and had risked his own and his brother's life for the royal cause at Nantes in 1214. As the younger son of the count of Dreux his expectations may not have been high originally, but his loyalty had seen him rise via his marriage to become one of the most powerful noblemen in France. Alas for Blanche and young Louis, it would appear that his ambition did not stop there. The dukedom of Brittany, previously held by members of the Plantagenet family, had long been associated with the earldom of Richmond in England, and Peter had entered into discussions with Henry III about the possibility of paying homage to him (thus effectively returning Brittany to English overlordship and removing it from French territory, which could have serious ramifications) in order to gain that title and its lands. Indeed, he may well have started these negotiations while Louis VIII was still alive, going behind the back of his king and liege lord. In an age which valued brotherhood-in-arms and chivalric companion-ship, this duplicity is all the more shocking. Louis's distress and anger, had he found out about this betrayal by his lifelong friend, would have been terrible.

Peter now joined Theobald and Hugh, and they were instru-mental in fomenting resistance to Blanche's regency and even to young Louis's kingship in the name of Philip Hurepel, the new king's twenty-six-year-old uncle who had been overlooked as regent. This was potentially dangerous: as the complex recent situations in England and the Holy Roman Empire had demonstrated, the claims of an adult male if he had enough resources to back him up could push aside those of a woman or child who had a better blood claim. In this case it appears that although banners were being raised in the name of Philip Hurepel, he was not actually the instigator of any revolt and did not press a claim to the throne himself. If he had done, it is difficult to see what he might have achieved: Philip Augustus's bigamous marriage to Philip Hurepel's mother meant that there were always going to be questions over his legitimacy, and this was France, not England – the Capetian dynasty was by now so well established that there was no real challenge to the idea that the eldest son of the previous king should inherit the throne.

Over the next seven years Blanche – who, as one modern histo-rian has opined, could really be classed among the kings of France rather than the queens – and her son Louis IX rode at the head of their loyal forces to subdue various uprisings from the rebels and their backers across the Channel. They were supported by the other nobles of France, including Robert III, count of Dreux, the last of Louis's boyhood companions, who had no hesitation in declaring for his king against his brother Peter. Simultaneously Blanche dealt with the remainder of the Cathar question: in 1229 she set her seal to the Treaty of Paris which officially ended the Albigensian crusade after Raymond VII of Toulouse submitted unconditionally to her and to the Church.

Any lingering resistance in the name of Philip Hurepel came to an end in 1234 when he was killed, accidentally, in a tournament. In the same year Theobald of Champagne became king of Navarre and so lost interest in internal conflicts in France; Peter de Dreux, the main instigator of the rebellion, realised his cause was hopeless, and he submitted to Blanche, offered up a number of his castles in recompense, and took a vow to go on crusade to the Holy Land. Blanche had triumphed over the enemies of her son, those supposed friends who had betrayed her husband's memory.

The regency was a success. Louis VIII's legacy in France had been to leave his realm in a strong position politically, administratively, militarily and financially, and to leave his dynasty in uncontested possession of the crown, despite the precarious circumstances. The sudden death of a king from dysentery, leaving a minor as his heir, had far less catastrophic consequences for France in 1226 than it had done for England a decade earlier.

Louis IX was declared of full age in April 1235, when he turned twenty-one; at this stage he took over personal rule, though he still relied on his mother for advice, and indeed left her as regent again when he went on crusade to the east. Blanche never remarried; she died in 1252 at the age of sixty-four and was buried at Maubuisson

Abbey, so her remains escaped the desecration of St Denis in 1793. Louis IX ruled peacefully and justly until 1270 and passed the throne safely to Philip III, the eldest surviving son of his eleven children by his queen, Margaret of Provence. Philip in turn would be succeeded by his own eldest son, and the Capetian dynasty continued its direct father–son line into the fourteenth century.

* * *

In England, meanwhile, the now-adult Henry III and his advisers had been keeping a close eye on developments across the Channel, hoping to regain both the lands conquered by Louis in 1224 and those lost to Philip Augustus before that. France under its warrior king Louis VIII was just too powerful for any meaningful attempt to be made, but Henry took advantage of Louis IX's minority and the support of Peter de Dreux to mount an invasion in 1230; it was easily repelled by Blanche's forces. A further attempt in 1242 was similarly unsuccessful, Louis IX by now at the head of his own army. Henry, who had grown into a devout man, came to recognise the piety and saintliness which Louis demonstrated during his life and reign, and the two of them – of a similar age and aided by their marriages to two sisters, Margaret and Eleanor of Provence – ended up enjoying a relatively cordial relationship.

Louis VIII's legacy to the English in France was thus the difficulty they found in trying to regain any lands there: thanks to his conquest of La Rochelle and the Poitou region, the English held no port further north than Bordeaux, which meant that any attempted landing on French soil involved a long sea journey along the French Atlantic coast and then, potentially, a hard march through well-defended French lands.

And what of Louis's legacy in England? He had, after all, come very close to emulating the feat of William the Conqueror. However, despite initial success he did not replicate William's final victory and his campaign was ultimately in vain. The Barnwell annalist, a sober monastic chronicler, puts it down simply to the fact that God was not on Louis's side, for how else could he have failed after gaining so much support and controlling such a large proportion of the country? Before sceptical readers dismiss this out of hand we should note that the effect of Louis's excommunication – the proof, to many contemporaries, that God did not support his cause – may have had a more substantial effect on morale than might seem thinkable now; added to this was the possibility that the papacy might step in to a greater extent to defend England (its own fief) if necessary. It would be difficult indeed for Louis to win a throne with the spiritual might and the practical resources of the papacy arrayed against him. Louis's status outside the Church contrasted with his opponents' positioning as crusaders against him, enjoying the support of the papal legate Guala (who had a violent antipathy to Louis); they could feel buoyant and confident that God was supporting them.

The opposition of the papacy may also have been a factor in Philip Augustus's decision not to support Louis overtly, therefore denying him the resources of the French crown. This certainly influenced the course of the war: had Louis been able to flood England with troops called up in the name of the French king, or had he been in possession of the substantial funds he needed to hire additional mercenaries, he might have had sufficient resource and momentum to tip the balance irrevocably his way. As it was, the lack of money and men meant that he had to leave England for over a month at a pivotal point in the campaign in order to beg his father for more. If this had resulted in immediate gain then the benefits of this tactic might have outweighed the disadvantages, but of course as it transpired he suffered the double blow of leaving the French court empty-handed *and* returning to England to find that William Marshal had broken the truce in the meantime and that many of his supporters had defected. Louis was thus forced to spend the next few months playing catch-up in order to regain his previous favourable position, and by the time the ever-loyal Blanche's reinforcements set out it was too little, too late, and the Henrician army had had time to prepare to repel them at sea.

One major factor in the campaign about which Louis could do nothing was the death of John, which as we have seen changed the complexion of the war considerably. Louis's portrayal by Guala and William Marshal as the foreign invader come to disinherit a blameless young boy, as opposed to the Christian prince invited by the barons to overthrow the tyrant John, provided a number of the war's waverers with the excuse to change sides and grab at the bait dangled by Marshal. The self-interest of the barons was of course another variable in Louis's equation; many of them were simply out for what they could get, swapping their allegiances back and forth whenever one side was in the ascendant. Even those English barons who supported Louis all through the war, such as Robert Fitzwalter and Saer de Quincy, had invited Louis to take the throne more because their own interests would be better served by having him on the throne than John, than out of any sense of personal loyalty to him.

But, however much Louis might have felt that some events were out of his hands, he would have known that all military leaders were liable to face unexpected setbacks, and that they needed to deal with them as they arose. What of those factors which *were* under his control? Could he have done anything differently which would have ensured his ultimate success? In Louis's favour was the fact that he was able to subdue so many castles in such a short space of time; his siege tactics proved effective over and over again and this gave momentum to his campaign. He was a whirlwind, taking the initiative and not sitting back and waiting for events to unfold: his personal presence gave heart to his men, with enemies retreating when they knew or even suspected that he was on his way at the head of his troops. But he could not be everywhere at once, and he needed to deploy his stretched resources to best effect – and this is where things went wrong.

Louis's forces, even without him, should have taken the decision to attack the oncoming army on the open ground outside Lincoln. Of course we cannot be completely sure of what Louis might have done had he been there in person, but his previous experience suggests, firstly, that he would not have made the elementary mistake of the young count of Perche in miscounting the enemy; and, secondly, that he would have been more inclined to opt for direct action. Although pitched battles were generally avoided by thirteenth-century commanders, in this particular case opting to fight outside the walls of the city would have been the more sensible option, and a more experienced leader might have chosen this course of action instead of staying within the walls with the attendant risk of becoming trapped in the narrow streets – something which had nearly cost Louis his own life at Bailleul in 1213 as the town burned around him. This personal experience would certainly have been a factor in any decision he might have made. But however we might speculate on this point, what remains indisputable is that if Louis had been present in person at Lincoln in May 1217 then his forces would have benefited from having one clear leader in command rather than a committee; this would have simplified matters considerably. However, as we have seen, Louis was not there: he was at Dover with the other half of his army.

Some historians have pointed to this division of his forces in May 1217, when he sent some north to Mountsorrel (from where they subsequently moved to Lincoln) and took the rest south to Dover, to be the decisive factor in the whole war; conventional wisdom says this is not a good tactic. But splitting his army had worked for Louis before, for example when he left part of it in London while he blazed a trail south and west to take Winchester – not to mention the division of forces in France in 1214 which led to success at La-Roche-aux-Moines and Bouvines – and he did not really have any choice. If he had committed all his forces northwards he could have lost his gains in the south, including any headway he had made at Dover. But if he had committed everything to Dover, the Henricians could have mustered unmolested further north and then marched to surround him. Even with the benefit of hindsight, if he were in the same situation again he would probably be forced to act in the same way.

Louis's greatest military error was his failure to capture Dover Castle, for having the huge fortress in enemy hands was a twofold problem. Firstly, it meant that the English had a stronghold from which they could launch attacks, meaning he had to deploy a substantial part of his resource to keep an eye on it. This would be the case with any major stronghold, but Dover's particular position caused a second difficulty in that it also commanded the Channel – which stopped Louis from bringing in reinforcements easily, which was what he needed to do in order to break through and end the siege, thus putting him in a vicious circle from which he could not escape.

But Louis's biggest mistake of all was not military. He was a fine leader of men and armies, and his military strategy was as good as it could have been given his situation and the resources available to him. He was, however, slightly less adept at politics and his greatest error was political: his failure to act on his proclamation as king and to get a crown put on his head in June 1216 when he first arrived in London and when it was there for the taking. He did not organise a coronation because of good reasons, or at least reasons which seemed good at the time: there was no archbishop of Canterbury, he could not use Westminster Abbey, and he was excommunicate. But under the circumstances half a coronation would have been better than none: it would have given him at least some legitimacy and enabled him and his supporters to position themselves differently. The Henricians, rather than fighting to repel an invader, would have been trying to depose a crowned and anointed monarch, a very different situation and one that had worked out well for King Stephen some eighty years previously. If Louis was going to be the sort of king who remained a few political and strategic steps ahead of the game (as his father had always done), he ought to have been able to foresee the consequences of his non-coronation and to act accordingly. As we noted in Chapter 4, this failure to do so may also indicate a hint of arrogance, for Louis evidently did not believe that his campaign was going to fail.

Louis's delicacy over the specific requirements of the coronation was not mirrored by William Marshal and his colleagues: they voiced no qualms about the legitimacy of the ceremony when they had Henry 'crowned' in October 1216 – not at Westminster, not by the archbishop of Canterbury, and not even with an actual crown. Later on they were to recognise that a more valid coronation was necessary, which was why Henry was crowned for a second time, in London in 1220. But the original ceremony served its purpose by giving Henry more of an official right to the throne than Louis; this proved to be a decisive factor in the war.

* * *

The English line of succession in the twelfth and thirteenth centuries was by no means clear; in the 150 years preceding Louis's invasion, starting with the death of Edward the Confessor in 1066, the English throne had been passed undisputed from father to eldest son only once, when Henry II was succeeded by Richard I in 1189. With no recent tradition of smooth transition, the backdrop to Louis's

campaign was that the throne could be claimed not only by hereditary right, but also by election or conquest – and he could make a
case on all three grounds, albeit that the most prominent blood claim
was Blanche's, his own descent from William the Conqueror being
overlooked. But a man's claim to rule territories in right of his wife
was a concept which was widely accepted at the level of the peerage
in both England and France, where earldoms and dukedoms were
held in this way. Louis's position should have been further strengthened when John died, as Henry III, being nine years old, could have
been deemed unfit to rule.

The closest parallel in terms of previous succession disputes is
that of Stephen and Matilda in the 1130s. As the only surviving
legitimate child and therefore heir of the previous monarch, Henry I,
Matilda's claim should in theory have taken precedence, but she was
deemed unfit to rule by some of her nobles on the grounds of her sex.
Stephen, with only a tenuous blood claim – made even more fragile
by the fact that he was not even the eldest son in his own family –
sailed from France, gained the support of the nobles and was
proclaimed king. Stephen got round his lack of hereditary right by
saying that he was the grandson (in the female line) of a great king
from the past, and that he could claim the throne by right of election
ahead of the closest blood heir.

On the grounds of becoming king of England by election, Louis
had a reasonable case; he was, after all, invited to take the throne by
representatives of the nobility, and he was openly welcomed and
proclaimed king when he arrived in the country. However, this was
not enough to secure his position, for he did not do what Stephen
had done within days of landing on English soil: he was not crowned
or anointed. In the thirteenth century it was the coronation ceremony that effected the transformation from man (or, in rare cases,
woman) to monarch. The crown was the all-important symbol of

kingship; the anointing with oil the sign of God's favour – hence the significance of the Capetians crowning their sons in their own lifetimes to demonstrate the validity and sacred nature of their dynasty, and the rush to hold a coronation, any sort of coronation, for Henry III.

The ritual outweighed all other factors such as conquest, primogeniture, heredity and election. If conquest and *de facto* control of the realm were all that were required, why would William I have bothered to have himself crowned? If primogeniture had been the paramount concern in the transmission of the crown then William would have been succeeded by his eldest son, Robert Curthose, and then by Robert's son William Clito; the coronation of Robert's younger brother William II put paid to this. If hereditary right was the principal criterion then Henry I would have been succeeded by his daughter Matilda, not his nephew Stephen; but Stephen's coronation made all the difference as it made him a king, and this could not be undone. Louis, as we have seen, could make quite a decent case for himself via the right of election, but this was not enough on its own: he might *claim* the throne by election, but he could only *succeed* to it by coronation.

Louis himself was aware of this distinction. While he was in England he assumed the right to distribute lands and castles as he saw fit, but he did not style himself 'king of England' – he referred to himself as the 'eldest son of the lord king of France'. There was recent precedent for similar nomenclature in John's actions: John technically claimed the throne of England as of 6 April 1199, the date of his brother Richard's death, but he was not crowned until the feast of the Ascension on 27 May. During the intervening seven weeks he issued charters which referred to him as *dominus Angliae*, that is, 'lord of England'; he did not change his style to *rex Angliae*, 'king of England', until after his coronation. In the early thirteenth century regnal years were counted from the day of a king's coronation, not from the date of the death of his predecessor, as that was the day he became king. There was no sense, as there would be later, of monarchy transmitting itself instantly ('the king is dead; long live the king') – instead the death of one king meant an interregnum until the coronation of his successor. The two examples of monarchs of England or Britain who are recognised officially but who were never crowned (Edward V and Edward VIII) date from the fifteenth and twentieth centuries when the principle of the transmission of monarchy was different. In the thirteenth century the coronation was paramount, and this is why Louis is not, and never has been, styled King Louis I of England.

* * *

Although Louis never succeeded in becoming the official king of England, he had a much greater influence on English history than he is generally given credit for. His story therefore needs to be included in the narrative of the development of England and its government in the Middle Ages, which too often moves in a deceptively smooth manner from John and Magna Carta to Henry III without examining the reasons for, or the background of, the transition.

Louis did not do all that much wrong during his campaign. His main problems were that he, personally, was the driving force behind his victories; that his absence was a significant factor in his defeats; that he could not be in more than one place at once; and that he was a better warrior than politician. Thus his quest for the throne of England was ultimately unsuccessful, but he did leave an important legacy in the form of a new and different constitutional situation. His campaign resulted in an increased Church influence over England for some time: the legates Guala and Pandulf both wielded great powers in the name of the pope. There is also an argument to be made that Louis's invasion permanently weakened royal power in England, as it (and the ongoing threat that he might relaunch it, given the chance) meant that Henry III swore to uphold Magna Carta so that he could retain the support of his barons.

Let us not forget just how startling this was. Sealed by Guala and William Marshal, the reissuing of the charter meant that the legate was supporting on behalf of the papacy the very cause which Pope Innocent III had annulled in such strong language ('shameful and base ... illegal and unjust ... we utterly reject and condemn this settlement ... null and void of all validity for ever') as soon as he heard of it; and also that the regent – and by extension the king – was voluntarily promising to uphold an agreement which his predecessor had gone to war to avoid just two years earlier. This would not have happened had it not been for Louis and his intervention in English affairs. Had Louis not invaded, it is likely that the baronial rebellion would have been crushed; Magna Carta might well have been annulled and forgotten, relegated to a footnote in history as the monarchy forged ahead unabated and unanswerable to the law. Louis's part in tempering royal authority therefore left a legacy to the English which is still being felt to this day.

CHRONOLOGY

1187 5 Sep	Birth of Louis in Paris; he is heir to the throne from birth.
1188 4 Mar	Birth of Blanche of Castile.
1190 Mar	Birth and death of twin brothers to Louis; death of his mother, Queen Isabelle.
1191 Jul	Health crisis for Louis who is suffering from dysentery; the clergy and people of Paris pray for his safe recovery.
1193 14 Aug	Marriage of Philip Augustus to Ingeborg of Denmark. He repudiates her the day after the wedding.
1193 5 Nov	Philip Augustus's marriage to Ingeborg is annulled.
1196 1 Jun	'Marriage' of Philip Augustus to Agnes of Merania, which is not recognised by the pope.
1198	Birth of Marie, half-sister to Louis.

1199
6 Apr
Richard the Lionheart dies. This interrupts the marriage negotiations in which Philip Augustus is engaging on behalf of Louis.

1200
26 Jan
The papal Interdict comes into force in France, having been proclaimed in December 1199.

1200
22 May
Treaty of Le Goulet between Philip Augustus and King John. Philip Augustus accepts John's offer of a dowry for Blanche; he also recognises John's claim to the English throne, abandoning his support of Arthur of Brittany.

1200
23 May
Marriage of Louis to Blanche of Castile. Due to the Interdict in France the marriage takes place in Normandy.

1200
Birth of Philip Hurepel, half-brother to Louis.

1200
31 Oct
Pope Innocent lifts the Interdict on France.

1201
Jul
Death of Agnes, 'wife' to Philip Augustus.

1201
Pope Innocent III legitimises Philip Augustus's children by Agnes, Marie and Philip Hurepel.

1203–4
Philip Augustus's campaign in Normandy, which he takes from John.

1205
Birth and death of a daughter to Louis and Blanche.

1206
Louis is present in Philip Augustus's army on campaign in Brittany.

1209
17 May
Louis is knighted at Compiègne during the feast of Pentecost.

1209
9 Sep
Birth of Philip, son and heir to Louis and Blanche.

1212
25 Feb
Treaty of Lens between Louis and Count Ferrand of Flanders. The treaty is recognised by Philip Augustus.

1212 Nov	Louis takes Philip Augustus's place at a meeting with Frederick of Hohenstaufen and a treaty is agreed.
1213 Jan	English prelates returning from Rome pronounce a papal sentence deposing King John and proposing a crusade against him.
1213 26 Jan	Birth of twins (possibly Alfonso and John), sons to Louis and Blanche. They die shortly after birth.
1213 Feb	Louis takes the cross for the crusade against the Cathars in the south. His expedition is delayed until 1215.
1213 8 Apr	Assembly of nobles and barons at Soissons. Philip Augustus engages his nobles for the projected expedition to England and declares he will confer the crown on Louis (with conditions).
1213 spring	Philip Augustus reinstates Ingeborg as queen, thus clearing last hurdle to papal reconciliation. He does not take her back as his wife.
1213 May	Philip and Louis gather their fleet for the invasion of England.
1213 22 May	Innocent cancels the invasion and threatens Philip Augustus with excommunication if he goes ahead with it. Philip Augustus agrees. Louis turns his attentions to Flanders instead.
1213 30 May	The earl of Salisbury attacks and destroys the French invasion fleet as it lies at anchor at Damme.
1213 Jun	Philip Augustus returns to Paris, leaving Louis in charge of the army in Flanders. Louis makes a brief trip to Paris in August but otherwise remains in Flanders several more months.
1213 autumn	Louis takes, pillages and burns a number of towns in Flanders.

1214 15 Feb	King John lands at La Rochelle.
1214 Feb/Mar	Ferrand of Flanders strikes a deal with John and they become allies. They go into coalition with Otto of Saxony.
1214 25 Apr	Birth of the future Louis IX, son to Louis and Blanche.
1214 spring	Philip Augustus and Louis leave Paris and head towards the Loire. Philip Augustus then turns northwards to deal with the situation there, leaving Louis in charge of operations in Poitou.
1214 25 May	Hugh IX de Lusignan betroths his son to John's daughter Joan. He and other Poitevin nobles join John.
1214 Jun	John makes an abortive attack on Nantes, then goes back along the Loire: he takes Ancenis on 11 June and Angers on 17 June.
1214 19 Jun	John begins a siege at La-Roche-aux-Moines.
1214 2 Jul	John hears Louis's army is a day's march away and flees. Louis pursues and defeats his forces at La-Roche-aux-Moines. Louis stays in the west until September 1214.
1214 27 Jul	Philip Augustus is victorious at Bouvines.
1214 18 Sep	Truce with John sealed at Chinon. Louis then returns to Paris.
1215 Apr	Louis sets off south on the expedition postponed from 1213. He meets Simon de Montfort at Vienne on 20 April. During a forty-day campaign the host takes Toulouse, then Louis returns to Paris.
1215 17 May	London opens its gates to the rebel barons in support of their cause.

1215
15 Jun

John seals Magna Carta.

1215
24 Aug

Innocent III rejects Magna Carta.

1215
Sep

John rescinds Magna Carta; Innocent excommunicates the rebel barons (though not specifically by name).

1215
autumn

English barons arrive in France to offer the throne to Louis.

1215
6 Dec

John takes Rochester Castle from the rebels.

1215
Dec

First 120 French knights cross the Channel and travel to London.

1215
16 Dec

Innocent excommunicates, by name this time, the rebel English barons.

1216
Jan

A fleet of approximately twenty ships travels to England carrying more supporters; John launches raids into northern counties.

1216
23–25
Apr

Assembly of Melun; Louis's arguments are put to the nobility of France and to the papal legate Guala.

1216
20 May

Louis sets sail from Calais for England.

1216
22 May

Louis lands in England on the Isle of Thanet.

1216
29 May

Louis and his followers are excommunicated by the papal legate Guala.

1216
2 Jun

Louis arrives in London, where he is welcomed and proclaimed king.

1216
7 Jun

Louis leaves London and embarks on a successful campaign in the south. He takes Winchester on 24 June.

1216 16 Jul	Death of Pope Innocent III; he is succeeded by Honorius III.
1216 July	Louis goes back to Dover. He starts a siege on 25 July.
1216 Aug	Homage of King Alexander of Scotland to Louis.
1216 Sep	Birth of Robert, son to Louis and Blanche.
1216 18–19 Oct	Death of King John of England.
1216 28 Oct	First coronation of Henry III, at Gloucester.
1216 25 Dec	A truce is agreed between Louis and William Marshal, from 25 December 1216 until 13 January 1217. Later the truce is extended to 16 April 1217.
1217 Feb–Mar	Louis goes back to France to ask his father for reinforcements. While he is away, the earls of Salisbury, Arundel and Warenne desert him for Henry, and William Marshal breaks the truce.
1217 22 Apr	Louis leaves Calais to go back to England; he arrives at Sandwich.
1217 23 Apr	On hearing news of other castles under siege, Louis makes a truce with Hubert de Burgh at Dover; he leaves Dover that evening and divides his army in two.
1217 3 May	Louis enters London; he leaves again on 12 May to go back to Dover. A fleet bringing help is prevented from landing.
1217 20 May	Battle of Lincoln; news of the defeat reaches Louis five days later.
1217 29 May	Another fleet arrives but does not bring many knights. Louis leaves for London, reaching it at the beginning of June.

1217
12 Jun   Representatives of Louis and William Marshal meet four prelates nominated by the pope to try and negotiate a peace. Guala exempts some clergy from the peace and Louis refuses the treaty.

1217
late Jun   Louis writes to Philip Augustus and to Blanche. Philip Augustus is reluctant to help; Blanche faces up to him and gets some money from the royal treasury. She raises troops in Artois.

1217
20 Aug   A new fleet leaves Calais. It gets near to Dover but is then blown back to France by a storm. It sets off again, arriving on the night of 23–24 August.

1217
24 Aug   Battle of Sandwich; Louis's fleet of reinforcements is defeated.

1217
26 Aug   Louis, in London, hears of the defeat at Sandwich.

1217
5 Sep   Louis meets William Marshal on an island in the Thames to agree terms. Several days of negotiation follow.

1217
11 Sep   Treaty of Lambeth ratifies the peace agreement. Among other conditions Louis is offered 10,000 marks of silver to leave.

1217
18 Sep   Peace is sworn at Merton by Louis, William Marshal, Isabelle of Angoulême and others.

1217
28 Sep   Louis leaves England.

1218
13 Jan   Pope Honorius lifts the excommunication on Louis and his followers.

1218
11 Aug   Pope Honorius asks Philip Augustus to help Amaury de Montfort in his crusade in Languedoc.

1218
20 Nov   Louis takes the cross, promising to fight the Albigensian heretics.

1218 Jun	Death of Philip, eldest son of Louis and Blanche. Their next surviving son, Louis, becomes heir.
1219 15 May	Honorius repeats his request to Philip Augustus for help with the Albigensian crusade. Philip Augustus does not want to go in person; Louis goes in his stead.
1219 May–Jun	Louis's army takes Marmande. Massacre of the population afterwards.
1219 16 Jun	Louis's expedition arrives at Toulouse and prepares for a siege. Many of Louis's forces leave after their forty days' service. Guérin heads back to Paris on 1 August.
1219 21 Jun	Birth of John, son to Louis and Blanche.
1220 11 Nov	Birth of Alfonso, son to Louis and Blanche.
1222 20 Feb	Birth of Philip-Dagobert, son to Louis and Blanche.
1222 Sep	Philip Augustus starts suffering bouts of a violent fever.
1223 6 Jul	Bishops in Paris are discussing the Albigensian question.
1223 13 Jul	Philip Augustus, who is at Pacy-sur-Eure, decides to try and travel to Paris for the discussions.
1223 14 Jul	Philip Augustus has to stop at Mantes after he is struck by another bout of fever. Death of Philip Augustus and accession to the throne of Louis as Louis VIII.
1223 30 Jul	Louis and Blanche leave Paris for Reims. They pass through Beauvais, Saint-Just-en-Chausée, Soissons, and arrive at Reims on 5 August.
1223 6 Aug	Coronation of Louis and Blanche in the cathedral at Reims.

1223 8 Aug	Louis and Blanche go back to Paris, where there are great celebrations for eight days.
1223 Sep	Louis and Blanche set off on a tour of his lands in Normandy, Anjou and Maine.
1223 Nov	A further trip for Louis and Blanche to Compiègne, Chauny, Saint-Quentin, Péronne, Arras.
1224 Mar	Birth of Isabelle, daughter to Louis and Blanche.
1224 Jul	Louis arrives at La Rochelle to campaign against the English. The siege begins on 15 July; La Rochelle surrenders on 3 August.
1224 24 Aug	Louis arrives in Poitiers and accepts submissions.
1224 Sep	Louis arrives back in Paris and is welcomed enthusiastically.
1225 27 Dec	Birth of Stephen, son to Louis and Blanche.
1226 28 Jan	Assembly at Paris, at which the excommunication of Raymond, count of Toulouse, is upheld; his lands are conferred on Amaury de Montfort, who cedes his rights to Louis.
1226 Easter	Louis's army assembles at Bourges and marches south along the Rhône valley.
1226 Jun–Sep	Siege of Avignon by Louis and his forces.
1226 8 Nov	Death of Louis from dysentery at the castle at Montpensier, Auvergne. He is later buried in the Basilica of Saint Denis in Paris. Blanche is pregnant with their youngest son, Charles, who will be born posthumously. Louis's eldest surviving son succeeds to the throne as Louis IX.

A NOTE ON SOURCES

Primary sources

The primary sources that have been consulted for this book were, of course, originally handwritten manuscripts composed variously in Latin, Old French (or the Anglo-Norman dialect thereof) or Occitan. Modern historians and writers are indebted to the great scholars of the nineteenth century who transcribed, edited and published these works so they could be appreciated by a wider audience; in recent years many of the texts have also been made freely available on the internet.

The principal series which contains the works dealing with French history is the *Recueil des historiens des Gaules et de la France* which initially ran to twenty-four volumes published in Paris between 1738 and 1865; a second series of another twenty-four volumes then followed between 1869 and 1904. The works of Rigord, William the Breton and Nicholas de Bray are all available both in their original Latin and in French translation in this series, which also includes the Latin-only *Ex Chronico Turonensi* (*Chronicle of Tours*) and the Old

French *Chronique des rois de France* (*Chronicle of the Kings of France*) by the Anonymous of Béthune. The entire *Recueil des historiens des Gaules et de la France* series can be freely consulted on the website http://gallica.bnf.fr/ hosted by the Bibliothèque nationale de France. The Anonymous of Béthune's other work, the *Histoire des ducs de Normandie et des rois d'Angleterre* (*History of the Dukes of Normandy and the Kings of England*), is available in its original Old French in a printed volume of 1840 and on the https://archive.org/ website. It is perhaps due a new edition, as is the anonymous *Vie de Louis VIII* (*Life of Louis VIII*; 1825) and the *Récits d'un ménestrel de Reims* (*Tales of a Minstrel of Reims*), also in Old French and also in printed form only, in a volume published in 1876. A rather melodramatic and not terribly reliable translation of the Minstrel's text can be found in Edward Noble Stone's 1939 *Three Old French Chronicles of the Crusades*; this gives a flavour of the Minstrel's writing, but for the purposes of the present volume I have carried out my own translations of his work. Other translations in this book are from the published English versions of works, where available, and my own where not, except for the long quote from the *Chronicle of Tours* in Chapter 9 assessing Philip Augustus and his life and reign, which appears in John Baldwin's book *Paris, 1200*.

The works relating to the Albigensian crusade are more widely available in modern printed editions; *La Chanson de la croisade albigeoise*, by William of Tudela and an anonymous continuer, is available in the original Occitan with a facing-page translation into modern French (1989), and also as *The Song of the Cathar Wars* in English (1996); Peter of Les-Vaux-de-Cernay's Latin *Historia albigensis* is available in both French (1951) and English (1998) translations, the latter entitled *The History of the Albigensian Crusade*.

The major series which collates the medieval historical writing of England is the Rolls Series, which comprises ninety-nine works in

253 volumes published between 1858 and 1911. The complete works or *Opera* of Gerald of Wales, the *Chronica Majora* of Matthew Paris, the *Flores Historiarum* of Roger of Wendover, and the monastic chronicles of Ralph of Coggeshall and the Barnwell, Dunstable and Waverley annalists are all in this series, although in Latin only. Roger of Wendover's work has been translated into English as *Flowers of History* and can be consulted on the https://archive.org/ website; a selection of the *Chronicles of Matthew Paris* (1986) is available in English, as are some of Gerald of Wales's texts, including the one which has been quoted in this book, *De principis instructione* or *On the Instruction of a Prince*, originally translated in 1858 as *On the Instruction of Princes* (reprinted 1991).

For many years the only available edition of the biography of William Marshal was Paul Meyer's three-volume *L'Histoire de Guillaume le Maréchal* (1891–1901) in the original Old French; this was superseded by the superb *History of William Marshal* of A. J. Holden, S. Gregory and D. Crouch (2002–6), also in three volumes, which includes both the original text and a facing-page translation into English, thus making the work more accessible to a much wider audience.

All of these primary sources, plus others consulted, are listed in the Bibliography. Further details on the English texts and their authors can also be found in Antonia Gransden's *Historical Writing in England*, vol. 1: *c.550–c.1307* (1974).

Secondary sources

No work on Louis could possibly be complete without owing a great debt to the French medievalist and scholar Charles Petit-Dutaillis, whose monumental *Étude sur la vie et le règne de Louis VIII 1187–1226* (1894) contains a list of all Louis's official acts as king and a complete itinerary of where he was during every month of his reign, as well as a myriad of detail about his life and government. Two more recent biographies also written in French are Gérard Sivéry's *Louis VIII le lion* (1995) and Ivan Gobry's *Louis VIII, fils de Philippe II, 1223–1226* (2009). The fact that the title of the latter needs to sign-post that Louis was Philip's son is indicative of the way his reign has been overshadowed in historical writing; the implication is that even the French public might not know who he was without the hint.

Most of Louis's life was lived during his father's reign, so biographies of Philip and works dealing with his era are very useful sources of information, although the details on Louis tend to be hidden in the background and need careful attention. I have found Jim Bradbury's *Philip Augustus* (1998) very valuable in this regard, and John Baldwin's immense *The Government of Philip Augustus* (1986) has been a constant companion. Equally, information on Louis can be gleaned from the early sections of the many available biographies of Louis IX; Jacques LeGoff's *Saint Louis* (2009) is the definitive text here. Louis VIII remains one of the few medieval kings to have a wife who has been the subject of more biographies than he has; I was able to gain many insights into their relationship from Philippe Delorme's *Blanche de Castille* (2002).

The Albigensian crusade is mentioned in passing in many books on the crusades generally, but the classic dedicated work is Zoe Oldenbourg's *Le Bûcher de Montségur* (1959), available in English translation as *Massacre at Montségur* (1961, 1998). More recent titles include Mark Pegg's *A Most Holy War: The Albigensian Crusade and the Battle for Christendom* (2008) and Sean McGlynn's *'Kill Them All!' Cathars and Carnage in the Albigensian Crusade* (2015).

There is a wealth of material available on the early thirteenth century in England. W. L. Warren's *King John*, in the Yale English Monarchs series (1961, 1997), remains among the most in-depth biographies of Louis's opponent, joined by those written by Ralph Turner (1994) and Stephen Church (2015) and Church's edited volume *King John: New Interpretations* (1999). Magna Carta is equally well documented, James Holt's seminal 1965/1992 volume being joined more recently by Nicholas Vincent's *Magna Carta: A Very Short Introduction* (2012) and David Carpenter's *Magna Carta* (2015), which looks set to become the definitive work on the subject. Carpenter's *The Minority of Henry III* (1990) is invaluable for information on Louis's invasion and on his later conflict with Henry's forces in France; Holt's *The Northerners: A Study in the Reign of King John* (1961) provides indispensable information on the barons and their reasons for rebelling; and, finally, McGlynn's detailed and thorough *Blood Cries Afar: The Forgotten Invasion of England 1216* (2011) is the first and so far only book dedicated solely to Louis's campaign.

Full publication details of these and all other works consulted may be found in the Bibliography.

BIBLIOGRAPHY

Primary sources

Anonymous of Béthune, *Histoire des ducs de Normandie et des rois d'Angleterre*, ed. F. Michel (Paris: 1840)

Anonymous of Béthune, *Chronique des rois de France*, in *Recueil des historiens des Gaules et de la France*, vol. 24, ed. L. Delisle (Paris: 1870)

Barnwell annalist, *Memoriale Walteri de Coventria*, ed. W. Stubbs, 2 vols (London: Longman, 1879–80)

La Chanson de la croisade albigeoise, ed. Henri Gougaud (Paris: Livres de Poche Lettres Gothiques, 1989)

Conon de Lausanne, *Cartulaire du Chapitre de Notre Dame de Lausanne*, ed. A. Jahn, F. Forel and F. de Gingins (Lausanne: Georges Bridel, 1851)

Delisle, L. (ed.), *Catalogue des actes de Philippe Auguste* (Paris: 1885)

Dunstable annalist, *Annals of Dunstable Priory*, in *Annales Monastici*, ed. H. Luard, 5 vols (London: Rolls Series, 1864–9), vol. 3

Epistolae Innocentii papae III, ed. J. P. Migne (Paris: 1855)

Ex Chronico Turonensi auctore anonyme S. Martini Turonensis canonico, in *Recueil des historiens des Gaules et de la France*, vol. 18, ed. Michel-Jean-Joseph Brial (Paris: 1822), pp. 290–322

Extraits d'un abrégé de l'histoire de France, in *Recueil des historiens des Gaules et de la France*, vol. 17, ed. Michel-Jean-Joseph Brial (Paris: 1818), pp. 428–32

Gerald of Wales, *Giraldi Cambrensis Opera*, ed. J. S. Brewer, J. F. Dimcock and G. F. Warner, 8 vols (London: Rolls Series, 1861–91)

Gerald of Wales, *Gerald of Wales: On the Instruction of Princes*, trans. Joseph Stevenson (London: Selleys, 1858; repr. Felinfach: Llanerch, 1991)

Gestes du roi Louis VIII, extraits des Grands Chroniques de France dites de Saint-Denis, in *Recueil des historiens des Gaules et de la France*, vol. 17, ed. Michel-Jean-Joseph Brial (Paris: 1818), pp. 417–21

Giles de Flagi, Prologue surviving from *Histoire de Philippe Auguste*, published by Paul Meyer, *Romania*, 6 (1877), 494–8

L'Histoire de Guillaume le Maréchal, ed. Paul Meyer, 3 vols (Paris: Renouard, 1891–1901)

The History of the Holy War: Ambroise's Estoire de la Guerre Sainte, ed. and trans. Marianne Ailes and Malcolm Barber, 2 vols (Woodbridge: Boydell, 2003)

History of William Marshal, ed. and trans. A. J. Holden, S. Gregory and D. Crouch, 3 vols (London: Anglo-Norman Text Society, 2002–6)

The Letters and Charters of Cardinal Guala Bicchieri, Papal Legate in England 1216–1218, ed. Nicholas Vincent (Woodbridge: Canterbury and York Society, 1996)

The Letters of Pope Innocent III (1198–1216) Concerning England and Wales, ed. C. R. Cheney and M. G. Cheney (Oxford: Oxford University Press, 1967)

The Life of Saint Hugh of Lincoln, ed. and trans. D. L. Douie and H. Farmer, 2 vols (Edinburgh: Nelson, 1962)

Matthew Paris, *Matthæi Parisiensis, Historia Anglorum*, ed. F. Maddern (London: Rolls Series, 1866–9)

Matthew Paris, *Matthæi Parisiensis, Monachi Sanctii Albani, Chronica Majora*, ed. H. R. Luard (London: Rolls Series, 1884–9)

Matthew Paris, *Chronicles of Matthew Paris*, ed. and trans. Richard Vaughan (Gloucester: Sutton, 1986)

Nicholas de Bray, *Gesta Ludovici VIII, Francorum Regis*, in *Recueil des historiens des Gaules et de la France*, vol. 17, ed. Michel-Jean-Joseph Brial (Paris: 1818), pp. 311–45

Nicholas de Bray, *Des faits et des gestes de Louis VIII*, in *Collection des mémoires relatifs à l'histoire de France*, ed. and trans. F. Guizot (Paris: Brière, 1825), pp. 385–463

Peter of Les-Vaux-de-Cernay (as Petrus Vallium Sarnaii), *Historia albigensis*, ed. and trans. Pascal Guébin and Henri Maisonneuve (Paris: Vrin, 1951)

Peter of Les-Vaux-de-Cernay, *The History of the Albigensian Crusade*, trans. W. A. and M. D. Sibly (Woodbridge: Boydell, 1998)

Philip Mousket, *Chronique rimée*, ed. Baron de Reiffenburg (Brussels: Academie Royale de Bruxelles, 1836)

Le Premier budget de la monarchie française. Le Compte général de 1202–1203, ed. Ferdinand Lot and Robert Fawtier (Paris: Bibliothèque de l'École des Hautes Études, 1932)

Pressutti, Petrus, *Regesta Honorii papae III* (Rome: 1888; repr. Hildesheim: Georg Olms, 1978)

Ralph of Coggeshall, *Radulphi de Coggeshall Chronicon Anglicanum*, ed. J. Stevenson (London: Rolls Series, 1875)

Récits d'un ménestrel de Reims, ed. Natalis de Wailly (Paris: Renouard, 1876)

Richard of Devizes, *The Chronicle of Richard of Devizes*, ed. and trans. John Tate Appleby (London: Nelson, 1963)

Rigord, *Vie de Philippe Auguste*, in *Collection des mémoires relatifs à l'histoire de France*, ed. and trans. F. Guizot (Paris: Brière, 1825), pp. 9–179

Rigord, *Gesta Philippi Augusti*, in *Oeuvres de Rigord et de Guillaume le Breton*, ed. H. F. Delaborde (Paris: Renouard, 1882), vol. 1

Rigord, *Histoire de Philippe Auguste*, ed. and trans. Elisabeth Carpentier, Georges Pon and Yves Chauvin, Sources d'Histoire Médiévale 33 (Paris: CNRS, 2006)

Roger of Hoveden, *The Annals of Roger of Hoveden*, trans. Henry T. Riley, 3 vols (London: 1853; repr. Felinfach: Llanerch, 1997)

Roger of Wendover, *Rogeri de Wendover liber qui dicitur Flores Historiarum*, ed. H. G. Hewlett (London: Rolls Series, 1886–7)

Roger of Wendover's Flowers of History, trans. J. A. Giles, 2 vols (London: Henry G. Bohn, 1849; repr. Felinfach: Llanerch, 1995–6)

The Romance of Eustace the Monk, in *Two Medieval Outlaws: Eustace the Monk and Fouke Fitz Waryn*, ed. and trans. Glyn Burgess (Woodbridge: Boydell, 1997)

The Sanctity of Louis IX: Early Lives of Saint Louis by Geoffrey of Beaulieu and William of Chartres, trans. Larry F. Field, ed. M. Cecilia Gaposchkin and Sean L. Field (Ithaca, NY: Cornell University Press, 2014)

The Song of the Cathar Wars: A History of the Albigensian Crusade, trans. Janet Shirley (Aldershot: Scolar Press, 1996)

Stone, Edward Noble, *Three Old French Chronicles of the Crusades* (Seattle: Washington State University Press, 1939)

Vie de Louis VIII, in *Collection des mémoires relatifs à l'histoire de France*, ed. and trans. F. Guizot (Paris: Brière, 1825), pp. 353–83

Waverley annalist, *Annals of Waverley Abbey*, in *Annales Monastici*, ed. H. Luard, 5 vols (London: Rolls Series, 1864–9), vol. 2

William the Breton, *Vie de Philippe-Auguste*, in *Collection des mémoires relatifs à l'histoire de France*, ed. and trans. F. Guizot (Paris: Brière, 1825), pp. 181–351

William the Breton, *Gesta Philippi Augusti*, in *Oeuvres de Rigord et de Guillaume le Breton*, ed. H. F. Delaborde (Paris: Renouard, 1882), vol. 1

William the Breton, *Philippide*, in *Oeuvres de Rigord et de Guillaume le Breton*, ed. H. F. Delaborde (Paris: Renouard, 1882), vol. 2

William of Puylaurens, *The Albigensian Crusade and its Aftermath*, ed. and trans. W. A. Sibly and M. D. Sibly (Woodbridge: Boydell, 2003)

Secondary sources

Allmand, Christopher, 'War and the Non-Combatant in the Middle Ages', in *Medieval Warfare: A History*, ed. Maurice Keen (Oxford: Oxford University Press, 1999), pp. 253–72

Allmand, Christopher, 'The Reporting of War in the Middle Ages', in *War and Society in Medieval and Early Modern Britain*, ed. Diana Dunn (Liverpool: Liverpool University Press, 2000), pp. 17–33

Asbridge, Thomas, *The Greatest Knight: The Remarkable Life of William Marshal, the Power behind Five English Thrones* (London: Simon & Schuster, 2015)

Audoin, Edouard, *Essai sur l'armée royale au temps de Philippe Auguste* (Paris: Champion, 1913)

Baldwin, John W., *The Government of Philip Augustus: Foundations of French Royal Power in the Middle Ages* (Berkeley: University of California Press, 1986)

Baldwin, John W., 'Le Sens de Bouvines', *Cahiers de Civilisation Médiévale*, 30 (1987), 119–30

Baldwin, John W., *Aristocratic Life in Medieval France* (Baltimore, MD: Johns Hopkins University Press, 2000)

Baldwin, John W., *Paris, 1200* (Stanford: Stanford University Press, 2010; orig. Paris: Flammarion, 2006)

Baldwin, John W., 'Master Stephen Langton, Future Archbishop of Canterbury: The Paris Schools and Magna Carta', *English Historical Review*, 123 (2008), 811–46

Barlow, Frank, *The Feudal Kingdom of England 1042–1216* (5th rev. edn, Harlow: Longman, 1999; orig. 1955)

Bartlett, Robert, *England under the Norman and Angevin Kings, 1075–1225* (Oxford: Oxford University Press, 2000)

Bartlett, Robert, *Gerald of Wales: A Voice of the Middle Ages* (Stroud: History Press, 2006)

Bartlett, W. B., *God Wills It! An Illustrated History of the Crusades* (Stroud: Sutton, 1999)

Bates, David, *The Normans and Empire* (Oxford: Oxford University Press, 2013)

Bautier, Robert-Henri, *La France de Philippe Auguste. Le Temps des mutations* (Paris: CNRS, 1982)

Bennett, Matthew (ed.), *The Hutchinson Dictionary of Ancient and Medieval Warfare* (Oxford: Helicon, 1998)

Berrou, Oliver, *The Contribution of Louis VIII to the Advancement of Capetian France* (Saarbrücken: Lambert Academic, 2013)

Berthelot, Anne, *Histoire de la littérature française du moyen âge* (Paris: Nathan, 1989)

Bliese, John, 'The Just War as Concept and Motive in the Central Middle Ages', *Medievalia et Humanistica*, 17 (1991), 1–26

Bloch, R. Howard, *Etymologies and Genealogies: A Literary Anthropology of the French Middle Ages* (Chicago: University of Chicago Press, 1983)

Bolton, J. L., 'The English Economy in the Early Thirteenth Century', in *King John: New Interpretations*, ed. S. D. Church (Woodbridge: Boydell, 1999), pp. 27–40

Born, Lester, 'The Perfect Prince: A Study in Thirteenth- and Fourteenth-Century Ideals', *Speculum*, 3 (1928), 470–504

Bradbury, Jim, *The Medieval Siege* (Woodbridge: Boydell, 1992)

Bradbury, Jim, *Philip Augustus* (London: Longman, 1998)

Bradbury, Jim, 'Philip Augustus and King John: Personality and History', in *King John: New Interpretations*, ed. S. D. Church (Woodbridge: Boydell, 1999), pp. 347–61

Bradbury, Jim, *The Routledge Companion to Medieval Warfare* (London: Routledge, 2004)

Bradbury, Jim, *The Capetians: Kings of France 987–1328* (London: Continuum, 2007)

Breisach, Ernst, *Historiography: Ancient, Medieval and Modern* (Chicago: University of Chicago Press, 1983)

Brereton, Geoffrey, *A Short History of French Literature* (London: Penguin, 1961)

Brooks, F. W. and F. Oakley, 'The Campaign and Battle of Lincoln 1217', *Associated Architectural Societies' Reports and Papers*, 26, part 2 (1922)

Broughton, Bradford (ed.), *Dictionary of Medieval Knighthood and Chivalry* (London: Greenwood, 1986)

Cannon, Henry, 'The Battle of Sandwich and Eustace the Monk', *English Historical Review*, 27 (1912), 649–70

Carpenter, David, *The Minority of Henry III* (London: Methuen, 1990)

Carpenter, David, 'Abbot Ralph of Coggeshall's Account of the Last Years of King Richard and the First Years of King John', *English Historical Review*, 113 (1998), 1210–30

Carpenter, David, *Magna Carta* (London: Penguin Classics, 2015)

Carpentier, Elisabeth, 'Les Historiens royaux et le pouvoir capétien. D'Helgaud de Fleury à Guillaume le Breton', in *L'Historiographie médiévale en Europe*, ed. Jean-Philippe Genet (Paris: CNRS, 1991)

Cassagnes-Brouquet, Sophie, *Les Métiers au moyen âge* (Rennes: Ouest-France, 2014)

Chamberlin, E. R., *Life in Medieval France* (London: Batsford, 1967)

Cheney, Christopher, *Pope Innocent III and England* (Stuttgart: Hiersemann, 1976)

Church, S. D., 'King John's Testament and the Last Days of his Reign', *English Historical Review*, 125 (2010), 505–28

Church, Stephen, *King John: England, Magna Carta and the Making of a Tyrant* (London: Macmillan, 2015)

Church, S. D. (ed.), *King John: New Interpretations* (Woodbridge: Boydell, 1999)

Coleman, Janet, *Ancient and Medieval Memories: Studies in the Reconstruction of the Past* (Cambridge: Cambridge University Press, 1992)

Contamine, Philippe, 'L'Armée de Philippe Auguste', in *La France de Philippe Auguste. Actes du colloque international organisé par le CNRS* (Paris: CNRS, 1982), pp. 577–94

Contamine, Philippe, *La Guerre au moyen âge* (Paris: Presses Universitaires de France, 1992)

Contamine, Philippe, *War in the Middle Ages,* trans. Michael Jones (Oxford: Blackwell, 1992)

Cormack, Margaret, 'Approaches to Childbirth in the Middle Ages', *Journal of the History of Sexuality*, 21 (2012), 201–7

Crosland, Jessie, *Medieval French Literature* (Oxford: Blackwell, 1956)

Crouch, David, *William Marshal: Court, Career and Chivalry in the Angevin Empire 1147–1219* (Harlow: Longman, 1990)

Crouch, David, 'Baronial Paranoia in King John's Reign', in *Magna Carta and the England of King John*, ed. Janet S. Loengard (Woodbridge: Boydell, 2010), pp. 45–62

Crouch, David, 'The Complaint of King John against William de Briouze', in *Magna Carta and the England of King John*, ed. Janet S. Loengard (Woodbridge: Boydell, 2010), pp. 168–79

Danziger, Danny and John Gillingham, *1215: The Year of Magna Carta* (London: Hodder, 2003)

Delorme, Philippe, *Blanche de Castille*, Histoire des Reines de France (Paris: Pygmalion, 2002)

DeVries, Kelly, *Medieval Military Technology* (Peterborough, ON: Broadview, 1992)

Duby, Georges, *Le Dimanche de Bouvines* (Paris: Gallimard, 1985; orig. 1973)

Duby, Georges, *The Chivalrous Society*, trans. Cynthia Postan (London: Arnold, 1977)

Duby, Georges, *The Legend of Bouvines: War, Religion and Culture in the Middle Ages*, trans. Catherine Tihanyi (Cambridge: Polity, 1990)

Duby, Georges, *France in the Middle Ages 987–1460*, trans. Juliet Vale (Oxford: Blackwell, 1994)

Duncan, A. A. M., 'John King of England and the Kings of Scots', in *King John: New Interpretations*, ed. S. D. Church (Woodbridge: Boydell, 1999), pp. 247–71

Faulkner, Kathryn, 'The Knights in the Magna Carta Civil War', in *Thirteenth-Century England VIII: Proceedings of the Durham Conference 1999* (Woodbridge: Boydell, 2001), pp. 1–12

Fawtier, R., 'Un fragment du compte de l'hôtel du prince Louis de France pour le terme de la Purification 1213', *Le Moyen Age*, 46 (1933), 225–50

Fawtier, R., *The Capetian Kings of France: Monarchy and Nation 987–1328* (Basingstoke: Macmillan, 1960)

Fleischmann, Suzanne, 'On the Representation of History and Fiction in the Middle Ages', *History and Theory*, 22 (1983), 278–310

Flori, Jean, *La Chevalerie en France au moyen âge* (Paris: Presses Universitaires de France, 1995)

Flori, Jean, *Chevaliers et chevalerie au moyen âge* (Paris: Hachette, 1998)

France, John, *Western Warfare in the Age of the Crusades 1000–1300* (London: University College London Press, 1999)

Galbraith, V. H., *Roger Wendover and Matthew Paris* (Glasgow: Glasgow University Press, 1970; orig. 1944)

Galbraith, V. H., 'Good and Bad Kings in History', *History*, 30 (1945), 119–32

Gaposchkin, M. Cecilia, *The Making of Saint Louis: Kingship, Sanctity and Crusade in the Later Middle Ages* (Ithaca, NY: Cornell University Press, 2010)

Gillingham, John, 'War and Chivalry in the *History of William the Marshal*', in *Thirteenth-Century England II: Proceedings of the Newcastle-upon-Tyne Conference 1985*, ed. P. R. Coss and S. D. Lloyd (Woodbridge: Boydell Press, 1986), pp. 1–13

Gillingham, John, 'Conquering the Barbarians: War and Chivalry in Britain and Ireland', *Haskins Society Journal*, 4 (1992), 67–84

Gillingham, John, 'Historians without Hindsight: Coggeshall, Diceto and Howden on the Early Years of John's Reign', in *King John: New Interpretations*, ed. S. D. Church (Woodbridge: Boydell, 1999), pp. 1–26

Gillingham, John, *The Angevin Empire*, 2nd edn (London: Bloomsbury, 2001)

Gillingham, John, 'At the Deathbeds of the Kings of England, 1066–1216', in *Herrscher- und Fürstentestamente im Westeuropäischen Mittelalter*, ed. Brigitte Kasten (Cologne: Böhlau, 2008), pp. 509–30

Gillingham, John, 'The Anonymous of Béthune, King John and Magna Carta', in *Magna Carta and the England of King John*, ed. Janet S. Loengard (Woodbridge: Boydell, 2010), pp. 27–44

Gobry, Ivan, *Louis VIII, fils de Philippe II, 1223–1226* (Paris: Pygmalion, 2009)

266

Goodall, John, 'Dover Castle and the Great Siege of 1216', *Château Gaillard*, 19 (2000), 91–102

Gransden, Antonia, *Historical Writing in England*, vol. 1: *c.550–c.1307* (London: Routledge & Kegan Paul, 1974)

Hajdu, Robert, 'Castles, Castellans and the Structure of Politics in Poitou, 1152–1271', *Journal of Medieval History*, 4 (1978), 27–53

Hallam, Elizabeth, *Capetian France 987–1328* (London: Longman, 1980)

Hanley, Catherine, 'Reading the Past through the Present: Ambroise, the Minstrel of Reims and Jordan Fantosme', *Medievalia*, 20 (2001), 263–81

Hanley, Catherine, *War and Combat 1150–1270: The Evidence from Old French Literature* (Woodbridge: D. S. Brewer, 2003)

Hanley, Catherine, 'Chivalric Biographies', in *Oxford Encyclopedia of Medieval Warfare and Military Technology*, ed. Clifford Rogers, 3 vols (New York: Oxford University Press, 2010)

Harvey, P. D. A., 'The English Inflation of 1180–1220', *Past and Present*, 61 (1973), 3–30

Hattendorf, J. and R. Unger (eds), *War at Sea in the Middle Ages and Renaissance* (Woodbridge: Boydell, 2003)

Hill, J. W. F., *Medieval Lincoln* (Cambridge: Cambridge University Press, 1948)

Holt, James Clarke, 'The Barons and the Great Charter', *English Historical Review*, 70 (1955), 1–24

Holt, James Clarke, *The Northerners: A Study in the Reign of King John* (Oxford: Oxford University Press, 1961)

Holt, James Clarke, *Magna Carta and Medieval Government* (London: Hambledon, 1985)

Holt, James Clarke, *Magna Carta*, 2nd edn (Cambridge: Cambridge University Press, 1992; orig. 1965)

Holt, James Clarke, 'The *Casus Regis*: The Law and Politics of Succession in the Plantagenet Dominions, 1185–1247', in *Colonial England, 1066–1215: Essays by J. C. Holt* (London: Hambledon, 1997), pp. 307–26

Howard, Michael, *War in European History* (Oxford: Oxford University Press, 1977)

Kaeuper, Richard, *Chivalry and Violence in Medieval Europe* (Oxford: Oxford University Press, 1999)

Keen, Maurice, *Chivalry* (New Haven: Yale University Press, 1984)

Keene, D., 'Medieval London and its Region', *London Journal*, 14 (1989), 99–111

Legge, M. Dominica, *Anglo-Norman Literature and its Background* (Oxford: Clarendon Press, 1963)

LeGoff, Jacques, *Saint Louis*, trans. Gareth Evan Gollrad (Notre Dame, IN: University of Notre Dame Press, 2009)

Lewis, Andrew, 'Anticipatory Association of the Heir in Early Capetian France', *American Historical Review*, 83 (1979), 906–27

Loengard, Janet S. (ed.), *Magna Carta and the England of King John* (Woodbridge: Boydell, 2010)

Luchaire, Achille, 'La Condamnation de Jean Sans-Terre par la cour de France', *Revue Historique*, 27 (1900), 285–90

McGlynn, Sean, 'Roger of Wendover and the Wars of Henry III, 1216–1234', in *England and Europe in the Reign of Henry III, 1216–1272*, ed. Björn Weiler and Ifor Rowlands (Aldershot: Ashgate, 2002)

McGlynn, Sean, *By Sword and Fire: Cruelty and Atrocity in Medieval Warfare* (London: Weidenfeld & Nicolson, 2008)

McGlynn, Sean, 'Louis VIII', in *Oxford Encyclopedia of Medieval Warfare and Military Technology*, ed. Clifford Rogers, 3 vols (New York: Oxford University Press, 2010)

McGlynn, Sean, *Blood Cries Afar: The Forgotten Invasion of England 1216* (Stroud: Spellmount, 2011)

McGlynn, Sean, 'The Real Robin Hood', *History Today*, 63 (2013), 22–8

McGlynn, Sean, *'Kill Them All!' Cathars and Carnage in the Albigensian Crusade* (Stroud: Spellmount, 2015)

Meuleau, Maurice, *Histoire de la chevalerie* (Rennes: Ouest-France, 2014)

Meyer, Paul, *'L'Histoire de Guillaume le Maréchal, Comte de Striguil et de Pembroke, Régent d'Angleterre*. Poème français inconnu', *Romania*, 11 (1882), 22–74

Morris, Marc, *King John: Treachery, Tyranny and the Road to Magna Carta* (London: Hutchinson, 2015)

Nicolle, David, *French Medieval Armies 1000–1300* (London: Osprey, 1991)

Nicolle, David, *Medieval Warfare Source Book*, 2 vols (London: Brockhampton, 1998)

O'Callaghan, Joseph, *A History of Medieval Spain* (Ithaca, NY: Cornell University Press, 1975)

Oksanen, Elijas, *Flanders and the Anglo-Norman World, 1066–1216* (Cambridge: Cambridge University Press, 2012)

Oldenbourg, Zoe, *Massacre at Montségur*, trans. Peter Green (London: Phoenix, 1998; orig. 1961)

Orme, Nicholas, *From Childhood to Chivalry: The Education of the English Kings and Aristocracy 1066–1530* (London: Methuen, 1984)

Orme, Nicholas, *Medieval Children* (New Haven and London: Yale University Press, 2001)

Painter, Sidney, *William Marshal: Knight Errant, Baron and Regent of England* (Baltimore, MD: Johns Hopkins University Press, 1933)

Painter, Sidney, *French Chivalry: Chivalric Ideals and Practice in Medieval France* (Baltimore, MD: Johns Hopkins University Press, 1940)

Painter, Sidney, *Medieval Society* (Ithaca, NY: Cornell University Press, 1951)

Painter, Sidney, 'The Lords of Lusignan in the Eleventh and Twelfth Centuries', *Speculum*, 32 (1957), 27–47

Papin, Yves D., *Chronologie du moyen âge* (Paris: Jean-Paul Gisserot, 2001)

Partner, Nancy, *Serious Entertainments: The Writing of History in Twelfth-Century England* (Chicago: University of Chicago Press, 1977)

Pegg, Mark Gregory, *A Most Holy War: The Albigensian Crusade and the Battle for Christendom* (Oxford: Oxford University Press, 2008)

Perry, Guy, *John of Brienne: King of Jerusalem, Emperor of Constantinople, c. 1175–1237* (Cambridge: Cambridge University Press, 2013)

Petit-Dutaillis, Charles, *Étude sur la vie et le règne de Louis VIII 1187–1226* (Paris: Bibliothèque de l'École des Hautes Études, 1894)

Power, Daniel, *The Norman Frontier in the Twelfth and Early Thirteenth Centuries* (Cambridge: Cambridge University Press, 2004)

Power, Daniel, 'Les Dernières Années du régime angevin en Normandie', in *Plantagenêts et Capétiens. Confrontations et héritages*, ed. Martin Aurell and Yves Tonnerre (Turnhout: Brepols, 2006), pp. 163–92

Power, Daniel, 'Who Went on the Albigensian Crusade?' *English Historical Review*, 128 (2013), 1047–85

Powicke, F. M., *The Thirteenth Century*, 2nd edn (Oxford: Oxford University Press, 1962)

Prestwich, J. O., 'Military Intelligence under the Norman and Angevin Kings', in *Law and Government in Medieval England and Normandy*, ed. G. Garnett and J. Hudson (Cambridge: Cambridge University Press, 1994), pp. 1–30

Prestwich, Michael, *Armies and Warfare in the Middle Ages: The English Experience* (New Haven, CT and London: Yale University Press, 1996)

Prestwich, Michael, 'The Garrisoning of English Medieval Castles', in *The Normans and Their Adversaries at War*, ed. Richard Abels and Bernard S. Bachrach (Woodbridge: Boydell, 2001), pp. 185–200

Richardson, H. G., 'Letters of the Legate Guala', *English Historical Review*, 48 (1933), 250–9

Riley-Smith, Jonathan, *The Crusades: A Short History* (London: Athlone, 1987)

Riley-Smith, Louise and Jonathan Riley-Smith, *The Crusades: Idea and Reality, 1095–1274* (London: Edward Arnold, 1981)

Rogers, Clifford (gen. ed.), *Oxford Encyclopedia of Medieval Warfare and Military Technology*, 3 vols (New York: Oxford University Press, 2010)

Runciman, Steven, *A History of the Crusades*, 3 vols (Cambridge: Cambridge University Press, 1951–4)

Russell, Frederick, *The Just War in the Middle Ages* (Cambridge: Cambridge University Press, 1975)

Sivéry, Gérard, *Blanche de Castille* (Paris: Fayard, 1990)

Sivéry, Gérard, *Louis VIII le lion* (Paris: Fayard, 1995)

Smith, J. Beverley, 'The Treaty of Lambeth, 1217', *English Historical Review*, 94 (1979), 562–79

Spiegel, Gabrielle, *Romancing the Past: The Rise of Vernacular Prose Historiography in Thirteenth-Century France* (Berkeley: University of California Press, 1993)

Spiegel, Gabrielle, *The Past as Text: The Theory and Practice of Medieval Historiography* (Baltimore, MD: Johns Hopkins University Press, 1997)

Strayer, Joseph, *The Albigensian Crusades* (Ann Arbor: University of Michigan Press, 1992)

Strickland, Matthew, 'Against the Lord's Anointed: Aspects of Warfare and Baronial Rebellion in England and Normandy, 1075–1265', in *Law and Government in Medieval England and Normandy*, ed. George Garnett and John Hudson (Cambridge: Cambridge University Press, 1994), pp. 56–79

Strickland, Matthew, *War and Chivalry* (Cambridge: Cambridge University Press, 1996)

Stringer, K. J., 'The War of 1215–17 in its Context', in *The Reign of Alexander II, 1214–49*, ed. Richard Oram (Leiden: Brill, 2005), pp. 99–156

Sumption, Jonathan, *The Albigensian Crusade* (London: Faber and Faber, 1978)

Thompson, Kathleen, *Power and Border Lordship in Medieval France: The County of the Perche, 1000–1226* (Woodbridge: Boydell, 2002)

Tilley, Arthur (ed.), *Medieval France* (Cambridge: Cambridge University Press, 1922)

Tout, T. F., 'The Fair of Lincoln and the *Histoire de Guillaume le Maréchal*', *English Historical Review*, 18 (1903), 240–65

Trotter, D. A., *Medieval French Literature and the Crusades* (Geneva: Droz, 1987)

Turner, Ralph V., *King John* (London: Longman, 1994)

Turner, Ralph V., 'England in 1215: An Authoritarian Angevin Dynasty Facing Multiple Threats', in *Magna Carta and the England of King John*, ed. Janet S. Loengard (Woodbridge: Boydell, 2010), pp. 10–26

Tyson, Diana, 'Patronage of French Vernacular History Writers in the Twelfth and Thirteenth Centuries', *Romania*, 100 (1979), 180–222

Vale, Malcolm, *War and Chivalry* (London: Duckworth, 1981)

Vale, Malcolm, *The Ancient Enemy: England, France and Europe from the Angevins to the Tudors* (London: Bloomsbury Academic, 2009)

Vaughan, Richard, *Matthew Paris* (Cambridge: Cambridge University Press, 1958; repr. 1979)

Verbruggen, J. F., *The Art of Warfare in Western Europe in the Middle Ages*, trans. Sumner Willard and S. C. M. Southern (Oxford: North Holland, 1977)

Vincent, Nicholas, 'Isabelle of Angoulême: John's Jezebel', in *King John: New Interpretations*, ed. S. D. Church (Woodbridge: Boydell, 1999), pp. 165–219

Vincent, Nicholas, *Peter des Roches: An Alien in English Politics 1205–1238* (Cambridge: Cambridge University Press, 2002)

Vincent, Nicholas, *Magna Carta: A Very Short Introduction* (Oxford: Oxford University Press, 2012)

Viney, William, 'The Significance of Twins in Medieval and Early Modern Europe', paper presented at the Annual Association for Medical Humanities Conference, 2013, available at http://thewonderoftwins.wordpress.com/2013/07/23/the-significance-of-twins-in-medieval-and-early-modern-europe/

Volkmann, Jean-Charles, *Généalogies complètes des rois de France* (Paris: Jean-Paul Gisserot, 1999)

Wakefield, Walter, *Heresy, Crusade and Inquisition in Southern France 1100–1250* (London: Allen & Unwin, 1974)

Warren, John, *The Past and its Presenters* (London: Hodder & Stoughton, 1998)

Warren, W. L., *The Governance of Anglo-Norman and Angevin England, 1086–1272* (Stanford: Stanford University Press, 1987)

Warren, W. L., *King John* (New Haven, CT and London: Yale University Press, 1997; orig. 1961)

Weir, Alison, *Britain's Royal Families: The Complete Genealogy* (London: Vintage, 2008)

Wilkinson, Louise, 'Women as Sheriffs in Early Thirteenth-Century England', in *English Government in the Thirteenth Century*, ed. A. Jobson (Woodbridge: Boydell, 2004), pp. 111–24

Wilkinson, Louise, *Women in Thirteenth-Century Lincolnshire* (Woodbridge: Boydell, 2007)

Zimmerman, Jean, 'Étude sur la *Chanson de la croisade albigeoise*', *La Nouvelle Tour de Feu*, 28 (1993), 123–38

Zink, Michel, *Littérature française du moyen age* (Paris: Presses Universitaires de France, 1992)

Online sources

Foundation for Medieval Genealogy, at http://fmg.ac/

Gallica (Bibliothèque nationale de France), at http://gallica.bnf.fr/

Internet Archive, at https://archive.org/

Magna Carta Project, at www.magnacartaresearch.org

Oxford Dictionary of National Biography, at www.oxforddnb.com

INDEX

Medieval people are listed by first name. Post-medieval people are listed by surname.